GOVERNING DEATH, MAKING PERSONS

GOVERNING DEATH, MAKING PERSONS

The New Chinese Way of Death

Huwy-min Lucia Liu

CORNELL UNIVERSITY PRESS   ITHACA AND LONDON

First published 2022 by Cornell University Press

Library of Congress Cataloging-in-Publication Data

Names: Liu, Huwy-min Lucia, 1978– author.
Title: Governing death, making persons : the new Chinese way of death / Huwy-min Lucia Liu.
Description: Ithaca [New York] : Cornell University Press, 2022. | Includes bibliographical references and index.
Identifiers: LCCN 2022010642 (print) | LCCN 2022010643 (ebook) | ISBN 9781501767210 (hardcover) | ISBN 9781501767227 (paperback) | ISBN 9781501767234 (pdf) | ISBN 9781501767241 (epub)
Subjects: LCSH: Funeral rites and ceremonies—China—Shanghai. | Funeral rites and ceremonies—Government policy—China. | Death care industry—Government policy—China. | Death care industry—Government ownership—China. | Shanghai (China)—Social life and customs.
Classification: LCC GT3283.S53 L58 2022 (print) | LCC GT3283.S53 (ebook) | DDC 393/.930951132—dc23/eng/20220603
LC record available at https://lccn.loc.gov/2022010642
LC ebook record available at https://lccn.loc.gov/2022010643

I would like to dedicate this work to Tsui-chuan, Szu-chi, Ming-how, Matt, and Mira.

Contents

Acknowledgments

I would not have been able to do this fieldwork without the help of many people I met during my time in Shanghai and other parts of China. Although I cannot thank them individually and by name here, I would like to express my deepest gratitude for their generosity. I especially want to thank those funeral professionals who took me in. I also would like to thank officials at the Shanghai Funeral and Interment Service Center. Without their initial support, I would not have had access to funeral parlors in the first place.

This book has gone through multiple lives: from being a research proposal to a monograph. Many institutions sponsored me financially during this reincarnation journey. These included the Anthropology Department and the Institute on Culture, Religion and World Affairs at Boston University, the Sociology and Anthropology Department and the Center for Humanities Research at George Mason University, the Humanities Division at Hong Kong University of Science and Technology and the University Grants Committee in Hong Kong, the Ministry of Education of the Republic of China in Taiwan, a Cora Du Bois Fellowship from Harvard University, and a Mellon/ACLS Fellowship.

Some of the most important people who made this book possible were my mentors at Boston University. Robert Weller is the best mentor anyone could ask for. His wisdom and warm personality (two things that often do not go together in academia) have been absolutely crucial in my life both before and long after I received my doctoral degree. Many parts of this book are in direct conversation with his mind. Although Charles Lindholm was "just" my second reader, he did so much for me that I cannot help but acknowledge him as a mentor, too. Although I would not categorize my work as belonging to psychological anthropology, he opened this door for me and has greatly expanded my horizons. I would also like to thank Kimberly Arkin. Perhaps due to our relative closeness in age, her mentorship was always mixed with a big-sister-like friendship. Her critical eye toward anthropological theory and sharp intellect have greatly improved how I frame my research. Finally, I would like to thank Robert Hefner and Donald J. Hatfield, whose feedback has greatly advanced my work.

From Boston University, I would be remiss if I did not thank "Fred"—the nickname of our writing group in the Anthropology Department at Boston University. Other than Chuck, Kimberly, and Rob, the wonderful people who were a part of "Fred" at that time included Tom Barfield, En-Chieh Chao, Andrea Chiovenda,

Melissa Chiovenda, Lynsey Farrell, Arianna Huhn, Jajang Jahroni, Eric Kelly, Adam Kuper, Mentor Mustafa, Paula Pryce, Chun-Yi Sum, Christopher Taylor, and Matthew West. Many of the foundational ideas of this book were formed and reshaped while we read and commented on each other's drafts and half-baked ideas in "Fred." All of these people together helped me bring this book to life.

There have also been a whole set of people who have helped me in various forms at different stages in this long journey, including Joseph Bosco, Matt Cartmill, David Cheng Chang, Siu-woo Cheung, Shannon Lee Dowdy, Flora Li-tsui Fu, Thomas B. Gold, C. Julia Huang, Paul Katz, Andrew Kipnis, Anru Lee, Haiyan Lee, Jianmei Liu, Gordon Mathews, Marc Moskowitz, Rebecca Nedostup, Evelyn Rawski, Joel Robbins, May-yi Shaw, Adam Seligman, Parker Shipton, Nancy Smith-Hefner, Jenny Smith, Siumi Maria Tam, Chee Beng Tan, Kellee Tsai, Peter van der Veer, Merry White, Keping Wu, and Angela Zito. I would like to offer a special thank-you to Ruth Toulson and Richard Madsen who later revealed themselves to be the reviewers of my manuscript. Without their critical reading and enthusiastic support, this book would not be able to see its light in the world. My editor, James Lance, at Cornell University Press also has my deepest gratitude for seeing something in my work worth sharing more broadly. He has been one of the best editors I have encountered. Finally, I would like to thank my colleagues in the Sociology and Anthropology Department at George Mason University—one of the most diverse universities in terms of student bodies in the United States. The collegial environment they provided has made me happy to make Mason my home.

There is an old saying that it takes a whole village to raise a kid. I think this statement is true for anthropologists as well. Indeed, it takes a whole village to raise an anthropologist. I have been extremely fortunate to have so many smart and kind people around me to help me navigate my professional life course in this long journey of becoming an anthropologist. Without the mentorship, friendship, and ongoing support of the above people, I would not have gotten nearly this far in my career. If there is anything good about this book, it is because of all the people and institutions I've mentioned above. Of course, if there are any mistakes, they are all mine, and I take full responsibility.

Several chapters in this book have been published previously with substantial revisions. An earlier and much shorter version of chapter 1 was published . under the title "The Civil Governance of Death: The Making of Chinese Political Subjects at the End of Life," *Journal of Asian Studies* 80 (1): 49–71, reproduced with permission. Chapter 5 was published under the title "Market Economy Lives, Socialist Death: Contemporary Commemorations in Urban China," *Modern China* 47 (2): 178–203, copyright © 2021, SAGE Publications, https://doi.org/10.1177/0097700419879121. Parts of chapters 6 and 7 were published in an article titled "Ritual and Pluralism: Incommensurable Values and Techniques of Commensurability in Contemporary Urban Chinese Funerals," *Critique of Anthropology* 40 (1): 102–24, copyright © 2020, SAGE Publications, https://doi.org/10.1177/0308275X19899447. The constructive comments of all the editors and reviewers involved in publishing those articles have influenced my thinking both in terms of the ethnographic descriptions and theoretical positions in my book.

I was very fortunate to deliver numerous talks based on the research that forms the foundation for this book in a variety of institutions. These included Appalachian State University, Barnard College of Columbia University, Boston University, Brown University, University of Cologne, George Mason University, George Washington University, Harvard University, Haverford College, the Hong Kong Anthropological Society, the Hong Kong Institute for the Humanities and Social Science of Hong Kong University, the Hong Kong University of Science and Technology, the Max Planck Institute for the Study of Religious and Ethnic Diversity, National Taiwan University, National University of Singapore, Northeastern University, and the University of Edinburgh. The stimulating conversations I had with people in these places across the United States, Asia, and Europe have improved my book greatly.

Doing fieldwork in China was a much bigger cultural shock than I had initially imagined even though my native language is Mandarin Chinese. As a Taiwanese studying China, I occupied an awkward position in my field. It is hard to explain the intricacies, complexities, and mine fields of this relationship in a few words to American readers who do not already know something about the complicated relationship between China and Taiwan. The best quick analogy I can come up with is to suggest American readers imagine me as a Puerto Rican anthropologist who studies white American working-class people in this book. On the one hand, there is a great geopolitical power difference between two sides. On the other hand, there is a class difference between the people who I relied on during my fieldwork and myself as an emerging anthropologist. Of course, there are also obvious limits in applying this Puerto Rican anthropologist analogy. For example, while the majority of Americans probably have very little interest in claiming Puerto Rico as a part of the United States, this is not how the majority of Chinese people feel. This is not even mentioning the additional racial implications in the Puerto Rican anthropologist analogy that emerge in the United States.

The reason I talk about this Puerto Rican anthropologist analogy is to help readers understand that I found that I was studying up and down at the same time during my fieldwork. Reflexive discussions on (if not in) classic anthropological works have helped many younger generations of anthropologists to recognize their privileged positions in their fieldwork. In response, we have seen the rise of native anthropologists and a trend of studying up. Anthropologists are slowly expanding the "we" for the better. Over the years, we have quite a lot of materials talking about studying up, studying down, the colonial legacies of anthropology, and of anthropologists studying their own culture. For Sinophone studies (Chinese-speaking societies), the most common kind of fieldwork power dynamics have long been Western anthropologists studying Sinophone societies, native anthropologists studying their own societies, and second (or later) generations of immigrants who were born in the global north studying their heritage cultures in the global south in anthropological literatures.

Yet we have had little discussion of issues resulting from anthropologists from the global south studying other parts of the global south. During my fieldwork in China, I found that while I was trained entirely by American anthropologists in Hong Kong and the United States, the kind of things Chinese people wanted to tell me or even the way people talked to me was based on their perception of Taiwan. Whether or not sovereignty was involved, these south-to-south encounters sparked very different kinds of power dynamics—ones that made me realize that I am studying up and down as well as studying self and other all at the same time. Such south-to-south interactions affect not only anthropologists' positionality and hence self-reflexivity but also the kind of data they gather. While this book does not directly deal with ethical issues in fieldwork, I hope it provides a glimpse for those global south anthropologists who study other global south places to see how such positionality might affect fieldwork.

Finally, I would like to thank my family. Thank you to my parents, Tsui-chuan Liu and Szu-chi Liu, who did not have a college education but who believed in my passion for anthropology. This was despite the fact that most parents in Taiwan wanted their children to be physicians, lawyers, or semiconductor engineers. Being stereotypical Taiwanese grandparents, my parent's self-sacrifice in helping me with child rearing has been crucial for me to continue to finish this book. Intergenerational support particularly came in handy in raising a preschooler in the era of COVID-19. I also appreciate the love and support of my brother, Ming-how Liu, from in Australia, my extended families in Taiwan and South Korea, my parents-in-law, Nancy and Tom West, sisters-in-law, Christina and Elizabeth West, and all the other extended families in the United States. This extended kinship network across space has kept me going both in my professional and personal life.

Last but not least, I want to give my deepest thanks to my partner, Matthew West. He is more than a spouse. He is my best friend and a fellow anthropologist. We met in our early twenties when we both studied anthropology at the Anthropology Department in the Chinese University of Hong Kong. Over the last two decades, we have gone through many ups and downs together as we went through our own mundane but profound struggles to become anthropologists and parents. Without his love, patience, and humor, I would not be who I am today. Together we are raising the best child anyone could ask for. Yu-pan, thank you for giving me such tremendous amounts of joy and affection, more than I had ever imagined possible before you joined my life. Like the character "pan" in her name indicates, she is already everything I have hoped for.

Abbreviations

CCP   Chinese Communist Party
CFIPL   Library of the Chinese Funeral and Interment Profession
FIA   Shanghai Funeral and Interment Administration
FIBA   Funeral and Interment Business Administration (the successor of the FIA)
FIS   Shanghai Funeral and Interment Service Center
KMT   Kuomintang (Chinese Nationalist Party)
PRC   People's Republic of China
PEC   Shanghai Poultry and Egg Company
ROC   Republic of China

Note on Anonymity and Transliteration

In conducting research for this book, I engaged in participant observation field-work in all three of Shanghai's city funeral parlors and several suburban ones, with one of these as a primary site. To maintain the anonymity of specific places and people, any time I refer to stories about particular persons or places within funeral parlors, I have described it as having happened within "Huangpu Funeral Parlor." However, to provide a clear picture of the differences between these parlors, I use their real names when describing public knowledge or character-istics of them, such as that the two centrally located city funeral parlors in Shang-hai were Longhua and Baoxin. One disadvantage in this writing decision is that Huangpu may seem, at times, somewhat inconsistent. For example, I sometimes described how the bereaved sent the deceased off in a car in Huangpu's parking lot, whereas at other times I described the bereaved walking with the deceased to an on-site cremator. Part of the issue here was that contemporary Chinese fu-neral parlors were places where the Chinese state implemented mandatory cre-mation. However, a new urban policy of the Shanghai government that was implemented after the 1990s moved the cremators of the two city funeral par-lors (Longhua and Baoxin) outside the city center to a third purpose-built fu-neral parlor, Yishan. In fact, as far as I know, Longhua and Baoxin are the only two funeral parlors in the People's Republic of China that do not have cremato-ria on site. There were also systematic differences between urban and suburban funeral parlors as well. Nevertheless, although various kinds of differences ex-isted, they shared enough similarities that using one name for all funeral par-lors in Shanghai in exchange for maintaining the anonymity of the people who were willing to participate in this study is appropriate.

In addition to the names of funeral parlors and in keeping with general an-thropological practice, I have also given pseudonyms to the individuals and pri-vate organizations I interviewed for this project. This group includes funeral brokers and their agencies, funeral banquet restaurants, religious leaders, and state funeral practitioners. I have also occasionally changed their gender or age depending on the specific situations. For government or government-like organ-izations (such as the Shanghai Funeral and Interment Service Center and the Shanghai Funeral and Interment Trade Association), I have used the organ-izations' real names. However, I have used pseudonyms for specific individuals within these and have changed their biographic descriptors to generic terms marking the general nature of their role in these organizations, such as "high-ranking government official," "prominent scholar in the funeral industry," or "quasi-government official from a private-public enterprise" even though many of these people accepted my interviews on the record and in their official capacity. In fact, some even expected me to quote their real names to gain credit or publicity. I have instead decided to use their organizations' real names but maintain their anonymity to hold them accountable for what they said as representatives of specific government bureaus and organizations without leaving them potentially accountable for what else I have said in the book.

Having laid out the work I did toward making people who interacted with me relatively anonymous, however, I also need to clarify that, following the general practice of historians, I have used real names for people and organizations when my descriptions were based on archival documents. All of the primary source, archival data cited and analyzed in my book are from documents stored in the Library of the Chinese Funeral and Interment Profession in Shanghai. I have translated all of the cited primary source documents myself.

As for transliteration, I have used the Pinyin romanization system prevalent in China to transliterate Chinese characters unless they already had well-known romanized names, such as the Chinese Nationalist Party, where I provide the more well-known "Kuomintang (KMT)."

INTRODUCTION

At the time of my fieldwork in 2010, Prosperity was one of the restaurants where Shanghai people ate *doufufan*, a phrase that literally meant "thick tofu soup" and metaphorically stood in to mean an entire funeral banquet. Thick tofu soup was one of the must-have dishes at funeral banquets in Shanghai and hence the name. After my first visit there, Liang Wan, a funeral broker who worked for a private funeral agency called Longevity, asked me if I had seen Chairman Mao's shrine in Prosperity.

"Shrine?" I asked, needing to confirm what he had just asked.

"Yes, shrine."

"No," I said, suddenly feeling quite upset about my apparent negligence during my first trip there. I had spent so much time observing everyone drinking their cup of sweet tea on the way from the parking lot to the restaurant as a purification ritual, the room for the deceased's tablets where the dead could also enjoy their meal, the banquet hall's decorations (a story that I tell in chapter 5), and the funeral banquet itself that I had somehow missed out on a shrine to Mao Zedong himself! I was resolved to return to Prosperity as soon as possible. On my next trip, I found the Mao shrine located prominently in the center of the front entryway. Most of the restaurant's customers, however, came and went through the back door because it connected directly to the parking lot. While the front entryway was indeed not a well-traveled space, Mao's shrine was nevertheless located at the symbolic center of the business itself. I had long heard of the existence of temples that worshipped Mao, especially in rural China—a phenomenon known in scholarly language as the cult of Mao (Barmé 1996). However, the reason why a funeral banquet restaurant was the subject of this cult I had no idea.

It turned out that Prosperity was originally located directly across the street from the Longhua Cemetery of Revolutionary Martyrs before moving to its then-current location. This cemetery was where Chinese Communist Party (CCP) veteran soldiers were buried and commemorated. Next to this martyr's cemetery was Longhua Temple—the largest and one of the most famous ancient Buddhist temples in Shanghai. Although this location generally attracted a large volume of foot traffic given the popularity of Longhua Temple, for some reason, all prior businesses on that particular spot had failed. In the 2000s, after the owners of Prosperity took over the spot from the previous shop owner, they opened a restaurant that targeted funeral banquets. Prosperity's decision to open a funeral banquet business at that location was partly because its location placed it next to Longhua Temple and only about a ten-minute drive from Longhua Funeral Parlor—one of only three funeral parlors in downtown Shanghai. The location was also selected because another funeral banquet restaurant nearby was doing quite well. Prosperity's management figured that its business should be able to quickly see success. However, for whatever reason, after Prosperity opened, just like all other businesses in that same place, it simply would not take off.

At the time of my fieldwork, restaurants in Shanghai commonly had a Laughing Buddha or Wealth God as their patron god. This practice survived the Cultural Revolution (1966–1976), during which the Red Guards enthusiastically destroyed religious practices, which were viewed as "feudalist superstition" (*fengjian mixin*). In 1978, following the death of Mao, the then leader of China, Deng Xiaoping, officially embraced a so-called socialism with Chinese characteristics, a socialist market economy. This process was also known as the Reform and Opening (*gaige kaifang*) or just the Opening Up in vernacular terms. However, in Shanghai, the full embrace of the reform policies did not happen until 1992 when Deng conducted his famous Southern Tour. On this tour, Deng not only reaffirmed the government's continued commitment to economic reforms but also put his stamp of approval on developing Shanghai's Pudong New Area— the key development project that revitalized the city as an economic center.

It was with this Opening Up that selecting a patron god returned openly to ordinary business practice in Shanghai. Prosperity was not exceptional in re-embracing a patron god. In the beginning, it also had a shrine for the Laughing Buddha. However, because Prosperity's business failed to take off, management changed to worshiping Guanyin, the bodhisattva of compassion. Unfortunately, this bodhisattva also failed to deliver the prosperity that the owners had hoped for. Finally, running out of options, the owners of Prosperity decided to hire a feng shui master to evaluate the restaurant and make recommendations to save it. The feng shui master came and, almost immediately, told the owners that Prosperity's problem was all of the spirits from the Longhua Cemetery of Revolutionary Martyrs who were resting across the street. Dealing with spirits was not the problem because either Guanyin or the Laughing Buddha could have held those back. The problem here was that these spirits were Communist Party members and must have been atheists. As such, regular gods or goddesses did not work—the communist spirits were not afraid of superstitious trickery. The only way to control these martyr spirits was to have someone that they were actually afraid of. The feng shui master suggested that the only possible solution was the Great Proletarian Cultural Revolution leader Mao himself, chairman of their party, to command these dead soldiers. Prosperity promptly replaced Guanyin with Mao as its patron god. And business subsequently took off. In fact, business was so good that Prosperity had to move to a larger location. I visited this location many times during my fieldwork. Although the new location was farther from the martyrs' cemetery, Prosperity kept Mao's shrine in the restaurant.

I once asked Tang An, another funeral broker who also worked at Longevity, if he thought that having Mao as the patron god of a restaurant made sense. He told me that, just as Chinese carpenters worshipped Lu Ban (507–440 BCE) as their occupational patron god because he invented several carpentry techniques, having a funeral banquet restaurant worship Mao made complete sense. After all, "Mao invented the memorial meeting [zhuidaohui]," he said. Memorial meetings were a kind of modern, secular, and civil funeral. Memorial meetings were modeled after memorial services in Euro-American societies with their Christian elements removed. Historically, however, it was the Chinese Nationalist Government—also known as the Kuomintang (KMT) or Guomindang—who established the format of memorial meetings. The KMT controlled China from 1911 to 1949 under the name the Republic of China (ROC). At that time, memorial meetings were more of a state ritual in a direct sense and represented a ritual for high-profile and high-ranking government officials (Nedostup 2010). They were never popular on the ground. The CCP was then not only responsible for the popularization of memorial meetings, but under their rule memorial meetings remained at the core of urban Chinese funerals for ordinary people in Shanghai all the way through my fieldwork in 2010 and 2011. As such, although Tang An's statement about Mao "inventing" memorial meetings was not entirely correct, it nevertheless revealed the deep connection between the CCP and memorial meetings.

After Mao became the patron god of Prosperity, its owners began throwing an annual banquet on the day of Mao's birth. Prosperity's annual banquet was meant to be a celebration of its patron god, Chairman Mao. Celebrating a deity's birthday was common practice in *minjian zongjiao*—a term that is often translated as "folk religion," "popular religion," or "diffused religion" (C. K. Yang 1961). This was an umbrella term for a kind of religion that contained a mixture of practices associated with Confucianism, Buddhism, Daoism, and others. Folk religion was not one of the five state-recognized religions in contemporary China, however. In both state discourse and vernacular vocabulary, popular religion was often referred to as "folk customs" (*fengsu xiguan*) at best or feudalist superstitions at worst. These vernacular terms in naming folk religion not only indicate the power the state held in defining the conceptualization of religions but also revealed the lack of a proper name for this kind of religion even in its own local language in the first place (Hatfield 2009). In this book, I use the terms *folk* or *popular religion* interchangeably. Traditional death rituals were part of this folk religion.

During Mao's birthday party, the primary living people invited to the banquet by Prosperity's management were funeral brokers (*binzang zhongjie*) like Liang Wan and Tang An. These brokers were self-employed private operators who mediated between the bereaved and funeral parlors. They are in contrast to people who worked at funeral parlors. In China, funeral parlors are state institutions. Although in some areas these state institutions were outsourced to private entities, this was not the case in Shanghai. I call people who were employed by funeral parlors *state practitioners*. I use the term *funeral professionals* when the distinction between state practitioners and funeral brokers is not important. While each of the three city funeral parlors in Shanghai have their own restaurants to host funeral banquets, private entities could establish restaurants like any other restaurant to host funeral banquets. As such, Prosperity's owner invited funeral brokers to thank them for bringing the bereaved to have their funeral banquets at Prosperity instead of at the funeral parlors' own restaurants. Mao's birthday banquet was a thank-you feast for funeral brokers.

How can we make sense of the centrality of Mao at Prosperity? How do we understand the odd coexistence of religion, especially folk religion, and secular socialism that allowed Mao to be honored for being the inventor of memorial meetings and for Mao's spirit to protect Prosperity from his atheist communist martyr soldiers as a patron god? How do we understand the role of Mao as the patron god of a private business that competed against state institutions over the funeral banqueting business? Following Robert Weller's (2006) concept of nodes of power, I found death to be such a node where governing power and other normative forces interacted with each other. Disentangling the work performed at this node requires both a thorough investigation of the changing political economy of the funeral industry in urban China (in Shanghai in this case) and an understanding of urban Chinese death rituals under the CCP. This book unpacks exactly how these different kinds of power, ideas, and practices came together in the making of funeral professionals, the bereaved, and the dead in Shanghai.

Commemorating the Dead in Urban China Today

One of the best departure points for unpacking death as a node of power is to start with identifying the unexpected. Not long after I started my fieldwork in Shanghai in 2010, I realized that urban Chinese death was not at all what I had expected. I went to Shanghai with two expectations about death in urban China today. I assumed that I would see an increase in personalized funerals and folk death rituals. The first expectation was based on the prior observations of many scholars of the rise of individuals since China moved toward an authoritarian market economy. In this book, I refer to this kind of self associated with the introduction of the market economy as *market subjects*. Scholars have analyzed the rise of market subjects from various angles and within the context of a wide variety of topics (cf. Farrer 2002; Hansen and Svarverud 2010; Hoffman 2006; Rofel 2007; H. Yan 2003; M. Yang 1994). While many saw the emergence of market subjects, they had very different interpretations of this phenomenon. They differed as to whether the emergence of market subjects should be seen as a triumph of individualism, globalization, and capitalism; as a loss of morality; or as growing commensurability between the market-driven ideas of a person (that were historically only tied to liberal democracy) and authoritarian states (Link, Madsen, and Pickowicz 2002; Yan 1996; Zhang and Ong 2008).

In urban China, the other side of this same story of change was associated with a dramatic decline in the work unit (*danwei*) (Davis 1995; Davis and Harrell 1993; Lu and Perry 1997). Work units were the lowest level of party organization that directly tied individuals to the state. Before the introduction of a market economy, such quotidian private life decisions as where to live, whom one could marry, or when to have children were subject to approval from these work units. All these studies in the world of the living led me to assume that I would see increasing numbers of personalized funerals in urban Shanghai. At the very least, I believed that I could find a strong desire for, if not actual moves toward, personalization even if the number of personalized funerals was still low.

My other expectation was that I would see the ongoing reemergence of folk death rituals. This second trend could be seen as the rise of individualism (market subjects), the reemergence of relationality (relational subjects), or the convergence of the two in contemporary China. Chinese folk religion is a locally based practice that operates through a series of exchanges among the living and between the living and the dead (and other nonhuman spirits). It is where relationality is created and maintained. Individuals who are embedded in such relationality are both obligated to fulfill their exchange duties and, at the same time, strategize around such relationships. Putting this in a temporal context, folk religion has enjoyed a widespread revival since the 1980s. Some scholars saw this revival resulting from local communal resistance to state power (Anagnost 1994; Bruun 1996; Dean 1998; Feuchtwang 2010; Jing 1996). Others emphasized state tolerance or ongoing state control such that, when the state believed that its legitimacy or stability was threatened by specific religious groups, it did not hesitate to crack down on them, whether successfully or not (Chen 2003; Madsen 2003; Palmer 2007). Still others focused on the psychological, spiritual, or ethical need for religious and ritual life after traumas, such as the Cultural Revolution, or to address the anomie of reform-era life (Mueggler 2001; Oxfeld 2010; F. Yang 2005). Although some argued that its rapid revival showed that religious and ritual life on the ground never truly disappeared, others emphasized that current religious and ritual practices were (more or less) traditions invented for individual utilitarian goals today (Chao 1999; X. Liu 2000; Siu 1989). The former indicated the revival of relationality while the latter stressed the rise of individuals.

As it turned out, however, in terms of death these expectations were either outright incorrect or required significant further exploration. First, the bereaved generally showed little interest in having personalized funerals. Personalized funerals that commemorate the dead as unique individuals only occurred when death was abnormal (any kind of young death) or when the deceased was a cultural celebrity (e.g., a film director). Instead, the core of urban death rituals was memorial meetings. This kind of funeral was repeated across classes, occupations, and genders during my fieldwork. Between June 2010 and January 2012, I attended more than seventy-five full funerals and many more in part. Regardless of whether the deceased was a humble retired worker, a petty capitalist (a small business owner), a university president, or a government official, people in Shanghai held memorial meetings as the core of their funerary rites. Memorial meetings were the most public event after the biological end of a person's life. In fact, these memorial meetings were the only event that had guests beyond the nuclear families of the deceased's children. Other death-related rituals might be held at homes, temples, or cemeteries but were confined in practice to only close family members. Although these family rituals may be more meaningful for the immediate bereaved (given differences in what meaningful means), they were less relevant in relation to the larger public.

The popularity of memorial meetings was surprising not only because they were secular rituals but also because they were socialist commemorative ceremonies. What I mean by "socialist" here refers to a set of specific moral characteristics promoted by the CCP. These socialist ethics include being selfless, frugal, and having endured bitterness. Although these moral characteristics were associated with the CCP's planned economy period, my usage of the word *socialist* is not meant to indicate a specific mode of production. While it made sense to see memorial meetings as the dominant type of death rituals in urban China when work units were the center of social and personal lives, it made little sense to me to see this in a time when we saw the decreased importance of work units and the rise of market subjects in daily life. My realization of the persistence of memorial meetings and the absence of personalized funerals was even more stunning once I discovered that Shanghai funeral parlors had been promoting personalized funerals in the hope of replacing memorial meetings since the early 2000s.

As for my expectation of an increase in religion at the end of life, although the general direction was correct, what happened in Shanghai had its own very instructive twist. Rather than a return to (or reinvention of) traditional death rituals to replace secular socialist rituals, Shanghai residents altered these socialist memorial meetings in a variety of ways to make religious versions of them. To be clear, plenty of cases throughout the world have shown that syncretism is not only possible but also, often, quite popular. The question here, however, is about the how. How did people create a mixture of a socialist, civil, secular ritual that denied any recognition of spirits and afterlife and folk funerals that were exactly based on spirits, ancestor worship, and reciprocal exchange without first throwing away the secular socialist civil parts? This question is made all the more significant for anthropology because it tackles the coexistence of seemingly incommensurable ideas of person and death. How does alterity become commensurable and in what context? At which points does such commensurability fall apart?

To sum up, I expected to see the rise of personalized funerals and the rise of traditional funerals given that existing studies on the world of the living all pointed to the rise of individualism and religious revivals since the Opening Up. However, I found instead the absence of personalized funerals, the continuity of socialist commemoration, and the growth of religious practices within and alongside secular commemoration. It is with these ethnographic puzzles concerning new Chinese ways of death that I suggest death is a node of power where different (yet particular) ideas and practices met at confluences and were remixed. Rather than being merely the end of life, death is productive of self.

Death as a Site of Subject Formation

To some degree, anthropologists have long treated death as something productive. For example, death rituals have restored the normal flow of community life that was interrupted by death (Durkheim [1912] 1965); funerals have helped individuals deal with psychological loss or fears associated with death (Becker 1973; Malinowski 1948); funerals have been a rite of passage that transformed living and dead participants from one stage to the next (Turner 1969; Van Gennep 1960); and they have been a moral obligation that regenerated society (Bloch and Perry 1982; Metcalf and Huntington 1991). Since the translation of Robert Hertz's *Death and the Right Hand* into English in 1960, scholars have come to pay greater attention to the productivity of dead bodies—how decaying dead bodies forced the living to reconceptualize their perceptions of the dead in terms of who they were before their death and of who the dead should be afterward, as well as of how the living should relate to the dead. In other words, the fact of death requires a new identity for both the living and the dead. The lasting life of dead bodies has continued to dominate the anthropology of death today (Engelke 2019).

Despite death rituals transforming people into culturally appropriate beings through socially and culturally recognizable means and establishing a new kind of relationship between self and other for both the bereaved and the dead, the productive nature of ritual in producing self has been largely absent from literature in the anthropology of subjectivity. Part of the reason for this absence was because people tended to have particular views on ritual. Since the rise of a set of empirical conditions and analytical approaches in the West highlighting the close links between modernity, individualism, and capitalism (Bellah et al. 1985; Giddens 1991; Taylor 1989), rituals have often been viewed as merely being about externalized social conventions outside of individuals—empty and meaningless at their best and hypocritical and inauthentic at their worst. Under this post-Reformation view of ritual, self was assumed to be articulated through the desire and pursuit of sincerity, authenticity, or both (Anton 2001; Lindholm 2008; Martin 1997; Trilling 1972). Whether or not a person needed to be envisioned as a kind of autonomous and independent subject, the effort to be who they are and then act accordingly was what mattered. The push was to match the internal state of being and thinking with external behaviors that created an authentic or sincere self (Seligman et al. 2008). Although this phenomenon did not exclusively align with the market economy worldwide, it nevertheless was emphasized. With this idea of self and rituals, scholarly work on the relationship between death and subjectivity tended to concentrate on the process of dying—the last phase before people have to deal with rituals.

Inherent in this tendency to avoid rituals in understanding subjectivity are the different assumptions scholars make about what subjectivity is and the kind of relationships that exist between subjectivity and normative structuring power. Some scholars have tended to treat agency as more or less innate to humanity. Human subjects are more like agents in these works. In this humanistic approach, humans are the center of action, being, and meaning making. As such, subjectivity then has become more like a product of the interaction between innate qualities and external structures (e.g., Luhrmann 2006; Parish 2008). While this humanistic approach usually presents complicated and multilayered accounts of the subjective experiences and feelings of human subjects as they navigate through political economic structures, if we take rituals as the antithesis of sincerity, authenticity, and individual autonomy, then ritual appears to have little to do with ideas of self.

Meanwhile, however, other scholars have tended to treat subjects more like objects by stressing how subjects become subjectified. In their diverse accounts, normative structuring power shapes (if not determines) individuals' senses of self even as the normative structuring power might refer alternatively to cultural meanings, social roles, or modes of production for different scholars. Among these, some have emphasized the role of external forces in shaping individuals; some have stressed how internal forces turned people into governable subjects. The former has its root in Emile Durkheim, while the latter often seeks inspiration from Michel Foucault (1991). While poststructuralists emerged to contest the cohesiveness and cohesion of structure (however structure was defined) and attempted to give space to agency, they nevertheless saw specific structures determining the subjective experience of individuals (e.g., Bourdieu 1997; Foucault 2003).

The differences between these two broad approaches indicate that scholars have opposing epistemological positions from which to view what subjects are and, therefore, how a subject becomes a subject. The humanistic approach has taken human subjects as an assumption to start with; the structuralist approach has viewed human subjects as a conclusion to end with. This is an epistemological dilemma—subjectivity is either a priori or not. To some degree, however, the need to choose an either-or epistemological position is at least partly the result of methodological constraints. That is to say, because the study of subjectivity is at the intersection between an individual and structure, scholars have examined subjectivity through either top-down (structural) or bottom-up (humanistic) processes.

However, as many of these scholars themselves have suggested, neither subjects nor structures are coherent and unitary entities in the first place. Moreover, the shaping processes might have been hierarchically top down or bottom up at some times and, at other times, various processes might simply have existed in competition or juxtaposition. I suggest here that a solution to this methodological quandary is to evaluate the circumstances under which more resonant or dissonant relationships between subjectivity and power develop.

In working to solve this dilemma, I tackle three specific empirical questions in this book concerning funeral professionals, the bereaved, and dead bodies in Shanghai. The first explores how the governance of death evolved in the first twenty years of the CCP in Shanghai. I examine how the specific details of governing funeral parlors, the bereaved, and dead bodies were meant to shape the identification and the relationships between the living and the dead. The second question is concerned with how the subsequent introduction of market economic principles brought about a new kind of governance for funeral professionals, the bereaved, and the dead and then how these differed from what were produced. While the former is about the intended consequences of governance on paper, the latter is about both the intended and unintended consequences in practice. Finally, the third question investigates how specific rituals emerged from these changing governance practices, how these rituals created ideas of self, and how these ritually constructed ideas of self were in resonance or dissonance with the normative structuring power of governance or ritual. These questions form the ethnographic backbone of this book.

By focusing on the concept of resonance or dissonance, I am able to identify a range of conditions of possibility that exist both for subjects acting as agents and for them to become subjected to normative structures. This resonant or dissonant approach to subject formation allows me to accomplish three analytical goals. Firstly, my findings challenge existing works on subject formation in China, especially referring to the arguments on the prevalence of market subjects since China adopted its market economy. Secondly, these specific findings about contemporary China also question the often taken-for-granted relationship between market governance and market subjectivity in anthropological studies on neoliberalism, neoliberal governance, and neoliberal subject formation. Finally, the resonant or dissonant approach allows me to establish the concept of ritually constructed subjectivity. Simply speaking, when analyzing contemporary urban Chinese funerals, I found that ritual constructs self through its ability to frame perceptions and actions. Ritual does this because, as Gregory Bateson ([1955] 2000) has shown, ritual is a type of cognitive framing that provides "a spatial and temporal bonding of a set of interactive messages." To use Bateson's examples, by evoking "this is a play," participants can understand the same act of fist fighting, for example, as part of a play rather than as a fight. The concept of ritually constructed subjectivity shows how the commitment to structuring power could be inherently self-reflexive. This characteristic of ritually constructed subjectivity bridges not only the epistemological differences within the anthropology of subjectivity but also the distance between the anthropology of subjectivity and ritual studies.

Doing Fieldwork on Death in Urban China

Chinese death rituals traditionally contained three interrelated sets of rituals: the *bin* (or *sang*), *zang*, and *ji* ceremonies. Bin originally referred to keeping a coffin in a temporary shelter before burial. Bin or sang ceremonies are rituals conducted during the period after death and before burial. Such ceremonies traditionally included activities like preparing bodies for burial, managing pollution, presenting offerings, mourning and hosting mourners, and making arrangements for follow-up rituals. Zang meant to inter or bury a body. Zang ceremonies are rituals conducted at the gravesite. The process of moving from bin to zang was the funeral procession (*chubin*), literally meaning "the leaving of the place where the body was encoffined." The funeral procession was both the defining moment and the most spectacular part of funerals throughout imperial China, the Republic of China era, and the period immediately after the establishment of the People's Republic of China (PRC) in 1949. The final part of Chinese death rituals was ji. Ji means to offer sacrifice. In the context of death ritual, ji particularly refers to ancestor worship. Sacrifice assured the continuous renewal of the relationship between living descendants and their deceased ancestors even long after biological death. It is with these offerings that we note that neither death nor burial were ends but rather intermediary points meant to transform the dead into new, ongoing relations with the living as ancestors.

In contemporary China, funeral governance was called "the administration of bin and zang" (*binzang guanli*). The death industry was called the *binzangye*—the industry for bin and zang. A funeral parlor was called a *binyiguan*, which literally means "bin ritual hall." In this sense, then, this book as a whole is primarily a story of bin ritual, bin governance, and the bin industry in contemporary China. For reading convenience, I call these three things *funeral ritual* (or death ritual, funeral, and funerary rites), *funeral governance*, and the *death (or funeral) industry*, respectively, throughout this book.

In the anthropology of Sinophone cultures (Chinese-speaking societies), death rituals have long been a key site in understanding what it means to be Chinese. Scholars have argued for the unity or diversity of Chinese culture all based on analyses of cults of the dead (Freedman 1974; Wolf 1974). This cult of death was based on a standardized set of death rituals among Han Chinese at least since late imperial China. Proper funerary rites (including ancestor worship) allowed the bereaved to transform dead bodies into a symbol of the lineage's fertility or the segment of an eternal patriline at the end of life (Ahern 1973; Fei 1946; Hsu 1971). Scholars differed, however, regarding whether correct thinking (orthodoxy) or correct performance (orthopraxy) was the major mechanism for such standardization and therefore the unification of Chinese culture (Katz 2007; Sutton 2007; Szonyi 2007)—the key debate addressed in the classic edited volume *Death Ritual in Late Imperial and Modern China* (Watson and Rawski 1988).

Despite the role that death rituals have long been said to play in understanding what it means to be Chinese in a general sense, there has been little interest in studying urban Chinese funerals in the CCP era. While some ethnographies of contemporary China have included a chapter or a section covering contemporary funerals in the postreform era, these short treatments have tended to have only a rural focus (e.g., Chau 2006; X. Liu 2000; Oxfeld 2010; Siu 1989). We have only very sporadic data in various book chapters on urban death so far (Aveline-Dubach 2012; Bellocq 2012; Goossaert and Palmer 2011; Ikels 2004; Kawaguchi 2012; Wakeman 1988; Whyte 1988).

Such an absence in studying urban death rituals was partially based on social scientists' imagination of the meaning of "Chineseness." Many simply considered contemporary urban funerals not to be truly Chinese and, therefore, not worth studying if we wanted to understand Chinese culture. For example, a professor in China who studied funerals once asked me why I wanted to do fieldwork in urban Shanghai if I wanted to study real Chinese funerals. He specifically asked why I did not go to a rural village instead. In fact, even my funeral professional interlocutors thought the same thing. Some told me directly that urban Chinese funerals had no Chinese culture. Some even went as far as to tell me that if I wanted to study real Chinese culture through funerals, I should go to Taiwan, where I am from, to do my research because people there "have kept more traditional funerals." However, if we accept, as I believe we must, that there is no need to assume some kind of essence for Sinophone cultures, then contemporary urban Chinese practices are just as Chinese (or just as un-Chinese) as their rural counterparts or other Sinophone societies outside the sovereignty of the PRC. The question of urban death ritual is then just as important in understanding what being Chinese means in the PRC (if not more so given population concentrations). After all, the CCP brought about dramatic and rapid changes in handling dead bodies and performing death rituals to urban China.

The lack of a monograph on death was also partly a result of methodological constraints. The vast majority of ethnographic works on death have been by anthropologists who went to villages to study something else. Then, when a funeral occurred, they wrote about it as part of their understanding of the larger networks and meanings of social life that the deceased had been embedded in within that community. As such, scholars who studied death tended to focus on rural life and the surviving family members in the contexts of the local community. Clifford Geertz's (1957) analysis of the death of a Javanese boy is one handy example of a similar strategy from beyond China. Purposeful research with the aim of becoming a monograph on death, however, cannot depend on spontaneity. One of the few remaining options then is to focus on death-management institutions, ranging from the religious to the medical. Among these death-related institutional settings, funeral professionals have probably been the least studied.

The larger academic indifference toward funeral professionals was rooted in a variety of different ethnographic and theoretical contexts. For example, in the United States, it was in part because funeral professionals came to be perceived as calculating, rational, profit-seeking individuals who exploited people at people's vulnerable moments ever since the *New York Times* best-selling author and journalist Jessica Mitford published *The American Way of Death* in 1963. This profiteering angle was partly rooted in the removal of death from domestic spaces and its placement in the hands of professional institutions in modern Europe and North America (Aries 1974; Laderman 2003). In Sinophone societies, however, paid funeral professionals have been crucial in folk death rituals at least since late imperial times. Yet they were usually analyzed (if they were examined at all) in terms of their symbolic structural position due to the strong presence of the concept of pollution around death (J. Watson 1988b). Overall, in the majority of work on death cross-culturally, funeral professionals were treated either as the nameless background workers to community social networks or as ritual experts guiding community participants as if the lives of funeral professionals themselves could tell us little about society at large or as if their lives were not worth studying. It has only been very recently that we have started seeing ethnographic works that take funeral professionals as the central focus of research (Dawdy 2021; Suzuki 2002; Toulson 2021). This book is one of the first ethnographies of urban death rituals and the funeral industry in contemporary China.

With these issues in mind, I focus on funeral professionals, their institutions, and the work they did as I trace changes in funeral governance, death rituals, and the Shanghai death industry. I do so based on participant observation fieldwork, extensive interviews, and archival research. In Shanghai, after someone died, the bereaved either contacted state practitioners at funeral parlors directly or hired a funeral broker to do so on their behalf. I started my fieldwork primarily working with state practitioners. I sat with those who worked in the sales department at Huangpu Funeral Parlor. I sat through countless business meetings to observe how they talked to the bereaved and to funeral brokers, how they made funeral arrangements with the bereaved and the brokers, and what they thought about the industry, funeral parlors, and urban death rituals. From the first day, however, my time conducting participant observations in Huangpu did not go smoothly. Even though I eventually figured out the power issues at play in Huangpu and developed a rapport with some state practitioners (especially grassroots workers), I never managed to navigate my way through the interpersonal politics of what was essentially a government bureau fraught with stratified (and sometimes monetized) tensions. Doing fieldwork in China at this time was probably never going to be easy (and I am not sure if being Taiwanese helped or worsened the situation), but doing fieldwork in a state institution was definitely worse.

As such, after seven months, I shifted my base to primarily working with funeral brokers, which represented the second stage of my fieldwork. I spent most of my time with funeral brokers from Longevity. I helped them set up memorial meetings and stood through these memorial meetings with them. Some days I attended three memorial meetings in a row because they needed some extra help. I also often accompanied brokers to the homes of bereaved to arrange funerals and to take the bereaved to crematoria or various private funeral banquet restaurants after memorial meetings. I am grateful that funeral brokers took me in, even though some had initial suspicions about my "real" motivations—they thought that I wanted to open my own funeral agency.

After changing my field base, I still frequently had to work in funeral parlors and interact with state practitioners. By working with funeral brokers, I became someone who worked from a structurally lower position within the funeral industry and closer to the "dark" (morally ambiguous) side of the Shanghai funeral industry. As it turned out, this actually made state practitioners more willing to open up to me. Rather than distancing me from the funeral parlors, this switch helped me understand funeral parlors from a very different perspective and placed me, socially, beyond the internal political struggles of those state institutions that I had been dropped into. On the whole, I learned more about funeral parlors, their internal and external politics, and their positions within the broader Shanghai funeral industry after the switch.

Another part of my fieldwork involved observing religious rituals at temples, in the homes of the deceased, and during burial and worship rituals in cemeteries. These religious rituals were either Buddhist or Daoist salvation ceremonies (most of those I observed were Buddhist). I also conducted interviews with Buddhist monks, Daoist priests, and Protestant pastors. Beyond fieldwork and informal interviews, I also conducted semistructured interviews with scholars, government officials, and industry leaders who were related to funeral governance or the death industry. These interviews included people from private commercial cemeteries (in Shanghai and Hunan), religious organizations (Shanghai), professional funeral associations (Beijing, Shanghai), the Civil Affairs College in Hunan Province, and some funeral parlor directors and brokers from Hunan and Sichuan Provinces.

Finally, I gathered together a historical study of funeral parlors and funeral professionals. I conducted ten life-history interviews and numerous semistructured interviews with funeral professionals. Three of these were with senior state practitioners who joined funeral parlors prior to the Cultural Revolution, in Shanghai and Hunan. I also documented the public-facing exhibition at the Shanghai Funeral Museum (that opened in 2008) and engaged in archival research at the Library of the Chinese Funeral and Interment Profession (CFIPL) in the museum. Most of the materials gathered from the latter were internal governmental documents from before the Cultural Revolution, especially between the 1930s and 1965. Chapter 1 and part of chapter 2 piece together a history of the industry in Shanghai largely based on these primary sources.

Organization of the Book

This book has two parts. The first part discusses the changing governance of the Shanghai funeral industry and its consequences for ideas of self from three perspectives: the Shanghai government, state practitioners, and funeral brokers. Chapter 1 describes how the CCP nationalized all funeral institutions and promoted cremation and secular civil funerals prior to the introduction of the market economy in urban Shanghai. I show how the CCP attempted to diminish religious, affective, and relational ideas in conceptualizing the dead and their relationship to the living in these policies. The goal was to produce political subjects—undifferentiated citizen subjects directly connected with the party-state. I call this logic of governing death the *civil governance of death*.

The next two chapters shift from analyzing funeral policies to funeral professionals. As China started to adopt an authoritarian market economy, the newly introduced logic of governing, *market governance of death*, came to affect state practitioners and funeral brokers very differently. Chapter 2 weaves history and ethnography together. It first describes how the state attempted to transform state funeral practitioners into individualist profit-seeking service providers to marketize state funeral institutions in the 1980s and 1990s. The goal was to create individualized self-managing market subjects. However, by diving into the life stories of funeral practitioners, I found that grassroots state practitioners have become working-class subjects instead. They fought for collective interests when the conditions were right. This chapter is a story of one emerging dissonance between market governance and market subjectivity.

Chapter 3 describes how funeral brokers occupied a fragile middle position in the funeral industry under the market governance of death. Their fragility transformed them into self-managing profit-seeking entrepreneurs despite the state having little intention to cultivate these mediators to be so. If chapter 2 is a story of dissonance, this chapter on funeral brokers is a story of resonance between market governance and market subjectivity despite such resonance being an unintended consequence of governance. Finally, despite being fragile, it was largely brokers who brought about structural change in the industry. The amoral and sometimes outright immoral practices of funeral brokers have successfully revived religious and relational rituals in commemorating the dead in Shanghai.

The second part of the book focuses on death ritual as shaped by governance and its intended and unintended consequences to understand how ritual constructs the self of the bereaved and of dead bodies. Chapter 4 is concerned with how and why state funeral parlors promoted personalized funerals that construct the dead as individuals. By analyzing a particular personalized funeral presented at a national funeral conference to inspire Chinese funeral professionals to learn about the personalization of funerary rites, this chapter shows how a personalized ritual could construct the deceased as a unique individualized self as well as how the state's attempt had, as of yet, failed.

Chapters 5 to 7 then explore contemporary Chinese funerals themselves in detail. Chapter 5 describes the meaning of memorial meetings and how they have been popularized in Shanghai. In tracing the history of memorial meetings and ethnographically delineating memorial meetings today, I show how performing memorial meetings created socialist citizen subjects. However, this ritually constructed socialist self is in dissonance with daily reality, which is marked by many kinds of moral discourses of self and death.

Chapter 6 describes how the majority of contemporary urban Chinese funerals were religious versions of memorial meetings. I explain how the deceased were commemorated as secular socialists, religious, and relational persons in conjunction and how the inclusion of popular religious and relational rituals within memorial meetings created a pluralistic idea of self. This possibility for pluralism began to shrink, however, as people came to emphasize a different way of viewing what rituals are (and should be). I show this process by describing and analyzing a Protestant version of memorial meetings in chapter 7. The concluding chapter, then, summarizes how marketization affected the emergence of these new Chinese ways of death and how the subject formation of funeral professionals, the bereaved, and the dead challenges current research on the assumed relationship between market economy and market subjects in both Sinophone studies and the anthropology of subjectivity.

Part 1

THE FUNERAL INDUSTRY AND THE MAKING OF MARKET SUBJECTS

CIVIL GOVERNANCE

On March 14, 1955, the Shanghai Funeral and Interment Administration (FIA) submitted a document to the Shanghai Civil Affairs Bureau. The FIA asked the Civil Affairs Bureau to approve one of the two propaganda samples included in the document. The FIA would then be able to print out the chosen one as campaign material and disseminate it through local Public Security Offices (police stations) and *lilong* (*linong* in Mandarin, meaning "residential alleyway") associations. The goal was to further reduce the number of dead bodies that were being left on streets. The two samples went as follows:

> [Propaganda Sample 1] Do Not Casually Dump Dead Children's Bodies
> After a person dies, his/her body will soon decompose. The process of decomposition is the best time for spreading germs around. The bodies of those who died from contagious diseases pose an even higher risk. This is even more so in urban areas in which the population is dense. Because some citizens today fail to understand this danger [of dumping bodies] and the proper protocol [of corpse disposal], they casually dump dead children's bodies on the streets. This practice has become an extreme threat to our city, its environmental hygiene, and its appearance. In order to correct such bad habits, we hope that all citizens work together. When such an unfortunate event happens, please call any nearby [funeral] branch or us. We will send a car to pick up the body.

[Propaganda Sample 2] Further Eliminating Body Dumps
Body dumping is a bad habit left over from previous counterrevolutionary governments. Since liberation, the people's government has cared
about the suffering of the people and has tried its best to facilitate the
handling of children's bodies. As a result, body dumps have decreased,
which has had positive effects on urban hygiene and the appearance of
the city. In order to further eliminate body dumps, we hope that all citizens work together to help us. If you encounter such issues, please call
any of our branches or us. (Shanghai Funeral Service Station 1955)

As these striking propaganda samples show, Shanghai was quite literally a city
of dead bodies until well into the mid-1950s. Since Shanghai became a treaty port
in 1843 and as the living flooded into this soon-to-be former fishing town looking
for economic opportunities, dead bodies ended up piling up on its streets. Many of
these bodies were of children since they were the population most vulnerable to
death. In Shanghai at that time, the proper way of taking care of the dead was to
send the deceased back to their hometowns and then bury them underground.
People often had to postpone the deceased's final journey home for a variety of
reasons. During this waiting time, the wealthy might place the dead in coffins and
then store them in coffin depositories or funeral homes. The less wealthy might
store coffins in places that cost less or were free, such as in empty houses or even
by the roadside. The former were what officials called accumulated coffins (*jijiu*)
while the latter were called above-ground coffins (*fucuo*). Finally, some of the dead
were discarded on the streets without coffins due to their loved ones' extreme pov-
erty or their own lack of any social support. Officials called corpses left on streets
exposed bodies (*loushi*). Exposed bodies were the target of elimination in the
above transcribed propaganda samples. These three—accumulated coffins, above-
ground coffins, and exposed bodies—were the core of Shanghai's dead body problem. The eight years of the Sino-Japanese War, mixed with an extended Chinese
civil war, had greatly worsened Shanghai's dead body problem, as food shortages,
dense populations, transportation blockage, and diseases took their toll, as did
violence perpetrated by guns, bullets, soldiers, and foreign occupations.

In Shanghai, dead bodies had been governed by the same authorities that
oversaw health, hygiene, and environmental matters in both the foreign conces-
sions and Chinese-administered areas. After Japan surrendered in 1945, the
Health Bureau of the ROC announced a series of new policies for cleaning up
dead bodies. By the time the CCP took over Shanghai in 1949, the new Health
Bureau of the PRC (largely consisting of the same people from the old bureau
under the ROC), issued their own proclamation, "Implementation Rules for the
Fifth Step of Cleaning Up Accumulated Coffins." This proclamation was the first

official document that the new bureau issued even though the order declared it-self as already on the "fifth" step of cleaning up unburied coffins (Shanghai Funeral and Interment Administration 1987).

While the CCP's Health Bureau and its concern for hygiene mitigated the im-mediate dead body problem after the wars had ended, the party believed that there was no way to solve the dead body problem at its roots without putting into effect a transformation that would fundamentally change people's prefer-ence for body burial. As such, in 1953, the CCP restructured the administrative position of the FIA by moving it from the Health Bureau to the Civil Affairs Bu-reau. Two years after this administrative change, however, in the text accompa-nying the two propaganda samples shown earlier, the FIA acknowledged that despite significant progress with wartime dead, the

> city still faces a serious issue in regard to the matter of exposed bodies. Taking January and February [1955] as an example, there were a total of 5,177 exposed bodies in January. This is an average of 172 bodies per day. Although the number of exposed bodies decreased in February, there were still 3,465 exposed bodies. That's at least 115 bodies per day. Many citizens do not understand the proper handling procedures or the special institutions that collect bodies, so they casually toss children's bodies on the streets. This has seriously influenced the hy-giene and appearance of our city. In order to further eliminate body dumping, we need to increase our propaganda. We propose to print out one sample to disseminate. (Shanghai Funeral Service Station 1955)

The continuation of the dead body problem reminds us that even a revolution does not always indicate a political and governing disjuncture at the ground level. The seemingly complete rupture of political ideology between the ROC and the PRC did not mean a discontinuity of social reality and governance: bodies were still on the streets, people's belief in an afterlife had not changed, and many of the people working in the various city bureaucracies were the same as before. Governing death was (and is) a rather continuous process even if official discourse from one side or another might link a particular policy to a particular period and only to that period. The coexistence of the two propaganda samples reflects these continu-ations despite the transition. The first sample has a negative, reprimanding tone, focused on hygiene, and describes the danger of abandoning dead bodies on the streets largely in terms of disease and public health. The second, while mentioning health, is written with a more optimistic, revolutionary tone, focusing instead on the emerging key word of the CCP, Liberation, and the need for ongoing revolu-tions in the habits of the people away from those of the "counter revolutionary" past to those of the "People" working together for the glory of socialist China.

However, the CCP was building its legitimacy on claims of being a radically different government. It intended to create a feeling of historical disjuncture despite any underlying continuities. "Socialist transformation" was an overwhelming movement that swept, albeit unevenly, all over China after the CCP consolidated its power. Death rituals and the funeral industry were just two of the many subjects for this socialist transformation. This chapter demonstrates that when the FIA shifted from being in the hands of the Health Bureau to the Civil Affairs Bureau, we started to see the emergence of what I call the *civil governance of death*. This new logic of governance aimed to reshape the conceptualization of the dead, relationships between the living and the dead, relationships among the living, and the key sources of authority in dead body management.

This chapter builds on Katherine Verdery's (1999) theoretical insight to explore the politics of dead bodies and Hikaru Suzuki's (2000) ethnographic concern with the practicalities of managing dead bodies. The goal is to reorient our understanding of dead body politics toward the doing aspects of dead body politics. I do so by documenting and analyzing how low-ranking quasi-government officials—state practitioners—interacted with Shanghai people in their quotidian encounters inside funeral parlors as they carried out Funeral and Interment Reforms (*binzang gaige*) (hereafter, Funeral Reform) in the 1950s and 1960s in Shanghai.

There are two key existing frameworks exploring Funeral Reform. The first examines Funeral Reform in the context of larger religious changes in Sinophone societies (Goossaert and Palmer 2011). Initiated during the republican era, Funeral Reform asked people to give up "processions, meat offerings, tablets (central to ancestor worship, and replaced with photographs), banquets, Buddhist and Taoist salvation rituals, and most other aspects of death rituals" (Goossaert and Palmer 2011, 228). Both the KMT and CCP promoted Funeral Reform because they saw these body burial related practices as wasteful, "superstitious" (as they were based on ideas of spirits and afterlife), and "feudalist" (since they maintained Confucian hierarchies). Funeral Reform was "one of the most salient aspects of the modern state's intervention in private religious practice so as to redirect filial piety from the limited circle of kin to the larger nation" (Goossaert and Palmer 2011, 227). While the elimination of rituals centered on dead bodies is indeed an essential part of understanding Funeral Reform, by focusing on religious change it is difficult to avoid overlooking the wider political and economic aspects of Funeral Reform.

The second key framework focuses on the infrastructure of dead body management: those civic associations and private companies that played crucial roles in managing dead bodies. In Christian Henriot's (2016) work, this focus on infrastructure allows him to reconstruct an economic history of dead body management in Shanghai. My analysis complements the religious change approach by showing how wider changes in politics and economics were also integral parts of Funeral Reform as a means for the CCP to exert control over dead bodies and change the rituals associated with them. Meanwhile, my work complements Henriot's comprehensive overview by piecing together and interpreting historical anecdotes and fragments to pull out personal and particular narrative threads about larger-scale changes happening in the governance of death in Shanghai after the establishment of the PRC.

Specifically, I examine three sets of policies crucial for understanding how Funeral Reform was operationalized. The first was to nationalize all funeral institutions. The second was to promote cremation. The third was to transform the (believed) unproductive and wasteful nature of the death industry into literal productivity: referring to the development of agricultural sideline businesses (including pig raising) in Shanghai funeral homes and cemeteries. The degree to which each of these policies was implemented varied: the first policy was implemented the most thoroughly; the second waxed and waned but eventually was implemented fully in Shanghai when the Cultural Revolution began; and the third was specifically executed around the time of the Great Leap Forward (1958–1961).

To foreshadow my analysis, in my discussion of the nationalization of funeral institutions in Shanghai, I show how the Chinese state attempted to eliminate alternative sources of identity that an individual might have (alternative, that is, to the state). This included cosmopolitan, associational, and religious aspects of being a person that had been prevalent in the handling of death and dead bodies at that time. Next, by analyzing how state funeral parlors promoted cremation, I show how quasi civil servants who worked at state funeral parlors tried to alienate individuals (in fact, both the living and the dead) from their kinship networks. This aimed to diminish the significance of relational ideas of self. Finally, by tackling funeral parlors' efforts at developing animal husbandry and agriculture as the Shanghai funeral industry's sideline businesses—turning plots of unused land into useful sites of production—I show how the state sought to transform everyone into (their imagination of) productive workers. Through an analysis of dead body politics in practice, I show how the CCP attempted to create a direct connection between governing death and cultivating citizenship for both the living and the dead at the end of life.

Nationalizing Objects of Identification

After the FIA was transferred to the Civil Affairs Bureau, one of its first new tasks was to nationalize the Shanghai death industry. While nationalization of funeral institutions was a part of changing the mode of production within China's larger socialist transformation, it involved more than a change of property ownership. It was also a part of a deliberate move to break nonparty ties and alternative sources of identity. Funeral institutions at the time had three common types of ownership: (1) foreign capital, (2) Chinese associations and Chinese capital, and (3) religious institutions. These three types of funeral institutions suggest three different directions for identification that were available and important for people in Shanghai at the time—foreign or cosmopolitan influences, associational ties, and religions. They thus provide a basis to think about what it meant to be a person then, both in China in general and in Shanghai in particular. These institutions were intermediate sources of identity between individuals and the state. As such, by nationalizing foreign influences, civic associations, and religious belonging, the nationalization of funeral institutions was meant to eliminate external Others, internal Others, and religious ideas of self that were enacted through dead body management. Herein, I discuss in turn how the FIA nationalized a funeral home owned by foreign capital, one owned by a native place association, and a crematorium owned by a Buddhist temple.

Nationalizing External Others

For most Chinese who did not live through the Shanghai of the 1930s, Wanguo Funeral Home will not ring any bells. However, many probably have heard about the funeral of Ruan Lingyu, then the most famous Chinese silent movie star, who committed suicide in 1935 at the age of twenty-five. Wanguo handled her funeral. Her funeral procession was three miles long, and three women committed suicide during it. The *New York Times* ran a front-page story, calling it "the most spectacular funeral of the century" (Cousins 2004). About a year later, one of the most important contemporary Chinese writers (one of the few claimed by both Communists and republicans alike), Lu Xun, died in Shanghai. Wanguo Funeral Home handled his funeral as well.

The story of Wanguo began when a funeral home in New York sent two people—the boss's son and an employee named R. O. Scott—to Shanghai in 1924. They started the China Casket Company there and named their funeral home the International Funeral Home in English and Wanguo in Chinese, which meant "ten thousand countries." This company originally served only foreigners. Wanguo marked the beginning of the institutionalization and professionalization of the care for dead bodies and of death rituals in China since it was the first modern funeral home. This marked Shanghai as the birthplace of the modern death industry in China.

To be clear, funeral professionals and funeral shops have long been a part of traditional Han Chinese funerals. In Shanghai prior to this, family members of the deceased generally handled funerals at home with help from specialized shops. These shops included both *guanqidian* and *hongbaigang*. The former provided rentals of ritual goods for both weddings and funerals, and the latter literally meant "wedding and funeral (sedan chair or coffin) carrier."[1] In addition to these kinds of shops, many temples also helped people organize funerals (Wang 2007). However, none of these kinds of places provided dead body care like funeral homes since such care was part of a death ritual performed by the family members of the deceased.

When Wanguo's business did not turn out as well as they had hoped, they extended their services to Chinese clients. However, not many Chinese used their services, at least partly because the operation completely followed then-current Euro-American funeral styles. In 1934, the company in New York decided to close the funeral home, and Scott took this chance to buy it from his former employer. After buying Wanguo, he shifted his target customers from foreigners to wealthy Shanghai businesspeople, celebrities, intellectuals, and artists. Through this switch, he also allowed many Chinese ways of operating funerals to intermingle with Western styles in Wanguo. The funeral of the movie star Ruan Lingyu made Wanguo a household name in Shanghai overnight. As Wanguo's business took off, many Chinese imitated it and many funeral homes, such as the China Funeral Home, the Centre Funeral Home, and the Shanghai Funeral Home, among others, suddenly sprang up in Shanghai (Lu 2013).

The Japanese regime that ruled the Chinese Administrative Area during Japan's wartime occupation of Shanghai took over Wanguo and made it state owned. The Chinese Nationalist government returned Wanguo to Scott after the war was over. By 1949, when the CCP took over Shanghai, Scott decided to return to the United States. He asked a Chinese man named Dong Shoupeng to continue to run the funeral home for him. On September 8, 1951, the Health Bureau submitted a request to take over Wanguo. This first request did not receive approval. On May 29, 1953, when the Civil Affairs Bureau wrote to the Health Bureau to discuss their impending receipt of the administrative functions of the FIA, they also revisited the issue of taking over Wanguo from its private foreign owner. In this document, the Civil Affairs Bureau suggested that, considering the excellent quality of the funeral home's equipment and the profit it generated, the Civil Affairs Bureau should continue to run Wanguo after the state takeover (Shanghai Civil Affairs Bureau 1953).

On December 7, 1953, the Shanghai Military Control Committee, the highest administrative authority at that time, ordered the Civil Affairs Bureau to take over Wanguo (Shanghai Civil Affairs Bureau 1954). This order stated that Dong Shoupeng should turn over all property belonging to this funeral home to the state without sabotaging, transferring, or hiding any of it. All workers were to be kept on working as usual. Two days later, the vice chair of the Civil Affairs Bureau had a meeting with Dong Shoupeng to inform him of the takeover. Later that same day, the head of the social unit (the FIA was underneath this unit within the Civil Affairs Bureau hierarchy), Fan Yuling, and five other people accompanied Dong Shoupeng back to Wanguo. As soon as they entered Wanguo, they called a meeting to tell all the employees about the takeover and to reassure them of their job security to assuage their fears about an uncertain future. In two days, the Civil Affairs Bureau had transformed a foreign private-capital-funded funeral home to a Chinese public funeral home.

One of my interviewees who worked at a funeral home in the early 1950s told me that Wanguo was responsible for introducing the American style of embalming to Shanghai. All of Shanghai's funeral homes' embalming fluids at that time were sourced either legitimately or illegitimately from Wanguo. Prior to the CCP takeover, most people who worked at Wanguo were Chinese except the vice manager Lonise Holte, a Jewish man, and two Russian embalmers, L. A. Kasikousky and Kosta Levchenko (Shanghai zangsu shihua wanguo binyiguan, 2003). When Levchenko left for Brazil in 1952, he taught Zhu Miaogen, Scott's private tailor, the embalming technique. After the nationalization of Wanguo, the Civil Affairs Bureau forced Zhu Miaogen to teach embalming techniques to other fellow Chinese funeral professionals.

As a cultural contact zone, Wanguo not only transmitted Euro-American techniques for handling dead bodies but also represented the colonial invasion that had made its existence possible in the first place. Wanguo represented an external Other that simultaneously stood for both cosmopolitan foreignness as well as colonial humiliation in the context of Shanghai. By eventually transferring this foreign cultural capital to the socialist collectivity, the nationalization of Wanguo was a part of the larger expulsion of foreign influences as both sources of cosmopolitan identity and reminders of colonial shame. Within a month of nationalizing Wanguo, the Civil Affairs Bureau changed the bilingual sign outside Wanguo to read (now only in Chinese) "Municipal No. 1 Funeral Home" (*shili diyi binyiguan*) (Shanghai Funeral and Interment Administration 1987). No longer marked as "ten thousand countries," which showed its global lineage, its new name emphasized its administrative status in relation to the beginning of the Communist period and to the municipal government. The only part that reminded the living about the particular history of Wanguo was perhaps the "No. 1" of its new name. After all, it was the first modern funeral home in China.

Nationalizing Internal Others

Whereas foreign capital institutions represented the invasion of the external Other, funeral institutions belonging to Chinese native place associations represented a type of internal Other to the new regime, one that united and divided people into different groups. Marie-Claire Bergère (2009, 84) described something of this in her description of Shanghai in the early twentieth century: "The population was fragmented into communities that had virtually no communication with each other. Shanghai was a Tower of Babel where provincial dialects created as many barriers between the Chinese as a national language did between the Europeans." Native places created community boundaries in an urban Shanghai where practically everyone was an immigrant. Most people viewed urban life as temporary at that time; urban residents thought that they would eventually return to be buried in their native places with their ancestors. This is the sojourning aspect of Chinese migration that carried over from imperial Chinese cities (Golas 1977; Skinner 1977). Alongside this was the traditional idea that a proper death was one in which one can be buried in one's hometown similar to "falling leaves returning to their roots" (*luoye guigen*). Coffin repositories thus were often attached to native place associations or guilds based on native place associations (Sinn 2003).[2] When these associations had enough coffins to fill up a boat, they would be transported together back to their hometown. Native place associations, empowered by this desire to be buried in hometowns, created strong institutional ties that stood in between individuals and the state. They therefore were the prime targets to be redefined and nationalized.

Similar to many other funeral homes prior to nationalization, Xijin Funeral Home was associated with Xijin Association—a native place association established in 1902 for people who came to Shanghai from the cities of Wuxi and Jinkui. As of a few years before Wanguo Funeral Home took off, the Xijin Association's coffin repository already contained several funeral halls and a funeral service department. These funeral halls and the service department were the predecessor of the Xijin Funeral Home. During the forty years of Xijin's operation, their services gradually expanded from providing only for people who came to Shanghai from the same area of origin to providing for-profit services to the general public. In 1954, the Civil Affairs Bureau and the Shanghai branch of the People's Relief Administration of China decided that all forms of native place associations counted as public property because they were established with social funds. As such, they were "public" entities that were improperly held for the private benefit of a small proportion of the public. In this sense, such a change was not framed as a change from private to state ownership. Rather, the nationalization of funeral parlors owned by native place associations was taken as a "return" of public property to the state. In July 1954, the Civil Affairs Bureau formed a four-person team to take over Xijin. Approximately four months later, the bureau officially finalized its takeover on November 13, 1954.

The FIA took over the funeral institutions of native place associations, disbanded them, and redistributed their property and employees elsewhere in the state apparatus. Even as the actual sense of emotional belonging and regional identities these associations emerged from were certainly more resilient, these regionally specific infrastructures of dead body management were a key part in facilitating ongoing identification with migrants' places of origin. Their nationalization was part of a larger process of dismantling the organizational power that such identifications gave these associations. After nationalization, employees were no longer employees of a private organization but were employees of the FIA—a state bureau reporting directly to the party-state. Although many owners stayed in their jobs early on, often working as day-to-day managers, the personnel assigned to the parlors by the FIA were the ones who held the real power in running the business. In March 1955, the Xijin Funeral Home was renamed the Shanghai Municipal Xijin Funeral Home (Shanghai Funeral and Interment Administration 1987). The funeral home's new name emphasized that it belonged to the municipality. Comparing the name change of Wanguo with Xijin, being a part of Xijin was fine as long people recognized that the Chinese socialist state was to be the first and foremost object of identification, ideally speaking.

Nationalizing Religious Others

Religious associations stood for transcendental and alternative sources of power that regulated relationships between humans and the larger cosmological world. Such characteristics gave religious affiliations the potential to compete with the party for group loyalty on the one hand and clearly linked them to "feudalism" and "superstition" on the other. At the same time, however, the CCP's new constitution legally allowed for religions. Although the state's definition of religion referred to institutional religions (subject to the party-state) instead of diffused religion (C. K. Yang 1961), the state's recognition of religion nevertheless created ambiguity for religious funeral institutions. Were they funeral institutions and, therefore, to be governed by the Civil Affairs Bureau, or were they religious institutions and, therefore, to be governed by the Religious Affairs Bureau? This uncertainty allowed interbureau politics to thrive and gave religious funeral institutions a much longer life span than any other funeral institution. Herein, I discuss in depth the story of Haihui Temple (*haihuisi*) to give a sense of the complicated texture of the Chinese state at that time, even in terms of nationalization.

In 1949, the sutra-chanting service business was not going well in the Haihui Temple. To gain additional income, the head monk Huikai got some money from a few fellow Buddhists to start the Haihui Temple Crematorium and register it with the Business Administration Bureau as a company serving the public. It officially started its business in January 1950. Although Haihui Temple and the crematorium were adjacent to each other, their finances, space (including land and houses), and personnel were separate. In addition to the seven monks assigned by Huikan to work there, Haihui Temple Crematorium hired around twenty other workers. Their business, however, was still not very good because most Shanghai people rejected cremation if they could afford body burial (Shanghai Religious Affairs Bureau 1957).

When the nationalization process started in 1956, in response to a Civil Affairs Bureau inquiry, the Shanghai Religious Affairs Bureau said that the Haihui Temple Crematorium was a business in nature and, therefore, should be included in the nationalizing project. As explained by the Religious Affairs Bureau, however, the problems only grew from there though. One document prepared by the Religious Affairs Bureau in 1957 said the following:

> Over the course of the nationalizing process, though, Comrade Zhu Jinfu, who was sent by the FIA to run the crematorium, seriously violated religious policies. He attempted to convert the Grand Hall [of the Haihui Temple itself] into a mourning hall. He also forced monks to stop being monks [*huansu*]. Some monks refused, yet they were told that the minority must obey the majority's decision. At the end of July 1956, the head of the sales department, Gu Jinshen called a meeting with nine monks. Comrade Gu told them in the form of an administrative order that there would be no Buddhist ceremonies [in the crematorium] and all religious activities were to be terminated in the temple. Those monks who did not want to return to the lay life soon came to our bureau [the Religious Affairs Bureau] in the Religious Affairs Department of the Luwan District Government, Shanghai Buddhist Association. Our bureau [the Religious Affairs Bureau] and the religious affairs department soon contacted Comrade Mao, the Division head of the Civil Affairs Bureau, Comrade Shu, the head of the FIA, and the representative Comrade Gu. We told them that they should not touch the Grand Hall. After several attempts at negotiations, although the Grand Hall was intact, they locked it up and suspended its usage. The above series of examples of violations of [the government's] religious policies caused many Buddhists unhappiness and even such that they mistakenly thought that the state had nationalized the Haihui Temple. (Shanghai Religious Affairs Bureau 1957)

Here, the Religious Affairs Bureau stepped in to halt nationalizing actions taken by the Civil Affairs Bureau given their conflict with the government's religious policies—the turf of the Religious Affairs Bureau. The two bureaus eventually sat down to negotiate and finally decided on a two-step plan. The first step was to make Haihui Temple Crematorium a privately run company as a sideline business of the temple. The temple itself would be subordinated to the Buddhist Association of China (which was itself subordinated to the Religious Affairs Bureau). The Civil Affairs Bureau would assist with the cremation business and the education of the workers in the crematorium. If this failed, the second step would be to separate the temple and the crematorium with the Buddhist Association supervising the former and the FIA taking over the latter.

However, the Religious Affairs Bureau later complained that the FIA did not conduct the right thought work to educate the workers in the crematorium and even told those workers who wanted to be nationalized that there was nothing they could do because their supervisor was the Buddhist Association, not the FIA. Thought work is an important technique in governing death—a topic I return to soon. From the Religious Affairs Bureau's perspective, this was a deliberate attempt to work against the existing agreement by suggesting that the problem lay in the workers' location within the Religious Affairs Bureau rather than the Civil Affairs Bureau. The tension between monks and crematorium workers worsened over the next few months given a continuing degeneration in the business of the crematorium—so much so that the workers blamed those monks who refused to return to lay life as the reason that the crematorium was not nationalized and ultimately did not do well. As a result, "five families of the workers, led by Gu Jinshen, moved into the crematorium (despite the fact that they all had their own houses in Shanghai and some even originally lived in the countryside). After they moved in, they even hung women's underwear in front of the Grand Hall [of the temple]. This disturbed and upset the monks very much" (Shanghai Religious Affairs Bureau 1957). Such a provocative act of forcing monks who had taken vows of celibacy to be exposed to women's underwear upset them greatly. The monks then made a formal request to the Religious Affairs Bureau to resolve the situation. When the Religious Affairs Bureau passed along the complaints to the Civil Affairs Bureau, the latter claimed that they did not own the property of the crematorium and could not deal with the issue. The Religious Affairs Bureau finally relented and requested that the Shanghai CCP Committee approve the separation of the temple and the crematorium (Shanghai Religious Affairs Bureau 1957).

The decision at the top levels continued to go back and forth, presumably as other political issues and policies changed. The Shanghai CCP Committee ap-

proved the Civil Affairs Bureau's request, submitted on August 22, 1960, to nationalize the Haihui Temple Crematorium and other religious cemeteries on
December 3, 1960. However, on May 18, 1961, this issue went back to the negotiating table. On June 11, 1961, the Shanghai CCP Committee approved a mo-
tion to suspend the Civil Affairs Bureau's nationalization of religious funeral
institutions. The issue was only finally solved at the end of 1965 on the eve of
the Cultural Revolution. At this time, Haihui Temple's crematorium along with
Shanghai's other religious cemeteries were finally nationalized by the Civil Affairs Bureau for good (Shanghai Funeral and Interment Administration 1987).

This vignette shows the complicated process that was necessary to eliminate
religious institutions in the management of dead bodies. The interbureau competition provided space for monks and crematorium workers to fight (via their
respective vertical backers) for their own interests, despite this occurring in the
midst of a seemingly overwhelming national project of socialist transformation.
While religious ideas of self and religious institutions are two distinct things,
their interrelations mean that tracking changes in the ownership of religious institutions nonetheless provides a window to see how the state tried to eliminate
religious ideas of self. It was much harder for the state to erase the infrastructure that supported religious ideas of self as compared with the state's elimination
of the infrastructure that sustained cosmopolitan and native-place-based ideas of
self. This separation of religion and funerals is also crucial to understanding the
eventual establishment of civil funeral institutions that were devoid of religion
in Shanghai.

Overall, whether we are talking about the nationalization of institutions controlled by foreign capital, native place associations, or religious organizations,
the nationalization of funeral institutions shows the state's desire to reduce horizontal ties among people in favor of vertical ties between the people (a single,
undifferentiated public) and the party-state in death and beyond. While all these
acts might seem to focus purely on changes in ownership, each says something
about how the state attempted to erase alternative possibilities for what being a
Shanghainese or Chinese person might mean. The nationalization of funeral institutions was thus a key part of the social and cultural engineering performed
by the state to atomize both funeral professionals and the bereaved. The ultimate
hope was to create a sole connection and single loyalty straight to the state without any dilution or competition from different possible ideas of self. In retrospect, while it is not hard to recognize the limits of such a state plan in shaping
actual identification, these policies nevertheless reveal what the intended consequences were in nationalizing funeral institutions.

Promoting Cremation: Eliminating Relational Self

In this section, I first provide a brief overview of cremation campaigns under the CCP. I discuss here the specific techniques they used in persuading the bereaved to accept cremation in Shanghai—persuasion, or "doing thought work" (*gao sixiang gongzuo*), to use the vernacular term. This description and analysis of state practitioners' thought work shows how these campaigns promoting cremation served to remove individual ties to extended kin relations at the micro level. Far from a policy implemented from on high by decree, like the nationalization of funeral institutions, these kinds of negotiations between the bereaved and the lowest rank of people within the hierarchy of funeral governance promoted cremation.

In modern Shanghai, cremation was associated with foreigners (Xiang 1992). The Municipal Council of the International Settlement established Jing'an Temple Cemetery in 1927 with a crematorium attached. This crematorium had gas-generated cremators in contrast to Buddhist temples' crematoria. Known as *huashenyao*, traditional Buddhist crematoria generally used a pile of wood to burn bodies (Ebrey 1990). The Jing'an Temple Crematorium was mainly for foreigners and was the first modern crematorium in China.

However, cremation as a choice of body disposal among Han Chinese people had long existed. Although its exact origin is still debated, its increase in popularity was linked to the popularization of Buddhism in China. Despite its popularity in places where Buddhism was popular, such as in Shanghai, imperial Confucian scholar officials objected to the practice and even criminalized cremation at various times (Chen and Chen 2008). This was because they believed that the deceased's body had to remain whole in death for a deceased parent to be a proper ancestor. Body burial rituals were a key location where the grieving family showed their filial piety, worshipped their ancestors, displayed their wealth and status, exchanged gifts in public, and repaired the disruption of normal community life caused by death. These rituals were the sites where relations among the living and between the living and the dead were constructed, articulated, and maintained.

This link between ideas of person and methods of interment can be seen in the FIA's work cleaning up dead bodies as well. For example, in 1953, the FIA declared that dead bodies of adults would be buried individually. The bodies of children and infants, on the other hand, would be cremated collectively at Xi Baoxing Crematorium (Shanghai Civil Affairs Bureau 1953). This difference in body disposal for adults and children shows how the former was recognized as a human subject even if individual identification was not possible. As such, they "deserved" body burials. On the contrary, the latter fell into a nonperson category. Their nonperson status made collective cremation a legitimate mortuary practice. Ways of interment provide a means to analyze how a subject is perceived.

While cremation was associated with a specific religion (Buddhism) and identity (foreigners), both the KMT and CCP promoted cremation because they saw cremation as the modern and secular form of interment. In Shanghai, in addition to these ideological underpinnings, the need to clean up dead bodies also played an important role. Under the CCP, there were at least two big waves of cremation campaigns. The first wave went on and off from 1954 to 1956. The second wave peaked between 1963 and 1965 (Shanghai Funeral and Interment Administration 1960a). The first wave was directly associated with the need to clean up dead bodies. Similar to its republican counterparts, the CCP saw the root of the problem of dead bodies accumulating in streets and warehouses in the customary preference of the bereaved for body burial. However, as explained earlier and in contrast to the KMT's focus solely on cleaning up already accumulated bodies, the CCP was determined to solve the dead body problem at its roots. Promoting cremation was thus the centerpiece of Funeral Reform under the CCP after the administrative authority of the FIA was transferred from the Health Bureau to the Civil Affairs Bureau.

The implementation of these cremation campaigns was more cautious and pragmatic than passionate and revolutionary, however. For example, when responding to the Civil Affairs Bureau's proposal to build more crematoria in Shanghai, the Shanghai Municipal Government said,

> [The Civil Affairs Bureau] should not solely depend on administrative orders to force the masses to accept cremation; they should not decrease the price of cremation so much that it is impossible to maintain crematoria. They also should not blindly and exaggeratedly campaign for cremation so that the current cremation facilities cannot meet the demand. . . . In approving all of the above, we should be well aware of the difficulty and the extended time needed to change the old customs. We should be reasonable, act accordingly and appropriately, we should not rush into things or force things with orders. We should not let private cemeteries freely charge people [whatever they like], yet we should also not allow public cemeteries to just go ahead and increase prices because this will cause the masses to feel upset and therefore lead us into a passive position (reacting rather than leading). (Shanghai Religious Affairs Bureau 1957)

Following this moderate spirit of the campaign, during the first wave of promoting cremation, the FIA set up a crematorium in Longhua Cemetery and another two crematoria, Xinlu and Lianxi, in rural Shanghai in 1954 to enhance the infrastructural aspects of promoting cremations (Shanghai Funeral and Interment Administration 1960a). Meanwhile, the FIA simplified the procedures for cremation and lowered the price of cremation by providing free funeral hall rental, free rentals of Western-style coffins (used during funerals but not to be cremated with the bodies), and lower prices for body transportation, embalming fees, and so on to people who chose cremation in June 1954 (Shanghai Civil Affairs Bureau 1956).

However, year to year cremation rates throughout the 1950s went up and down with no general trend showing substantial changes in Shanghai residents' habits. It was only as particular campaigns were emphasized on the ground that the numbers would see a modest increase; then as soon as the enthusiasm for the campaign waxed, the numbers similarly returned, more or less, to a baseline of around 10–15 percent of adult deaths (Shanghai Funeral and Interment Administration 1960c, 1964). By 1957, the Shanghai government had shifted away from the promotion of cremation toward its work on nationalizing funeral institutions (Xu and Xu 1999). In fact, by National Day (October 1) 1959, many Shanghai citizens had begun to complain of feeling tired of the cremation campaign itself. Some people in the Shanghai Municipal Committee of the CCP even criticized the FIA. Consequently, the "comrades in the FIA felt that they had had cold water thrown on them. The citywide cremation campaign thus stopped" (Shanghai Funeral and Interment Administration n.d, 35–36). These incidents show that even though the promotion of cremation was a central government decision, this political support translated into neither interbureau consensus at the levels above the FIA nor lasting changes in personal preferences among the people at that time.

At the time of my fieldwork, however, the China Funeral Association's official website described 1956 as a "watershed moment for promoting cremation." Marking the year of 1956 was to highlight a famous speech Mao Zedong had given proposing universal cremation. Along with the other 151 functionaries in the Central Work Conference, Mao approved *A Proposal that All Central Leaders Be Cremated after Death*. Mao then made the following exhortation when he signed it: "To chant 'Long life!' is to contradict natural laws. Everyone has to die sooner or later, whether they be killed by germs, crushed by a collapsing house, or blown to smithereens by an atom bomb. Anyway, one way or another everyone ends up dead. After people die, they should not be allowed to occupy any more space. They should be cremated. I will take the lead. We should all be burnt after we die, turned into ashes and used for fertilizer" (Barme 1996). In retrospect, the statement was rather ironic because Mao's cremation proposal came to be recorded on the official website of Mao's mausoleum in Tiananmen Square: the very place at which his body remains unburied, uncremated, and taking up significant space.

Leaving the irony aside, while the first wave of the cremation campaign happened in the context of cleaning up dead bodies, the second wave was situated in the larger context of mass political movements. In 1961, alongside the final year of the Great Leap Forward, the Ministry of Internal Affairs of the central government (the predecessor of the Ministry of Civil Affairs) requested all civil affairs bureaus at local levels to prepare for a new nationwide promotion of Funeral Reform. This new promotion had four specific requirements: (1) promote cremation and establish crematoria starting from the large cities and then moving on to medium and smaller cities, (2) use barren mountains and deserted lands to build public cemeteries to reform body burial, (3) break the old funerary customs and institute frugal funerals, (4) use administrative unit divisions as the basic units to promote unity in Funeral Reform. This new nationwide plan developed into the second wave of cremation campaigning (Shanghai Civil Affairs Bureau 1996).

Starting in July 1963, the Ministry of Internal Affairs of the central government in Beijing issued a nationwide document to reassert the central government's determination to promote cremation. As such, on March 10, 1964, the Shanghai municipal government approved the FIA's proposal to renovate Longhua and Xi Baoxing Crematoria. These two crematoria are the predecessors of today's Longhua and Baoxing Funeral Parlors (Shanghai Civil Affairs Bureau 1996). By the end of 1964, a citywide Transforming Customs and Promoting Cremation Committee (Yifeng yisu, tuixing huozang gongzuo weiyuanhui) was established (Xu and Xu 1999). Several months later, in July 1965, the Internal Affairs Bureau of the central government announced its formal "opinions about Funeral and Interment Reform." These opinions finalized the CCP's effort to, again, promote Funeral Reform in general and cremation in particular at a nationwide level. In March 1966, the Ministry of Internal Affairs even organized a national meeting in Nanhui County of Shanghai City to discuss the technical issues of building crematoria and installing new, cutting-edge gas cremators as part of promoting cremation. The Ministry of Internal Affairs' ambition to promote funeral reform nationwide was an "arrow just being shot from the bow" (Shanghai Civil Affairs Bureau 1996). Prior to everything changing with the start of the Cultural Revolution, then, Shanghai had the highest cremation rate nationwide (and all the way up to the time of my fieldwork, it kept this spot). While I return to the Cultural Revolution by the end of this chapter, for now, we move on to a description of how state practitioners on the ground went about "promoting" cremation during these campaigns. In this analysis of what state practitioners did to promote cremation, I show that promoting cremation was achieved by alienating individual mourners from their kin relations.

Cremation Campaigns in Practice

In the beginning, promoting cremation involved disseminating printed campaign materials throughout hospitals, police stations, alleys, neighborhood communities, charity organizations, and funeral parlors. After 1955, the FIA expanded its propaganda tools to include a slideshow that promoted cremation that was shown in all movie theaters in Shanghai for an entire month, setting up giant billboards in such landmark areas as the Bund and the People's Avenue for the entire year, creating a "walkway" promoting cremation in the downtown district and inviting people to visit crematoria. In 1959, the FIA even campaigned at the temple festivals of Qibao Temple, Longhua Temple, and Jing'an Temple (Shanghai Funeral and Interment Administration 1960a). During the second wave, the Transforming Customs and Promoting Cremation Committee not only campaigned in temple festivals as before but also turned the month of the Tomb Sweeping Festival (April) into a Campaign for Cremation Month in 1964. By this time, six more crematoria had been built in rural Shanghai, and each funeral parlor was to compete against the others to determine the one with the highest cremation rate at the end of the month (J. Fan 2000).

Whereas these methods were important in promoting state-sanctioned ideas about funeral and interment, this did not mean that those people who needed to arrange funerals at that time accepted these ideas. Therefore, within funeral homes, state practitioners were tasked with persuading those bereaved who went to the funeral homes to accept cremation. For example, in 1965, government figures recorded 13,930 bodies being cremated, or 50.46 percent of that year's deaths in Shanghai. Among these, 1,285 households were persuaded to accept cremation by funeral practitioners—a threefold increase from the previous year (Shanghai Funeral and Interment Administration 1987). One of my interlocutors told me that persuading the bereaved to accept cremation was not easy. He said that some bereaved became so upset that they threw shoes at him.

I transcribe below a document I found that describes the process of persuading the bereaved to agree to cremate their loved ones (Xijin Funeral Parlor Funeral Service Team n.d.). State practitioners wrote these documents as work reports to their superiors, who then collected them for use in their annual reports and other documents. While these documents were written for government authorities, they nevertheless give us a unique, partial look at how persuasion was carried out, especially at how state practitioners persuaded the bereaved.

No. 2. Taking different strategies with different people

I: Combining the scatter and gather method

Sun Xinwu. Male. 41 years old. Died from a car accident. In the past we usually did not campaign for cremation in this type of case. The deceased lived with his wife and his parents. When they came to our funeral home to organize the funeral, more than 20 people came (even though these people did not, in general, interact socially). The deceased's wife thought about cremating her husband but was unsure. This possibly open attitude, compared with the objections from the parents-in-law [of the deceased's wife] and other relatives, stood in strong contrast to the other people. The Comrades working in the memorial meeting halls were not discouraged. On the one hand, Comrade Zhu Xifu invited the Public Security Bureau to assist [in their persuasion work]. On the other hand, Comrade Qiu Genchu and other comrades talked to the deceased's wife several times. They analyzed for her the intentions of those relatives and encouraged her to stick to the truth and stand firmly in her position. They told her, "As long as you are willing to stand up, the Party and the masses all support you." Then, funeral practitioners talked to the relatives together to explain the Party's policy and that they [the relatives] had no right to stop other people's progress—they [the relatives] were politically criticized. Among these relatives, one woman was particularly negative. She kept talking to the wife, telling her not to agree. Therefore, we had an individual meeting with [this woman] to more strongly pressure her so that her negative influence would be ineffective. As soon as we found a man among these relatives who seemed to change his mind a little, we took the chance to encourage him to help us by conducting an inside job to turn things toward a good direction. After using this method many times, we succeeded.

II: The Three Catches: Catch the organizer; catch the major conflict; catch the thought

August 30. The deceased was Zhang Aidi. Female. 60 years old. Her husband, Xu Jiji, was a petty capitalist. Unemployed. He planned to buy a coffin [meaning using body burial]. He originally intended to have her funeral at his house. However, because his lilong [neighborhood community] did not allow this [because doing so has a very negative influence], he came to us [a funeral home]. Xu Jiji insisted on transporting her body back home [to her hometown] to be buried. His oldest son also insisted. After Comrade Kong [a funeral practitioner] learned more about the situation, he found out that the father most favored his second son and, therefore, believed most strongly in his [second son's] words. When the second son returned from the army, Comrade Kong focused on persuading him [the second son] to persuade the father. Through memory contrast methods (comparing how the second son treated his mother before and after he joined the army) and other persuasion methods, the father finally changed his attitude. He said, determinedly, "My good son, I will listen to you. I certainly will cremate your mother." His other sons asked him to think seriously again. He said, "I certainly will do this. There is no way that I will change my mind." Finally, [the bereaved family] had one request—to bury her ashes nicely [meaning to still have a nice plot in the cemetery]. We agreed and helped them return the coffin. They were also very grateful.

III: Cooperate Closely with the Lilong

April 1. The deceased Wei Gendi. Female. 31 years old. Her husband was Chen Pingling. Their three children and the mother-in-law of the husband [the deceased's mother], who came from Wuxi, lived together. Because the work unit did "thought work" with the husband in advance, he had already agreed to accept cremation. The main obstacle was the mother-in-law. She said to him, "If you cremate my daughter, I will not take care of these three kids." The husband was worried about this situation because he did not have parents to take care of his kids. Comrade Hua Xingshen actively persuaded the mother-in-law (because they all came from Wuxi and shared a language, which made persuasion easier). Comrade Hua used himself as an example. He said, "When my wife died, she was cremated. According to my understanding of what is happening over in Wuxi, there were many tombs that were dug up. If you buried your daughter's body, I'm afraid that it wouldn't be too long before it too is dug up. Then, you would have to spend more money to deal with it all again. What trouble. I will not lie to you. If you agree to cremate your daughter, it will be good for your son-in-law [his work unit will have a very good impression of him]." After several persuasion attempts and the cooperation of the work unit, the mother-in-law finally changed her mind. The childcare issue was solved.

In this report, the key technique used to persuade people to accept cremation was to identify and isolate the chief mourners in their decision making to ensure that the state formed a direct bond (through state practitioners) with chief mourners. The chief mourner could be the spouse or the children of the deceased. This direct bond was intended to move the chief mourners out from the influence of their extended family. For example, the wife in the first story—the outsider in a patrilineal family yet also "the partner" of the deceased within her nuclear family—was chosen to be the target of persuasion. The state practitioner working in the meeting hall stood at the wife's side when fighting the patrilineal family of the deceased, particularly the parents of the deceased. When this support did not work, the state practitioner, Comrade Zhu Xifu, recruited people from the Public Security Bureau to persuade the patrilineal family of the deceased. Meanwhile, Comrade Qiu Genchu continued to talk to the wife to affirm her position by "analyzing the intentions of those relatives." Although the report did not state these intentions, Qiu Genchu stated that the deceased's patrilineal family refused cremation based on its lineage interests instead of the wife's interests. Thus, the report stated, "As long as you [the wife] are willing to stand up, the Party and the masses all support you." Moreover, one woman who asserted a "bad influence" from the state practitioners' perspective and who was a moral upholder of extended family values was singled out. State practitioners had a separate and individual meeting with this woman to stop her from standing up for traditional values.

We see this strategy of choosing a target and then using a divide-and-conquer technique in the second and third cases as well. In the second story, state practitioners persuaded the husband of the deceased by making the second son of the deceased persuade the father. This placed the father and second son in alliance against the other sons. In the third story, the state practitioners made sure that the widower was strong enough to resist his parents-in-law. This task was easier compared with the first one. After all, the first case was to persuade the wife to stand up against the patrilineal side. The second was to support the husband to push back against the matrilineal side, which, however significant childcare labor was to the husband, nonetheless still existed within a patriarchal society. Although the general campaign might have had an impact on people's perceptions of and initial openness to cremation, cremation was more successfully promoted in the direct interaction between the bereaved and funeral practitioners working on the front lines of the funeral parlors precisely because the decision was always also made alongside influential relatives. What made changes to cremation possible were these negotiations between the bereaved and the lowest rank of people within the hierarchy of funeral governance.

While families as a group have historically had rights and obligations in deciding how funerary rites and body disposal should be performed, we see a shift begin here whereby it now became the specific individuals, backed by the state, who had the right and obligation to make such decisions. All three cases show not only the divide-and-conquer technique but also purposeful acts of atomizing individuals in making funeral decisions. As a result, if the nationalization of funeral institutions was meant to remove associational ties or ties via religious belonging, campaigns promoting cremation aimed to remove individual ties to extended kin relations at the micro level. Promoting cremation was not just about changing the default way of handling corpses. It articulated, too, the state's desire to discourage relational ideas of persons to construct a new kind of subject who was directly tied to the party-state. This was not done by authoritarian decree, however. Rather, since the promotion of cremation relied on persuasion, it gave the bereaved more space to negotiate with the state, and both increases in cremation and this atomization process proceeded at slower rates.

Turning Uselessness to Usefulness: Constructing Productive Socialist Workers

I have excerpted and translated the following quote from a six-page document (Funeral and Interment Administration 1960).[3]

> Why is there such a high death rate for the pigs? Is it because the quality of the pigs was bad [in the first place] or is it because of the quality of our subjective management?[4] I think it is because, subjectively, we did not work hard enough, and this caused the pigs' death even though Qingpu pigs' quality was indeed not good. From our work unit to other work units, we can all observe this. Now, let's examine this more specifically.
>
> 1. Our cleaning job is not good enough. . . . Pigs are similar to humans. If they live in a humid environment, they get sick. Pigs die from being sick.
> 2. Because we did not find the right interval to feed the pigs, they got sick. Even when this happens to humans, such as eating a full meal this time but not enough the next meal, we too will have stomach problems in the long term.
> 3. In general, we were not attentive enough to our pigs. If we pay more attention to them, we will know which pigs are getting sick and can treat them right away. Then, we might be able to keep them alive. However, many people in the work units did not notice that the pigs were ill until they were dying. How can you treat pigs when you do not have enough time to diagnose them?

4. Because we did not protect against epidemics or quarantine pigs, contagion caused significant death.

5. Because we failed to engage in a thorough examination of the pigs when we first bought them, new sick pigs lived with the old, healthy ones. Contagion then brings death.

6. We did not classify the pigs and raise them accordingly. When you put large and small pigs together, the food is not distributed evenly. . . .

7. We have to admit that our bad management was the primary cause of their deaths. Subjectively, we did not work hard enough and lacked experience. The bad quality of the pigs was just one of the objective factors. From now on, we should pay attention to the subjective factors to overcome the objective factors.

Perhaps the first question this report raises is why it even exists. Why in the world would someone in a funeral governing institution need to write a report to explain why pigs died? It turns out, though, that pig raising was intimately related to funeral and interment governance in certain periods in Shanghai. Not only this, but pig raising also represents one of the crucial ideas of funeral governance: the desire to transform something that, to the party, was inherently unproductive into something productive in a literal sense. Master Gao, for instance, worked in a funeral home during the 1950s and 1960s. He told me how, at that time, because he was one of the younger ones in his work unit, they always sent him to collect grass to feed the pigs—this task involved two or more hours of walking with a pushcart filled with grass. I met him early on in my fieldwork. At that time, my Shanghainese was not very good, and Master Gao did not really speak Mandarin. I had to ask him to repeat several times what he had just said in various ways to confirm that he was indeed talking about collecting pig feed as part of his job at a funeral home. I certainly did not expect a funeral professional to need to know how to raise pigs. In the following sections, I show that if the nationalization of funeral institutions and promotion of cremation illustrate the state's attempts to eliminate previous and competing aspects of being a person in favor of a single, direct relationship with the state, developing such sideline industries as the struggles here describes the introduction of new criteria for being a proper citizen—being productive workers. Governing death and funerals was an effort to alchemize uselessness into usefulness.

After the first wave of the cremation campaign and the nationalization project, Shanghai funeral governance's own objectives fell victim to the bigger wave of the Great Leap Forward, which aimed to turn unproductive cemeteries and the death industry's labor force toward productive enterprises through technological innovation. The FIA started its experiments with growing agricultural products in cemeteries at least as early as 1954 (Shanghai Funeral and Interment Administration 1956). Around the time of nationalizing funeral institutions in 1956, the FIA submitted a proposal for how to distribute profits earned from agricultural products planted in these same cemeteries. This proposal described eighty mu (thirteen acres) of land that was being used to grow cotton and thirty mu (five acres) for soybeans among the graves. The FIA even planted potatoes and fava beans in various places to "make sure that no land [in cemeteries] was wasted" (J. Fan 2000). The next year, the FIA divided the management of all twenty-four nationalized cemeteries into four large ones: Lianyi, Longhua, Ji'an, and Dachang (Huang, Liu, and Wang 2005). This consolidation of ownership laid the foundation for funeral governance during the Great Leap Forward.

The Great Leap Forward represented Mao's first attempt to move away from a Soviet-style centrally planned economic model to a mass-based, self-reliance, and self-energizing model of economic development (Schirokauer 1989). Simply put, Mao mobilized the masses to devote themselves to rapid industrialization and modernization. The most famous part of the Great Leap Forward was probably the effort to set up smelting furnaces in every corner of China. People put their cookware and farming tools into backyard furnaces to produce steel (often of questionable quality) for industrial usage. Consequently, the Great Leap Forward brought about massive deforestation and a disastrous famine nationwide between 1959 and 1961—the so-called Three Years of Natural Disasters, as some of my interlocutors (as well as current official discourse) called this period.

For the Shanghai death industry, the FIA asked its employees to grow fruits trees and commercial forests at their respective funeral institutions (including funeral parlors, crematoria, and cemeteries) in 1958. In 1959, they initiated a pig-raising project as a key sideline enterprise for funeral institutions (Huang, Liu, and Wang 2005). To give a sense of this from a different angle, an internal document from 1960 records some examples of the FIA's focus on revolutionizing funeral and interment technologies (Shanghai Funeral and Interment Administration 1960a). This included a list of technological innovations like "the addition of an automatic cutting machine for pig feed, special canvas body bags, electronic embalming machines, [and] pig feed mixtures." While what exactly these innovations entailed (or even if they were real beyond the documents they were listed in) was unclear from the report, my point here is to show how technological innovations in funeral institutions (at least in people's imagination) were, in fact, a jumbled mixture of human- and pig-related technologies.

When the dead were forced to share their resting place with domesticated animals, the two did not necessarily coexist in peace. I encountered many reports in the archive pointing out recurrent problems with high death rates of pigs at the

FIA's properties. For example, one report written in February 1960 recorded a 19 percent death rate for pigs raised in Longhua Cemetery, 0.9 percent in Lianyi Cemetery, 5 percent in Wan'an Cemetery, 12.8 percent at the Xijin Funeral Home, 20 percent at Anle Funeral Home, and 19.4 percent at Guohua Funeral Home. Since they only had 640 pigs and their goal was to have 1,350 pigs by August 1960, the FIA tried hard to meet their quotas (Shanghai Funeral and Interment Administration 1960a). These high death rates were serious business. Several of these reports, like the one quoted above, explored the causes of the pig's deaths through the by then classic Chinese Communist genre of self-criticism.

I suggest that the FIA's workers used these self-criticism reports as allegories. For example, reason two describes how pigs are like humans and how both died from unstable food sources. While these workers might have been novices at pig raising, they certainly knew a great deal about human death. To wonder why so many pigs died is, in a way, also to ascertain why so many fellow human beings were dying. During the latter years of the Great Leap Forward, the fate of the pigs merged with the fate of human beings, and these report writers, while certainly trying to redouble their efforts, did not know what they could do to keep the pigs (and themselves) alive. Given the seemingly odd intermixing on the technological innovation list and the parallels between the pig's fate and the simultaneous disasters of the Great Leap Forward, it is not too far-fetched to argue that pigs were an analogy for humans in this case.

To be clear, I am not saying that there is only one way to read the symbolic meaning of pigs in the history of China or in some sort of abstract "Chinese culture." Pigs are animals and therefore stand, too, as the opposite of humanity. As such, one way to curse people in Chinese is to name someone a pig. For example, when the KMT took over Taiwan from the Japanese, local Taiwanese described this change as "after pigs left, dogs came" (*zhuqu goulai*). By evoking pigs as the opposite of humanity this phrase was meant to describe how both regimes were animal-like, and therefore neither one was all that much better than the other. However, pigs have long occupied a privileged position in Chinese family life, as a source of sideline cash in subsistence economies. They have enjoyed a kind of status in terms of measuring wealth that other domestic animals, such as chickens, just did not have. In Sigrid Schmalzer's (2016) documentation of the development of socialist and scientific agricultural practices in China, she not only shows a deep connection between humans and pigs in Chinese rural villages in general but also, in particular, the privileged position of pigs, as opposed to other animals, in the CCP's imagination and attempts to increase economic development. Pigs were also the default meat in Han Chinese diets. The centrality of pigs in the meat category of Han Chinese meant that eating pork was a crucial identity marker for both Han and Muslim Chinese in distinguishing between one another as well as among different degrees of Muslimness (Gladney 1991). In this sense, pigs play a key role in sustaining humanity rather than just being the opposite of it. Such a close relationship between humans and pigs for Han Chinese, complete with both positive and negative connotations, makes pigs an easy, at-hand analogy for human lives.

In her own early work, Emily Martin Ahern (1973) too suggested that pigs were a key analogy for humans in Han Chinese popular religion because of pigs' close connection to humans. While I am hesitant to go quite as far as Martin to say that pigs symbolize or stand in for the human more generally, I do think that in the context of the Great Leap Forward, when raising pigs was at the center of its movement to increase agricultural productivity, this link is quite strong. Given the parallels between human and pig suffering on top of these analogical connections within funeral professionals' cultural repertoire and the fact that, as funeral professionals, they would have been most clearly aware of the upticks in human death by this point, it is not far-fetched to interpret this striking example of funeral professionals' self-criticism as allegory questioning why humans were themselves dying—a question that was officially explained away as a "natural disaster," therefore needing no further explanation, rather than a human disaster.

The path and fate of humans and animals finally diverged as the Great Leap Forward campaigns faded out in Shanghai's governance of death. On March 12, 1961 (after the Great Leap Forward had just been terminated), the FIA submitted a letter to the Civil Affairs Bureau and cc'd it to the Shanghai Poultry and Eggs Company (PEC). In this letter, the FIA requested that the Civil Affairs Bureau force the PEC to clean up the cemetery that was on loan to it so that it would be clean prior to the April Tomb Sweeping Festival. The FIA also proposed to terminate its lending out of this cemetery to the PEC. The letter says, "According to our most recent investigation, there were 157 tombs that have lost their burial mounds. Among these, five coffins were exposed in the ground. Another 690 burial mounds are now filled with small and large holes." This was in addition to the fact that many tombstones had been moved. The Funeral Office thought that as far as plans were concerned, it was "inappropriate to use cemeteries to raise chickens because when chickens scavenge, they dig into the burial mounds. Chickens scavenge the earth every day and every hour so there is no way to fix the holes in the burial mounds. There are just too many holes" (Funeral and Interment Administration 1962).

When a state funeral practitioner's job turns into the raising of pigs and when the sideline enterprises of funeral institutions are agricultural production and animal husbandry, it goes to show how the funeral industry had been moved toward being a productive site in the most literal sense. This is not to say that other Chinese ideas or funeral and interment practices have nothing to do with increasing the material welfare of the living or fertility as commonly observed in funerals cross-culturally. Quite the opposite, traditional Chinese funeral rituals—such as choosing an auspicious cemetery plot based on feng shui, burying the deceased at a certain time and date, and burning ritual money and other goods for the use of the deceased—all aimed to make the dead happy. This was in return for calling on the dead, as ancestors, to protect and bless the living with material benefits. Moreover, this was not just a practice in imperial China. Marc Moskowitz (2011) shows in his documentary film on the popularization of funeral strippers since the 1980s a deep connection between fertility, production, and death in contemporary Taiwan as well. The difference under CCP rule during the 1950s and 1960s, however, was the deliberate removal of the mediation and supernatural role of the dead. The magical protection and blessings from the dead did not bring wealth. Instead, it was to be the work of the living under the CCP's supervision—quite literally on the fertile backs of the dead—that was to increase productivity and bring wealth to the whole of society. The CCP was turning "feudal" ritual spaces into productive fields for all to see. As such, by turning the useless to usefulness, the state's development of agricultural and animal husbandry sideline industries especially strived to cultivate a particular sort of work ethic for funeral professionals as a new kind of citizen.

The Great Proletarian Cultural Revolution

While the exact starting point of the Cultural Revolution is not uniformly agreed upon, the Cultural Revolution as it related to the Shanghai death industry and funeral governance began with an exact date: August 22, 1966 (J. Fan 2000). On that day, the Red Guards broke into the Shanghai coffin transportation station located at a port. They opened all the coffins, took out their human remains, and burned them right then and there. This incident was not only the end of coffin transportation in Shanghai but also the dramatic turning point between the predominance of body burial and cremation as the primary form of interment. After this incident, the Red Guards started to "break the Four Olds" (*puosijiu*): old customs, old culture, old habits, and old ideas. The "breaking" here was both physical and metaphorical, paralleling the CCP's earlier efforts at nationalization from the start of this chapter. Where the CCP aimed to remove alternative identities by nationalizing related institutions, the Red Guards hoped to change habits by literally destroying the objects associated with the Four Olds. The Red Guards went to cemeteries to destroy tombs, crypts, and gravestones and went to funeral homes to smash coffins and unceremoniously scatter the remains. By 1958, only five funeral homes remained in Shanghai after nationalization: Wanguo, Anle,

Xieqiao, Xijin, and Guohua. They survived nationalization but not the Cultural Revolution, however. All were shut down a few months after the Cultural Revolution campaign began.

In early December, many peasants from Jiangsu and Zhejiang (the two nearby provinces) started a one-month-long raid on Shanghai cemeteries. They dug up tombs, broke tombstones, opened coffins, and abandoned the remains on the grounds.[5] By the end of 1966, at least 400,000 tombs were estimated to have been destroyed (J. Fan 2000). The Communist Party branch of the Shanghai Civil Affairs Bureau submitted a document to the Communist Party of the Shanghai Municipal Committee on December 24, 1966. This report had a vivid description of these raids:

> In recent months, wave after wave of Red Guards and little Revolutionary Vanguards, especially those revolutionists in rural communes, stood up and took revolutionary acts to crush tombstones and tear down tomb mounds. According to partial statistics, excepting only those tombs of veterans, all tombstones have been pushed down or destroyed so far (half of the foreigners' tombstones have also been crushed). Tombs in the Buddhist Cemetery and Zili Cemetery [a Christian cemetery] were all or largely destroyed. Hundreds of the tombs of bloodsuckers and parasites ["enemies of the masses"] were dug out and some foreigners' tombs as well. The rural masses who are close to Dachang, Jiangwan, and Lianyi Cemetery are preparing for an even more comprehensive set of revolutionary acts (Shanghai Civil Affairs Bureau 1966, 1).

As this description indicates, the first targets of destruction were tombs of foreigners, religious practitioners, and class enemies—external and internal Others. This initial period of the Cultural Revolution campaign (also the most radical period), for the first time, left little room for the coexistence of plural ideas of the person in death. This contrasted with the pre–Cultural Revolution era when there was space for different ideas of commemorating the dead to coexist despite various Funeral Reform campaigns aiming to destroy cosmopolitan, religious, and relational bases for parallel conceptualizations of the dead.

Many Shanghai people were not happy with these revolutionary developments. The abovementioned report thus continued:

> However, many tombs have owners [meaning that they belong to someone]. For those owners, . . . most of them have been persuaded and agree. But some people have not strengthened their thoughts. Recently, many family members [of the deceased] have individually or collectively filed complaints to the FIA, asking the party committee to immediately take

action to make related units and rural communes act in organized ways and to pick up the remains and cremate them, among others. Thought work is a difficult task. In any case, we cannot wait a single second to solve the problem of cemeteries. Without immediate and active actions to handle this, it might cause internal conflicts and quarrels among the masses; therefore, leading to unsolvable chaos. . . . As far as destroying all cemeteries, we suggest the Bureau of Urban Planning, Civil Affairs, and the district and county governments [of Shanghai] work together to form a work team to carry out this task in an organized way. At the same time, we should inform the owners of the tombs to do thought work right. We should also have the FIA supervise the tearing down of the tombs.

It was in this way that the party branch of the Shanghai Civil Affairs Bureau attempted to regain its control of dead body governance from the Red Guards by suggesting to do thought work with the bereaved, to close off all cemeteries, and to supervise how the Red Guards would tear down the tombs if needed. On July 1, 1967, however, the Shanghai Civil Affairs Bureau handed all cemeteries over to the Revolutionary Committee of the Municipality of Shanghai—the highest governing authority of Shanghai during the Cultural Revolution.[6] After shutting down all funeral homes and cemeteries by the end of 1966, only two crematoria, Longhua and Baoxing, were left to handle all of Shanghai's deaths. Almost overnight, cremation became the only possible way to inter dead bodies. The implications of this were not just about the form of interment, however. Once the Red Guards took full control of these two crematoria, no traditional death rituals were allowed there either. As such, people needed to figure out a new form of commemoration. I discuss the formation of the new commemoration rites that emerged from this in chapter 5.

It was in this way, then, that the Cultural Revolution realized universal cremation—the goal of Funeral Reform. However, the Cultural Revolution also terminated the institutional life of both the Shanghai Civil Affairs Bureau and the FIA. The Red Guard shut down these bureaus because they saw these organizations as part of the Four Olds due to their involvement in governing death rituals. After these institutions were officially abolished, authority over funeral governance was then transferred at the national level to the Ministry of Finance in 1972 with little actual administrative work enabled on the ground. In other words, Shanghai had been a pioneer of Funeral Reform that, thanks to the Cultural Revolution, came to successfully exemplify the goal of funeral governance without having a funeral governing institution to carry out any Funeral Reform policies. The irony is clear here—the FIA's lifelong goal of funeral governance was achieved only through the death of itself and the very institutions it had created.

Conclusions: The Making of Political Subjects

Throughout this chapter, I have delineated the birth of the civil governance of death through an examination of how funeral governance in Shanghai was carried out, based on the mundane work of state funeral professionals. After the CCP took over China, funeral governance was first occupied with the task of nationalizing funeral institutions. The goal of nationalization went well beyond shifts in economic wealth or power, this despite the acts themselves appearing to focus purely on changes in ownership, right down to the inventory lists recorded when each parlor was nationalized. While the "objects" to be nationalized were foreign capital, Chinese capital, and religious-owned organizations, each of these says something about how the state went about erasing possibilities for being a Shanghainese or Chinese person alternative to the CCP's own vision of proper citizen subjects. The destruction of horizontal ties and the relationships between a person and private companies, native place associations, and their religious affiliations was the first step in constructing socialist citizenship.

The state's effort to diminish alternate sources of identification was also carried out by its cremation campaigns at the level of kin groups. While persuading the chief mourners to accept cremation, funeral practitioners worked to alienate specific individuals from their larger kinship- based social networks. The governing techniques used in deploying the civil governance of death were meant to eliminate previously strong intersubjective (such as links to ancestors as well as to family and lineage members) and associational (such as native place or cosmopolitan/colonial) ties within the world of the living and between the living and the dead. With the removal of various funeral institutions that built on differentiated group identities, the state's intention was to leave individuals with only the choice of linking themselves and their dead more directly to the state without any intermediation. As such, individuals were being atomized even as they were "liberated" in the CCP's venture into creating political subjects.

Finally, where nationalization and cremation promotion illustrate the CCP's endeavors in creating political subjects by eradicating institutional ties and intersubjective ties, the discussion of the radical socialist period explains how the CCP also attempted to manufacture a new kind of citizen. That is, the Great Leap Forward era enacted changes to funeral homes and cemeteries attempting to transform them from places of ritual, remembrance, and grief to sites of production where agricultural products flourished, pigs thrived, and, eventually, socialist citizenship would be realized and reaffirmed. As the centrality of the dead there receded, new socialist workers were produced and advanced. Instead of being an end, death was to become a productive site where New China's new citizens were grown.

These funeral governing policies were a key part of the larger social and cultural engineering performed by the state to reduce horizontal ties among people in favor of vertical ties between the people (a single, undifferentiated public) and the party-state. By managing the boundaries between civic and kin groups within China and between humans and spirits, the civil governance of death aimed to create political subjects who were directly linked to the socialist state. This new kind of citizen-subject was supposed to articulate a collectively shared singular socialist citizenship. Midlevel formal institutions and practitioners—such as funeral homes, their frontline practitioners, and the FIA—played key roles in carrying out such dream works of governance.

My analysis suggests, however, that prior to the Cultural Revolution, there was a degree of ambiguous space that allowed different ideas of a person to continue to coexist even at the level of state discourse. Such space was particularly obvious regarding religious ideas of self. As such, although both funerals as rituals and the funeral industry itself were fundamentally changed, as with a "revolution" where, on the ground, one era and the next tend not to be separated by clear and distinct lines but, rather, bleed across those boundaries from one into the other, the boundary between the state's efforts to construct citizenship and the actual discourse and attempts to create such projects was porous and contingent. One of the many factors for such dissonant relations between state discourse (and social structure) and human subjects was based on the fact that the state itself was heterogeneous and the abstract concept of the state was composed by actual living people who were situated in different chains of command. Religious institutions thus could call on the state's own religious affairs bureaucracy, and cremation policies from above had to be enacted within real family politics by actual practitioners on the ground. Having said this, however, the shift of the FIA from the Health Bureau to the Civil Affairs Bureau did indeed mark a boundary whereby, going forward, the primary focus of funeral reform was on creating citizen-subjects and not simply dealing with the dead. This logic of civil governance and its intended construction of socialist citizenship would later be contested by a second competing logic of governing death and making persons. In the next chapter, I explore the emergence of a form of market governance as China moved from a planned to a market economy.

MARKET GOVERNANCE

The dead cannot afford to die. The living cannot afford to live.

(A popular saying in contemporary China)

On September 9, 1976, Mao Zedong died. Two years later, Deng Xiaoping won the post-Mao power struggle to lead the party and nation. Deng Xiaoping's eventual consolidation of power meant that within only a few short years after Mao, China entered a new era of what Deng called "socialism with Chinese characteristics," or a socialist market economy. These economic reforms would again radically transform China over the next three decades, including in matters relating to death. I call the process of introducing market economic principles in governing death the *market governance of death*. Through both archival and interview data, this chapter explores what the market governance of death was, how it was operationalized, and what the intended and unintended consequences of it were.

I depict here an unfamiliar example—the Shanghai funeral industry—of what at least starts off looking like a familiar narrative of privatization in China since the 1980s. Simply speaking, the goal of the market governance of death was to transform funeral parlors into profit-making businesses for the state (and for the Shanghai Civil Affairs Bureau, to be exact). To achieve such a goal, state funeral practitioners had to be cultivated in specific ways so that they would care about their personal bonuses, parlors' profits, and customer satisfaction. In other words, state practitioners had to change from their roles as government officials solely responsible for disciplining the bereaved and dead bodies to their emergence as service providers who were self-motivated and risk-taking entrepreneurs—some of the key characteristics of market subjects that are often assumed to be direct results of market governance.

However, in-depth fieldwork among state funeral practitioners three decades after the introduction of the market governance of death in Shanghai revealed a more complex picture of this seemingly familiar narrative of privatization in China. The next part of this chapter thus explains the unexpected consequences that emerged from the creation of the market governance of death. Specifically, out of the contradictions between the new market governance and still present civil governance and between state funeral practitioners' roles as officials and service providers within a state monopoly, I found that some grassroots state funeral practitioners have turned into working-class subjects whose collective actions were driven by both socialist moralities of equality and capitalist logics of market competition. When the conditions were right, these people even took collective action to fight against the interests of the state. The state's attempt at turning state funeral practitioners into entrepreneurs was only partially realized.

Finally, although my ethnographic findings question whether the institution of a market economy in contemporary China was a sufficient condition for the rise of market subjects, I am by no means saying that the state somehow failed to marketize funeral parlors. The Shanghai funeral industry changed dramatically after two decades of implementing market economic principles in governing death. In showing what it became, I also show how governing death via funeral parlors in contemporary China morphed from being a state-led moral project of remaking persons (vis-à-vis regulating people's moral obligations to tend to dead bodies) to being an economic project geared toward generating profit.

The Market Governance of Death

In Shanghai, the market governance of death included restructuring funeral parlors, transforming state funeral practitioners, and reshaping the relationship between government bureaus and the death industry. Before these could happen, though, the bureau that governed funerals had to first be resurrected. As described in the last chapter, one of the key goals in Funeral Reform, universal cremation, was realized in Shanghai as the very governing bureau that promoted these policies ceased to exist at the beginning of the Cultural Revolution. The FIA was first reinstituted on paper as a subunit of the Service Department of the Shanghai Civil Affairs Bureau in 1976. Then, in 1978, a new FIA was finally reestablished with twenty personnel in Shanghai. The mandate of this newly resurrected FIA, however, was again revoked after only a year of life in 1979. This time, the FIA became a part of the Third Unit of the Social Welfare Department of the Civil Affairs Bureau—a two-level decline into obscurity, institutionally speaking. The FIA finally regained its institutional life for good in October 1981 (J. Fan 2000).

The institutional life of the FIA, oscillating between life and effective death, points to the uncertainties that dominated funeral governance in the immediate post–Cultural Revolution period. The key issue here was that officials were trying to decide whether civil governance was to remain the only mode of governing death under the newly established socialist market economy. The debate over whether or not Funeral Reform was a product of extreme leftism (and therefore should be suspended) was finally settled in December 1981 at the First National Work Conference on Funeral and Interment. The Ministry of Civil Affairs affirmed that the future direction of funeral governance was to continue to promote Funeral Reform, including promoting cremation, modifying body burial practices, eradicating old funerary customs, and promoting frugal funerals (State Council of the People's Republic of China 1982).

In this spirit, in February 1982, the Ministry of Civil Affairs promulgated a document asking all local governments to improve the problem of decreasing cremation rates and the resurgence of old funeral customs—a nationwide phenomenon after the Cultural Revolution ended. To echo the Ministry of Civil Affairs' call, the Shanghai FIA held its own First Shanghai Work Conference on Funeral and Interment two months later. However, since cremation was already well established in Shanghai, the Shanghai FIA's primary task was "to break the old funeral customs, to handle funerals in an economic way, and to promote new social behaviors" (Ministry of Civil Affairs 1982, 1). The goal of the civil governance of death in Shanghai at that time was to fight the revival of funerary practices and associated religious and folk death rituals (Shanghai Funeral and Interment Administration 1984a).

To be clear, when I use the word *revival* in describing these practices, I am not saying that folk and religious funeral customs had completely disappeared in Shanghai. Except during the peak of the Cultural Revolution campaign, people continued to carry out certain preexisting funerary practices in their homes. In fact, by the mid-1970s, before the introduction of the market economy, Shanghai people even started to hold funeral banquets again—something that usually happened outside of their homes. Thus, my usage of revival does not imply discontinuity and disruption. Rather, it refers to a shift back toward public performance and an increase in such performances. Meanwhile, even though I describe these practices as having been revived, I also do not mean that they all were direct copies of past actions. Rather, I consider ongoing improvisation and invention as inherent parts of repetition and growth.

On July 12, 1982, the FIA made a public announcement geared against these increasing public performances to reaffirm that there should be no more "superstitious activities" in crematoria. In October 1982, Shanghai crematoria in both urban and rural areas conducted a (new) "changing customs" (*yifeng yisu*) campaign that did not appear too different from campaigns in the 1950s and early 1960s. On October 5, 1982, the Civil Affairs Bureau further promulgated its "Provisional Measures on the Management of Crematoria of Shanghai." This seemingly ordinary policy was in fact the first funeral policy in Shanghai since Mao's death. All these events indicated that civil governance would continue to be an important orientation of funeral governance in the future.

However, this orientation toward civil governance was not the only orientation for governing death in this new era. In the spirit of the nascent market economy, a new competing orientation for funeral governance emerged. At the end of 1983, the Ministry of Civil Affairs organized a national work conference in Weifang City, Shandong Province (B. Fan 1989). This conference had two goals. The first task was to make sure that all local FIAs understood the need to continue to implement Funeral Reform (Shanghai Funeral and Interment Administration 1984a). The second task of this conference, however, was to make all local FIAs exchange their experiences with experiments in various "contract responsibility systems" in funeral and interment management. The contract responsibility system in funeral parlors, simply speaking, was a way to tie salaries to new measures of merit. I explain this further when I later describe changes that happened to state practitioners. In any case, the first goal of the conference pointed to the continuity of the civil governance of death while the second established the foundation for this new market governance of death.

Despite an intention to implement market governance of death, no one really knew how marketization should work in China at that time, either in general or in the death industry in particular. Deng Xiaoping once said that developing China's market economy was a matter of "crossing the river by feeling your way from rock to rock" (Kipnis 2008). The Weifang conference was essentially a place where state funeral professionals from various places went to share their experiences of initial ways of "feeling for rocks." One crucial conclusion from this Weifang conference was that all crematoria should soon adopt the contract responsibility system. All local FIAs then went home with basic guidelines for how to operationalize the contract responsibility system. During the next year, in September 1984, the Shanghai FIA held a Second Shanghai Work Conference on Funeral and Interment. This conference officially approved the implementation of the contract responsibility system in all Shanghai crematoria (including both city and district crematoria) and therefore marked an official beginning of the market governance of death in Shanghai.

As a part of embracing the spirit of a market economy, the FIA announced the renaming of Longhua and Baoxing Crematoria as Longhua and Baoxing

Funeral Parlors on October 6, 1984. Officials believed that such renaming might mitigate people's fears and generally negative impressions of crematoria and cremation (Shanghai Funeral and Interment Administration 1984b). Officials also hoped that this name change would show the public that they, as governing institutions, were sensible and capable of "humanistic" thinking. Since then, on all official documents, funeral governance changed from being about governing the "cremation industry" (*huozang shiye*) to being about governing the "funeral and interment industry" (*binzang shiye*) in Shanghai. The return of the word *bin* in self-descriptions turned out to also be a prelude for the return, reinvention, and reemphasis of religious and relational rituals in commemorating the dead—something that had been drastically simplified during the Cultural Revolution.

On November 5, 1984, the Shanghai Civil Affairs Bureau approved the renaming of the FIA's full name from the Shanghai Funeral and Interment Administration to the Funeral and Interment Business Administration (FIBA) (J. Fan 2000). This one additional word, *Business*, stood for the Shanghai government's effort to define funeral governance not only in terms of civil administration but also as business administration. From this moment on, funeral governance officially shifted from being only a matter of civil governance to having a dual orientation toward both civil and market governance. This name change was more than rhetorical—it reflected how state discourse on funeral governance changed with the introduction of a market economy. To operationalize such changes, the Shanghai state had to transform both funeral parlors and those who worked in funeral parlors so that they were suitable for carrying out market economic operations of death. In the following sections, I explain how the state operationalized this market economy shift, in turn, at institutional and personal levels.

Marketization of Funeral Parlors

To transform funeral parlors from being a part of the state apparatus to being a part of a profit-making business, the government needed to first identify what the key is to generating profits according to local conditions. In China, the cremation rate has been directly tied to the profitability of funeral parlors regardless of whether a market economy was involved or not. This was because funeral parlors were the direct products of promoting cremation. For locations with low cremation rates, funeral parlors were an outright financial drain on local governments. As such, two years prior to the decision to marketize all funeral parlors in China, in 1981, 85 percent of crematoria operated at a loss due to low cremation rates (Ministry of Civil Affairs 1989). However, given the high acceptance rate of cremation even before the introduction of market economic principles, Longhua and Baoxing Crematoria together already earned RMB 1,300,000 (USD 498,084) for the Shanghai Civil Affairs Bureau in 1983 (Shanghai Funeral and Interment Administration 1984a).[1] In contrast, even about a year after adopting the contract responsibility system, only 23 percent of crematoria made any profit in China in 1984.[2] The causation between cremation rates and profits meant that for many funeral parlors, one of the easiest ways to increase profits was to promote cremation. However, this also meant that such methods would not work for Shanghai funeral parlors since their cremation rates were already high. They thus focused on expanding available services and product sales instead.

As mentioned, there were only two funeral parlors in downtown Shanghai: Longhua and Baoxing. Baoxing had been initially established by the Japanese for handling Japanese deaths. It was located in the more working-class parts of downtown Shanghai. Longhua was located in the more middle- and upper-class areas. In the 1990s, the FIA built a third funeral parlor, Yishan. Yishan was located just outside downtown Shanghai. Yishan was established to provide cremation services for Longhua and Baoxing (in addition to its nearby areas) after new urban planning policies prohibited cremation facilities in downtown Shanghai itself. By the time of my own fieldwork, Longhua, Baoxing, and Yishan were still the only three city funeral parlors in downtown Shanghai. They together served about 12 million or so residents—about half of the total Shanghai population. The monopoly they thus held on death turned out to be crucial for state practitioners to resist state-initiated plans to reshape them into market subjects—a point I return to soon.

Among these three, Longhua was the most well-known one. From high-level cadres to humble factory workers, from popular cultural celebrities to ordinary people, from the CEOs of international companies to owners of mom-and-pop recycling companies, and from serving and retired members of the People's Liberation Army (PLA) to former "counterrevolutionaries," many Shanghai residents made their last stop in Longhua. Next, I use Longhua as a case study to portray various steps the FIA took in their parlors to expand services and products.

From Longhua Crematorium to Longhua Funeral Parlor

Despite its fancy look today, Longhua started as just a set of crude cremators within Longhua Cemetery. These cremators were built in 1952 to cremate the abandoned—dead children, infants, and the homeless. In 1954, the FIA approved the official establishment of the Longhua Crematorium (J. Fan 2000). Four years later, the FIA renovated Longhua. However, the renovated crematorium was by no means grand. By 1958, Longhua Crematorium still only had two coal-run cremators, three body transportation cars, and one meeting hall (Shanghai Funeral and Interment Administration 1978). In 1965, the FIA rebuilt Longhua Crematorium during the second wave of cremation promotion.[3] On May 1, 1966, Longhua Crematorium gained its independence from Longhua Cemetery.[4] With all cemeteries and funeral homes closed at the end of 1966 when the Cultural Revolution began, Longhua began to turn a profit by 1969 as one of the only two funeral facilities remaining in Shanghai. In 1975, Longhua made an annual profit of RMB 161,780 (USD 87,448).[5] By 1977, profits were up to RMB 227,080 (USD 122,745).[6] Longhua had gone from being a drain on state resources to a by no means insignificant source of funding for the Shanghai Civil Affairs Bureau well before China's change from the planned economy to the market economy.

With cremation as the main profit-making factor, the key income revenues for Longhua were associated with the infrastructure of crematoria and cremation-related fixed costs. As table 2.1 indicates, in 1978, meeting hall rentals were its highest profit-generating item. The other profitable items included cremation fees, rent for space in their cremains depository, sales of funerary merchandise (in particular, referring to the cremains casket that people used to store cremated remains), and body transportation (e.g., a hearse) (Shanghai Funeral and Interment Administration 1985).[7] It is with this revenue structure in mind that we might understand why one of the first steps taken to generate even more profit was to sell more merchandise and expand services—these were areas where there was still lots of space for growth.

Officials therefore expanded Longhua's Business Department and added a new department, the Merchandise Management Department. By 1985, the Business Department contained six subunits: sales, body transportation, body cosmetics, cremator, meeting hall, and cremains depository. People in this department provided labor needed for funerals. The newly established Merchandise Management Department had three subunits: the business administration, funeral merchandise services, and wreath units. This department provided commodities needed for funerals. In addition to continuing to sell cremains caskets, this newly added Merchandise Management Department also sold mourning dress (shouyi, lit. "longevity garments"), wreaths (both rentals and sales), food and drink, small decorative items, and other miscellaneous funerary goods that had not been sold previously (Shanghai Funeral and Interment Administration 1985).

However, an institutional reorganization by itself is not sufficient to operationalize market governance because, in the end, it is people who must carry out marketization in practice. Prior to the above-described administrative restructuring, Longhua only had three departments: a Political Work Department (the

TABLE 2.1 Longhua Crematorium profit distribution in 1978

CHARGE ITEMS	PROFITS (RMB)	PRICES[1] (RMB)	NOTES
Meeting hall rentals	96,000 (USD 39,024)[2]	Large hall 40/half day Medium hall 10/1.5 hours Small hall 3/1.5 hours	
Cremation[3]	90,000 (USD 36,585)	10 per body	Low-income households exempted
Cremains depositary	84,000 (USD 34,146)	10, 7, or 4 per body every three years	The price depended on the height of the spot—the higher, the better and the more expensive
Merchandise handling fees	35,000 (USD 14,227)	10% of merchandise purchased	Items included cremains caskets, black armbands, and yellow flowers (a hair accessory for women mourners to wear on their head)
Body transportation	20,000 (USD 8,130)	3 per body per 5 km	After 5 km, every 1 km was charged at 0.30
Body preservation	Not available	3 per body for the first day 2 per body per day after the second day	Bodies were preserved in crematorium refrigerators

[1] The exchange rate was 1:2.46 (USD to RMB).

[2] The profit from cremation fees was calculated after deducting a maintenance fee for the cremators and an RMB 4 per body gas fee. The profit generated through the body transportation fee was calculated after deducting hearse maintenance fees and an average RMB 0.85 per body fuel charge.

[3] A total of ten subunits existed under these departments, including the business, body transportation, body cosmetics, cremator, meeting hall, cremains depositary, maintenance, gardening, security and miscellaneous affairs, and cafeteria (for employees) units (Shanghai Funeral and Interment Administration 1985).

predecessor of the Human Resources Department in all state institutions), a Funeral Service Department, and a General Affairs Department.[8] Each department was led by a chief and a vice chief (*guzhang*), and each subunit had its own head and vice head as well. Although the three preexisting departments still had a chief and a vice chief after the administrative restructuring, the newly added Merchandise Management Department had a manager and vice manager. These personnel title changes were meant to reinforce the need to reconceptualize state workers from being "chiefs" in the administrative sense to being "managers" in a business sense. As such, in the following sections, I explain the other side of the marketization of funeral parlors—the state's attempt to transform state practitioners from being administrators to entrepreneurs.

The Making of Market Subjects

At the beginning of marketization, the FIA identified one of the fundamental flaws of funeral parlors as the fact that their employees were "eating from the public pot" (*chidaguofan*)—meaning everyone got paid more or less the same disregarding individual performance. To resolve this issue, officials designed a variety of new ways to transform state practitioners at the leadership level and then at the level of the rest of the employees. At the leadership level, the FIA ordered Longhua (and all other funeral parlors) to adopt a Chief Directors' Contract Responsibility Based System (*guanzhang chengbaozhi*) in 1985 (Shanghai Funeral and Interment Administration 1985).[9] This system required the chief directors of funeral parlors to take individual responsibility for their parlor's costs and benefits in the form of their salaries. The system divided the director's salary into two parts: a basic salary and a bonus calculated on a yearly basis. This system eventually evolved into an annual salary system (*nianxinzhi*)—a common employment scheme among chief directors and other senior managers in large state enterprises or international companies in China beyond the funeral industry.

In contrast to the previous salary system that basically followed a fixed scale, did not make such a distinction, and did not reward people based on revenue outcomes, the new system tied the director's salary to the effectiveness of management. The director's bonus was determined by the parlor's revenue. As such, this new salary system encouraged funeral directors to take risks by disproportionally rewarding their risk-taking behavior (as long as it was successful). Finally, the introduction of an annual salary system also created a dramatic economic inequality between leaders and employees working in these funeral institutions where there hadn't been before. I return to the point of the widening income gaps within funeral parlors shortly.

Creating responsible, motivated, and risk-taking chief directors, however, was not enough to transform funeral parlors because state funeral practitioners on the ground carried out the parlor's day-to-day business. Taking Longhua Funeral Parlor in 1985 as an example, it had a total of 183 employees (Shanghai Funeral and Interment Administration 1985).[10] The Shanghai government needed to make all 182 nondirector employees work in self-motivated and self-responsible ways and to learn to willingly take risks. As a result, the Financial Bureau and Civil Affairs Bureau initiated a series of changes targeting frontline workers in 1985. The most important aspect of these changes was to modify funeral parlors' universal bonus distribution into one that rewarded individuals and groups of funeral practitioners based on a commission system. This commission system involved several moving parts. First, the Civil Affairs Bureau removed the previous maximum limit on bonuses. Second, it assigned different basic quotas to different funeral parlors and then instituted different ratios for calculating commissions over the quotas. The differentiation existed because urban city parlors and rural district parlors were dealing with different kinds of customers and different cremation rates. As long as funeral practitioners met the basic quota assigned to their parlors, they received a bonus (Shanghai Funeral and Interment Administration 1984b). These policies worked well in terms of increasing the profits of the funeral parlors. Within a year of adopting the contract responsibility system, by 1986, Longhua employees as a group were making a total of RMB 760,000 (USD 220,289) in annual profit (Shanghai Funeral and Interment Administration 1985).[11]

This process illustrates the way that Chinese officials clearly attempted to turn state practitioners into market subjects. The most important spirit of the contract responsibility system was to provide personal financial incentives to both leaders and workers. Instead of "serving the people," they now worked for themselves and were encouraged to take personal risks. The more quantified work that a person accomplished, the higher his or her earned income. Moreover, the more risk that leaders and workers took, the more they would likely earn. Leaders were rewarded on a similar basis, except that the potential bonus available was set at a higher level to reflect the perceived greater risks at the managerial level. Employees' income became the result of sales outcomes and individual risk-taking. As a result, state practitioners were no longer treated merely as government officials with both the right and the obligation to work and who received more or less equal pay despite differences in administrative rankings. Rather, they were envisioned to be market subjects whose values hinged on differences in efficiency and differences in the degree of risk they took on.

So far this is a familiar narrative—one told by many ordinary people and scholars. However, we still need to ask whether these state funeral practitioners became market subjects in resonance with the logic of market governance. If not, then what did they become?

The Formation of Class-Based Subjectivity under Market Governance

Rather than the formation of market subjects as the state had planned, my fieldwork, conducted three decades after the initial implementation of the market governance of death, found the formation of working-class consciousness among grassroots state practitioners. This working-class consciousness was largely built on income inequality created by the previously described salary scheme. Moreover, their sense of being working class was not a replica of "class labels" implemented prior to the introduction of market economy. Rather, this working-class subjectivity was developed from the bottom up and was articulated through two different sets of ideas. The first was a cultural idea of class distinction that separates manual labors from intellectual labors. The second was the market logics of competition. When the conditions were right, this working-class subjectivity could turn into collective action for class interests. Such an unintended consequence in implementing the market governance of death was possible because these state practitioners worked for quasi-state institutions within a state monopoly. In the following sections, I unpack these findings with the lived experiences of state practitioners.

Ma Haiming was a senior funeral practitioner who was close to retirement age when I met him. I asked him what the parlor was like when he first started working there in the 1970s. Instead of giving me an answer about the past, though, he chose to tell me about the present:

> "Funeral parlors have changed so much since I started in the late 1970s," Haiming began. "Today, many leaders in funeral parlors are 'tuochan'— not just leaders but also other people, such as accountants and cashiers. All they do is sit in their offices and have meetings. They do not produce [shengchan], but they get a salary—a large salary. In fact, a higher salary than we who produce—"
>
> "Tuochan? What is that?" I interrupted. "How do you write those two characters?" I was unsure if I was missing something here because of his strong Shanghainese accent or some other issue, but I could not understand what he meant.
>
> "Oh, of course, you do not know this," Haiming continued. "You are from Taiwan. I think that tuochan is a [Chinese] Communist Party

phrase. *Tuo* is the *tuo* for *tuoyifu* [meaning 'taking off clothes'], and *chan* is the *chan* from *shengchan* [production]. If someone is tuochan, then it means that they have left production."

I had never heard of *tuochan* being used in this way. In Taiwan, *tuochan* describes the act of selling property to avoid liability (more along the lines of "shedding property"). Although the word still uses the same *chan* character as in "production," in this meaning, the *chan* takes its meaning more from *caichan* (property).[12] Unable to elicit any more information about tuochan other than what Haiming had just provided, I carried out the rest of the interview. Later, I asked a Chinese scholar about the term. He said that *tuochan* is an employment category in China—usually a temporary stage and often associated with going back to school. For example, when he left his original job to pursue his doctoral degree, his employment record showed that he was then "tuochan." Dictionary definitions are consistent with this scholar's explanation. For example, a Chinese-English dictionary published in the PRC indicated that *tuochan* means "to be released from production or from one's regular work to take on other duties; to be disengaged from work; to divorce oneself from one's work."[13]

According to these definitions, however, it seems that Haiming did not use this term correctly. Funeral parlors' leaders and other administrative staff to which Haiming referred as tuochan still remained in production. They were not in school and had not in any sense left production similar to scholars leaving their original work units to pursue PhD degrees. These people might have different kinds of jobs, but that did not mean that they "do not work but receive a salary." The scholar with whom I consulted thought that Haiming just misunderstood this word probably because of his lack of education. However, I felt that Haiming's mistake might have meant something more despite not being able to pinpoint exactly what that was at that time.

This puzzle was finally solved for me when I found out that some cadres in rural China would be released from field labor once they were promoted to the party secretary position of a commune. For these cadres, by taking on administrative duties and leaving field labor, they were said to "leave production" even though they still worked (Jiang and Ashley 2013). As such, whether someone remains in production has less to do with whether or not he or she works, even if this was indeed how this word, *touchan*, is used as an employment category. Instead, it had more to do with the nature of the work. To further unpack what kinds of work counted as production, we need to know what working in a funeral parlor meant to Haiming.

Haiming graduated from junior high school in 1977 in Shanghai, the same year that all sent-down youths from all over China desperately attempted to return to the cities from which they came. Sent-down youths were urban youths who were either forced or volunteered to leave their home and be relocated in rural areas during the "Up to the Mountains and Down to the Countryside" (*shangshan xiaxiang*) movement (Ebrey 2005).[14] However, once in rural areas, given the country's household registration system and overcrowding in the cities, it became nearly impossible for these youths to go home. With the death of Mao in 1976 and the resumption of college entrance exams in 1977, these sent-down youths made a series of petitions and other actions calling for permission to go home, including briefly going on strike.[15] Shanghai was home to many of these youths, which made job assignments particularly difficult for anyone in Shanghai that year. Given the long line caused by these returnees, Haiming waited at home for two years to finally get his job assignment. He was told that he had two choices. He could either work on a farm in rural Shanghai or a crematorium in urban Shanghai. Haiming had lived in the urban part of Shanghai for a long time and had an urban household registration. He thus explained that he felt that farming would be too bitter. Furthermore, "worker" (*gongren*) was a much more prestigious class category even though the funeral industry was a historically stigmatized profession.

When Haiming first started work at a crematorium, he was assigned to work at the cremator unit (*luzijian*). Back then, cremators relied on coal for their fuel. At the time, there were five cremators in his crematorium, and his unit had a total of six employees. When they worked, they did so in pairs. Therefore, they could keep only three cremators working on normal days. Haiming's job was to keep adding coal to maintain the fire's temperature. Haiming said that it only took about a week for someone to learn when to add coal and how much was needed. Working in the cremator unit was very hard, hot work, not so much because of the psychological aspect—although Haiming said that he was well aware that he was burning dead bodies (*shao siren*) and even more aware of how other people might think of him. Rather, the work was difficult because it took significant physical strength to shovel the coal up into the cremator. The heat and smoke also made the work extremely uncomfortable.

In fact, even during Shanghai's notoriously cold and wet winters when the temperature often hovered just around freezing, Haiming would sweat profusely. Shanghai people pointed to the winter's humidity and cold as one reason the winter solstice was the time ghosts came out to wander around among the living. Whether or not ghosts were wandering around, winter was definitely the high season for funeral parlors. The cremator unit needed four or even five cremators running full-time in the winter without any increase in employees. Haiming recalled that he did not have a single piece of clothing that was white while he worked in the cremator unit between 1979 and 1988. The smoke always left him with a layer of dust coating his skin. Not surprisingly, his work choice also affected his marriage prospects. He did not get married until 1988, when he was twenty-eight, which was very late for men in Shanghai at that time. Haiming's wife was from rural Shanghai. He said that her parents were quite open-minded and decided that Haiming's stable job and regular salary were much better than a livelihood that depended solely on heaven's will (meaning being a farmer).

For Haiming, working in funeral parlors was to be plunged into the hard labor of dealing with decaying corpses by shoveling coal. Only manual labor counted as production. I suggest his misuse of the CCP's employment category, tuochan, indicated his conscious realization of the formation of class distinctions along the manual and nonmanual types of work within funeral parlors. Aunt Wang, another senior state practitioner, articulated a similar view to me. She said that she remembered how the chief director of her crematorium went into the cremator unit to determine what was wrong with the machine in the 1960s. Today however, "all directors wear white shirts and ties and sit in their air-conditioned offices and have 'meetings' instead," she said. For these grassroots workers, merchandise sales and having meetings were not production. Dressing dead bodies, shoveling coal, and cleaning up meeting halls counted as production. By describing leaders, salespeople, and certain office job holders as having already left production, these grassroots practitioners showed a realization of their economic position as a part of the collective that remained in production.

To be clear, I am not saying that hierarchy was somehow new in funeral parlors. Quite the opposite, hierarchy had always existed in funeral parlors. However, before the Opening Up, hierarchy was built on political domination because funeral parlors were part of the government in a more direct sense. The relationship between leaders and other people was defined administratively through their positions in the bureaucracy. Moreover, this politically dominating relationship was tempered by a general sense of economic equality. The difference between the lowest- and the highest-paid employee was moderate. For example, a report from 1985 listed level 1 employees as receiving RMB 41–46. Level 2 received RMB 52–57. Level 3 received RMB 63. Level 4 received RMB 70. Their average salary was RMB 62.69 (USD 25) per month (Funeral and Interment Administration 1985). Add to this relative equality Aunt Wang's recollection that funeral parlors' leaders were not exempt from physical labor, and you had a very different system. When funeral governance changed from civil governance to market governance, however, economic inequalities within funeral parlors increased along the divides established by administrative hierarchies and market-oriented divides.

This working-class consciousness is both old and new. To begin with, using manual labor for class distinction indicated the resilience of deep-rooted cultural ideas of class found more broadly in Sinophone societies. In my prior work on the relationship among substance use, class, and gender among Taiwanese men (H. Liu 2011), I found that Taiwanese working-class men talked about class differences by distinguishing people who "work with physical force" (*laoli*) from those who "work with their minds" (*laoxi*) rather than, for instance, income. This way of distinguishing social classes echoes Haiming's (mis)usage of *touchan*. This is the part of Haiming's working-class consciousness that was old.

Meanwhile, however, Haiming's way of thinking about class and class distinction (and the very capacity to do so) was very different from the CCP's discourse of class (*jieji*). The CCP assigned class labels to everyone during the land reform movement they implemented in the early 1950s, and out of this the CCP claimed to have removed class from China. Recognizing that Haiming's way of thinking about class diverged from this history of class labels is not meant to minimize the many ways that class categorizations had a profound effect on all aspects of personal life; nor does it negate the importance of a subjective dimension to belonging to a class. Yet it does highlight how the newly articulated sense of being part of a (working) class was necessarily a bottom-up realization process rather than a top-down labeling process. We see this most clearly from the fact that this newly formed working-class subjectivity is often articulated through the market discourse of competition, self-reliance, and risk. For example, Master Gao described to me how when the then chief director of Huangpu called a meeting to announce that he was going to take a "personal risk" and implement the contract responsibility system, he felt strongly that the director was lying. Gao said there was no "risk" there because Shanghai funeral parlors are a state monopoly, and everyone dies eventually. This meant that Huangpu would always have business, and given the high cremation rates in Shanghai, it always would make money regardless of how poorly the leader performed. "Exactly what kind of 'risk' was he taking?" Gao half-jokingly said to me. "I would love to take that 'personal risk' as well if I had a chance." For Master Gao, class distinction between directors and practitioners on the ground was not justifiable because he saw no risk in running funeral parlors. Instead of challenging the concept of risk as a basis for salaries itself, Gao bought into the argument and turned it back on itself.

The absence of risk in operating funeral parlors was also why some grassroots state practitioners felt that class distinction was unjustifiable within funeral parlors. Here I provide a long quote from my interview with a grassroots state practitioner:

> From the funeral parlors' perspective, it is a monopolized business. If you asked me to point out where competition exists, it only exists among the sixteen or seventeen funeral parlors . . . and they are not in

real competition in the sense that they are generally far away from each other geographically. Among these, it only exists in the three city funeral parlors because suburban parlors simply cannot compete against these three city ones. Every year, Longhua, Baoxing, and Yishan City Funeral Parlors announced their annual statistics, including the number of bodies they handled. These numbers were strange sometimes. For example, a funeral parlor might have handled fewer bodies compared with its previous year but yet its net profit increased because many service items were monopolized. People have no choice. They have to buy these services from the parlors. . . .

From one perspective, a monopoly may not be a bad thing. However, it is important to recognize that these profits are not the result of some individual's self-initiated hard work and achievement. Individuals did not fight to get sales done. Business came to your door directly. Thus, profits here have nothing to do with certain individuals striving to offer more or better services. This is why I think that salespeople [in the sales unit] should not have such high commissions. Their "sales" result from their "sitting and facing the south" [*chao nanzuo* in Mandarin, *shao noeshu* in Shanghainese]. In the past, an emperor sat on the south side to wait for his people to come to see him. In modern times, this means that our salespeople merely sit in their offices and wait for the bereaved to come to them directly. This is very different from what people do in your Taiwan, for example. Taiwanese funeral professionals need to go out to find dead bodies. If we had to do this, giving salespeople high commissions makes sense. However, they simply wait for dead bodies to come to them. Their "sales" are simply side expenses that occurred around dead bodies. This is not "sales" (*yeji*). Market competition in the funeral industry should be about competing for dead bodies.

For this person, there was no real market competition in the business of funeral parlors since parlors are a state monopoly. As such, making every state practitioner work for a personal bonus was unfair. The revenue generated in the sales unit of funeral parlors should therefore not be viewed as the result of individual salespeople's hard work and risk-taking. In this sense, the market logic of competition as well as that of self-management, ironically, became the foundation for this newly formed class consciousness. The formation of this working-class consciousness under the market economy was thus not a resurrection of these state-assigned labels.

Finally, when conditions were right, some grassroots state practitioners took class interest-based action using classic socialist protest methods to counter the effect of market governance, even if they also partially bought into the market logic of competition and risk taking. Elsewhere I have described the life story of an unusual state practitioner, Wang Wu (H. Liu 2022). Here I would like to tell the story of a protest he organized. In the late 2000s, a "big character poster" (*dazibao*) hung outside the staff cafeteria at Huangpu. This type of poster was a common genre of protest, self-criticism, and propaganda prior to the end of the Cultural Revolution. The poster explained why people who worked at the cosmetics unit deserved better pay since there was a big income gap between people working at the cosmetics unit who handled the dead bodies and people who worked in the sales department who just had sales meetings with the bereaved. One of the immediate causes of this protest was because funeral parlors reduced subsidies that had been given to workers who handled abnormal deaths. The state reinterpreted these subsidies as gray income because they claimed that it was difficult to have an exact way to determine what counted as a body in abnormal condition and thus who should get the subsidies. However, from the perspective of people who worked in the cosmetics unit, preparing bodies who had died in abnormal circumstances took a lot more work and was certainly something they should get compensated for.

During the protest, Wang Wu and other organizers threatened to release the content of their posters online. They even considered performing a "work slowdown" (*daigong*) for half a day. A half-day slowdown would have had immediate repercussions because there were only three funeral parlors in Shanghai. If the people in the cosmetics unit of a funeral parlor refused to handle dead bodies for half a day, then it would affect one-third of urban residents who needed these services during that time. As a state monopoly, if all three parlors' cosmeticians joined the half-day work slowdown, then the effect would have an immediate impact citywide. In the end, these protestors more or less got what they demanded (although some midlevel leaders who had sided with the workers got punished later).

Beyond showing the possibility of collective class action, even given that parts of their working-class consciousness were based in market logics, this incident clearly revealed that, somewhat ironically, the key factor for these grassroots state workers to be able to resist the state was the fact that they worked for a state institution that was also a state monopoly. This structurally advantageous position of state practitioners was the precondition for a striking dissonance between market governance and market subjectivity. This unintended consequence of the market governance of death regarding state practitioners was in contrast to the fate of private funeral brokers, who were situated in a structurally fragile position—a topic I explore in the next chapter.

From Death as a Moral Project to Death for Profit

By questioning the extent to which there was a creation of market subjectivity among state practitioners, I do not mean to say that funeral parlors somehow failed to become profit-making businesses. Quite the opposite: Shanghai funeral parlors (and cemeteries) were doing very well in terms of generating profits. As mentioned, the state restructured funeral parlors by disentangling the civil from the business administration. As the range and scale of commodities expanded in funeral parlors, the contradictions between civil administration and business administration increased as well. The same group of people were responsible both for funeral parlors turning a profit and for ensuring they continued implementing Funeral Reform. As someone working on the government side told me, "You cannot be a referee and at the same time also be a player" (*qiuyuan jian caipan*). This was not only unfair but also created a situation in which he felt that being good at both was impossible. Another person said directly that if you perform too much civil management (*xingzheng guanli*), you lose at business management (*qiye guanli*).

Theoretically, generating profits and Funeral Reform policies need not be incompatible. However, the reality in Shanghai was that most of the funerary merchandise being revived in funeral parlors to increase profits were exactly the same items that were repressed under Funeral Reform policies (such as having cemeteries, coffins, banquets, and other markers of social and economic status)—not to mention that Funeral Reform emphasized a commitment to frugal funerals. In contrast, the goal of market governance was to bring in revenue through reliance on expanding and elaborating funerals, whether or not they were related to religious and folk ritual practices.

The Shanghai Civil Affairs Bureau, too, was well aware of this contradiction. However, rather than privatizing funeral parlors, as had happened in many industries, the Shanghai government ordered the formation of a new and separate organization in 1998 directly under the Shanghai Civil Affairs Bureau. This new organization was the Shanghai Funeral and Interment Service Center (FIS). FIS was designed to completely take over the business functions of the Shanghai FIBA (formerly the FIA). FIS was approved in February 1998 and officially began operations in August of the same year. FIS can be viewed as the mother company for the three city funeral parlors. Figure 2.1 shows how by 2011, following this change, FIS also owned several funerary merchandise companies and a large number of cemeteries (the number of these properties has continuously grown since then). These entities ranged from other public nonprofits (such as funeral

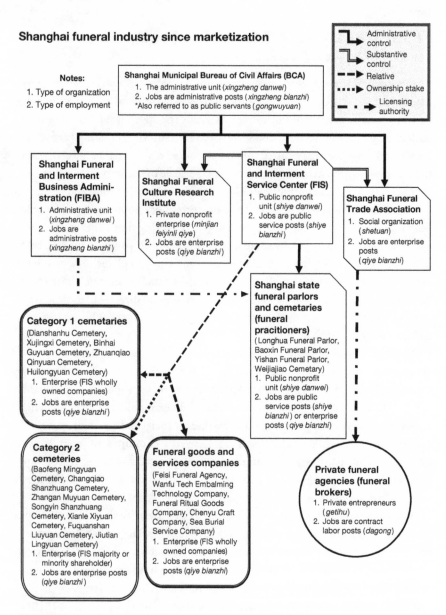

FIGURE 2.1. Structure of Shanghai funeral governance and death industry. Used with permission from Matthew West.

parlors) to wholly owned subsidiary companies, shareholding companies, and participating stock companies.

Administratively, FIS is parallel to FIBA because both report directly to the Shanghai Civil Affairs Bureau.[16] Therefore, the FIBA as an institution lost much of its power with the establishment of FIS. One of the few powers that the FIBA retained during my fieldwork was that of renewing the licenses of funeral parlors. However, even this was more of a formality than any real threat. I was at Huangpu Funeral Parlor when officials from the FIBA came to carry out their annual inspection. Everyone involved acted as if the visit had real significance, but when I asked a relatively senior person at Huangpu whether it was possible for the FIBA not to renew Huangpu's license, she laughed at me for asking such a naive question. She told me that it was not possible. In fact, she added, considering the amount of money that Huangpu contributed annually to the Civil Affairs Bureau, the FIBA's direct boss, the FIBA would not dare revoke Huangpu's license. Huangpu Funeral Parlor earned enough profit that the portion they passed along to the Civil Affairs Bureau in 2010 was in the region of RMB 80 to 100 million (USD 13 to 16 million) according to several interviews.

As a result, the establishment of a separated business managing institution—FIS—did not solve the contradictions between the goals of civil and market governance but merely shifted the original issue up a level from the FIBA to the Civil Affairs Bureau. In fact, FIS was still charged with executing Funeral Reform even though it was not, strictly speaking, a government bureau. Moreover, the leadership of FIS consisted of exactly the same employees who had worked in the old FIBA. The Civil Affairs Bureau made the then chief director of the FIBA (and others) retire from their government posts and "dive into the ocean" (*xiahai*, meaning "going into business") to become the first generation of FIS leadership.[17] The interchanging of personnel between FIS and the Civil Affairs Bureau (including the FIBA) then continued through the period of my fieldwork.

Although the kind of hierarchical relationship outlined here with few horizontal interactions between government bureaus and organizations (communications moved upward and then back down through common parent bureaus) was a defining characteristic of the Chinese government, we must also keep in mind the cross-branch movement of personnel among FIS, funeral parlors, and the FIBA and how such actions affected governing death even under a market economy.[18] The establishment of a separate business managing institution (i.e., FIS) did not allow the state funeral government industry to escape the "one crew with two signs" (*yitao renma liangkuai paizi*) trend that then characterized the so-called privatization of Chinese state institutions across an entire range of sectors. The fundamental problem of governing funerals remained constant as FIS was charged with both executing the ongoing civil governance of death and the often-contradictory task of making a profit. If somehow this ambiguity is less of an issue today than in the past, it is only because profit has so clearly won out.

Profiteering in the funeral industry had become a major public concern in China at least by the early 2000s. In 2004, the journalist Wei Yahua published an article titled "The Top 10 Industries with Exorbitant Profits [*baoli*] in China in 2003." The funeral industry was number 3 on this list.[19] This article immediately caught the nation's attention. The word choice of *bao* here implied that these profits were unreasonable. The usage of the word also hinted that people who profited from such an industry did so through immoral means. Profiteering is a common framework to understand the death industry cross-culturally. In China, however, the affordability of taking care of the dead took on another layer of meaning—one that questions the state's legitimacy. In imperial China, the fact that subjects of a specific emperor could not afford a proper funeral was seen as a clear indication that the current regime must have lost the Mandate of Heaven— the primary source of (divine) political legitimacy (Zhao 2009). This concept of legitimacy emphasized the state's performance in providing provisions for its people. With this idea in mind, Chinese media outlets routinely published new articles on the matter in which some people "make money from the pockets of dead people" (*zhuan sirenqian*). In this context, the contemporary public sentiment that "the dead cannot afford to die"—the quote with which I began this chapter—was a statement that had the potential to make people wonder whether the current state that was profiteering from death still holds the Mandate of Heaven (or, at least, legitimacy to govern).

To be clear, I am not saying that immoral profits from funerals today have led to a loss of political legitimacy for the CCP. What I am saying is that the market governance of death has led to questions concerning the state's legitimacy around governing death. This observation is supported by a consideration of how the central government reacted to public accusations of profiteering from death. Since the turn of the century, considerable internal debates (especially at the national level) have occurred among government officials who were involved in governing death over whether the funeral industry should be further marketized or, instead, maintained "for the common public good" (*gongyixing*). Han Shen from Huangpu Funeral Parlor told me:

> The full marketization of Shanghai funeral parlors was truly the result of trying to get ready for China's entrance into the WTO [back then]. People were worried that foreign capital would flood the Shanghai funeral and interment industry on a large scale, thereby destroying state enterprises. This was why they decided to fully marketize the three parlors and five cemeteries we had at that time. The idea was that we can monopolize the

market similar to a trust [before we enter the WTO] so foreign companies would not be able to compete. However, ten years after entering the
WTO, we realized that we were wrong [then]. It turned out that the approval department [the Civil Affairs Bureaus] would in no way approve
the idea of foreign capital entering the Chinese funeral market. This is
particularly true in Shanghai. The concern about the WTO bringing
open competition was certainly unfounded. Meanwhile, the general
public is becoming more and more unhappy with soaring prices. . . . [As
such,] they think the right goal is to increase "public satisfaction."

Consequently, the Ministry of Civil Affairs officially declared in 2011 that the
Chinese funeral industry is an industry for the "public good"—a position that it
still holds in 2019. In implementing this new responsibility to the public good,
the local institution, FIS, decided that public satisfaction could be measured using three indexes: the general impression of funeral parlors, the impression of
their services, and their honesty and trust (*chengxin*). To enhance the general
impression of funeral parlors and their services, for example, funeral parlors created a new service called the "accompaniment service" (*peitong fuwu*). Purchasing this service ensured that the bereaved were accompanied by the same
practitioner throughout the entirety of the funeral organizing and hosting process regardless of whether they were arranging funerals in a sales unit or carrying out the funeral in memorial meeting halls. This way, if any unpleasantness
or doubts emerged during the process, the funeral practitioners could immediately solve or clarify issues. Regarding personnel training, funeral parlors asked
state practitioners to take classes on how to build honesty and trust into their
business practices. They even had an open book test after every class!

The outcome associated with defining the funeral industry as being for the
public good was a slight decrease in cremation rates at the national level. The
Ministry of Civil Affairs published *The Green Book of Funerals: Report on Funeral Development of China (2012-2013)*, which showed that a "second return
of old customs" (meaning a slight decrease in the national cremation rate) in
approximately 2006 was related to the launch of human-centered concerns
with customer satisfaction. In fact, the national cremation rate dropped from
53 percent in 2005 to 48 percent in 2006. This latter rate remained more or less
steady through the primary year of my own fieldwork in 2011. At the local level,
because cremation rates were not an issue in Shanghai, the influence of this campaign was expressed through a slight decrease in profits as funeral parlors reviewed their pricing policies item by item.

Whereas *The Green Book of Funerals (2012-2013)* stated that the decrease in the
cremation rate was a result of funeral government officials misunderstanding

the true meaning of human-centered funeral and interment, it nevertheless showed the ultimate impossibility of governing death as a form of both civil and market governance. Whereas market governance seemed to have lost its voice on the front stage of the funeral policy (because, at least since 2011, the funeral industry should be run for the public good), thinking that profits lost their role in governing the death industry is a complete misunderstanding. Looking a bit deeper, we find that this "public good" characterization limits only four aspects of funeral and interment: transportation of the deceased, refrigeration of the deceased, cremation, and cremains storage. In these four areas, the state carefully controls prices to aid the public. Anything else, however, is left to market competition. In fact, the Chinese state has even purposefully allowed cemetery plot prices to increase as a means to discourage people from burying cremains (and the Civil Affairs Bureau owns many cemeteries). As such, the dead still cannot afford to die so long as the living hope to find a more or less permanent resting place for them ("permanent" in China's cremains cemeteries means seventy years). The marketization of Shanghai funeral parlors was not a story of privatization.[20] Funeral parlors have continued to be a state monopoly and were still the only destination for dead bodies in Shanghai before the cremains found their final resting place.

Conclusion

This chapter started with the resurrection of the civil governance of death following the Cultural Revolution and alongside the introduction of market reforms and ends with the triumph of the market governance of death. The conjunction of these two modes of governance after the introduction of market economic principles in China shows that marketization was not a teleological transition from civil to market governance. Instead, it is a change from treating death only as a matter of civil administration to a dual matter of both civil and business administration. The uneasy relationship, if not outright tension, between these regimes of civil and market governance has been a defining feature of funeral governance in Shanghai since the death of Mao.

Within the market governance of death, marketization operated at least at two levels. The first was through the reorganization of funeral parlors, especially through an emphasis on merchandise sales. The second, perhaps most important level, was through policies aiming to remake state funeral practitioners. At the leadership level, funeral parlor directors were rewarded disproportionately for their performance outcomes based on imagined risks. All other state funeral practitioners were encouraged to become entrepreneurs who generated profits and who were self-managing. The marketization of funeral parlors generated new subject formation processes to transform funeral practitioners from comrades who received more or less equal pay, who worked for the people, and who were government officials implementing funeral reform policies into entrepreneurs who were to be self-motivated to pursue maximal benefits at their individual level, who were to take risks, and who were supposed to be self-disciplined.

However, as these subject formation processes unfolded, what we saw was only a limited development of market subjectivity, the formation of class-based subjectivity, and the reconfiguration of such class-based subjectivity among some grassroots state funeral practitioners. My analysis of state funeral professionals shows how funeral practitioners on the ground were simultaneously formulating class-based ideas of self through rhetoric that described who was still "in production" and who was not. They recognized how this marketization created an entire set of class distinctions. While some parts of this working-class consciousness were based on a traditional divide between manual and intellectual labor, this working-class subjectivity was new because it was also embedded in the market discourse of risk, competition, and self-governance. The irony is that the reality of the state's monopoly over dead bodies helped these people identify the lack of risk in their business. The value they imagined markets gave to risk and competition then became justification for collective class action. Their position as essential workers in an essential state monopoly, in turn, enhanced the possibility for their actions to see some degree of success. Consequently, the marketization of these state funeral practitioners challenges the often taken-for-granted link between market governance and market subjectivity in the study of privatization in China.

Despite the only semisuccessful creation of market subjects under market governance in death, however, funeral institutions themselves by no means failed to generate profits. As a result, the contradiction between civil and market governance here was not because "the market" was the opposite of "the state" (if we momentarily essentialize both "market" and "state"). Quite the opposite: this contradiction emerged because "the state" wanted to be simultaneously the governing body and "the market." If we see dissonance between market governance and market subjectivity for state practitioners as an unintended consequence of the market governance of death, then the next question we need to ask is whether private funeral brokers also came to see themselves as members of a working class or instead were turned into market subjects. If they did shift toward market subjects, then what might the context for the rise of private funeral brokers tell us about the conditions of possibility that transformed this group into market subjects. In focusing on private funeral brokers, the next chapter takes on a group of people that the state had no intention of cultivating into market subjects, who, nonetheless, became self-motivated entrepreneurs pushing the death industry in new directions in Shanghai today.

THE FRAGILE MIDDLE

Q: Why has the Chinese table tennis team always been so amazing?
A: Because every Chinese citizen is an expert at playing edge balls.

(A popular joke in China)

Chen Yu grew up in rural Jiangsu Province. She started working in various factories in Suzhou after she turned sixteen, as did most of the other young women she grew up with in the countryside. Several years later, she came to Shanghai to escape her unhappy marriage to a fellow villager. When I met her in Shanghai, she was a private "funeral broker." In Mandarin, funeral brokers or their companies were called binzang zhongjie (funeral agents) or *binzang daili* (funeral representatives). When I conducted my fieldwork in 2010, more than 60 percent and 80 percent of memorial meetings held in Longhua and Baoxin Funeral Parlors, respectively, were operated through funeral brokers.[1] Sometimes people referred to funeral brokers as *binzang yitiaolong* (lit., "funeral dragons") because they were known for providing a comprehensive package-style service known as "dragon service" (*yitiaolong fuwu*). Although the dragon metaphor probably best resonates with the English phrase "one-stop shop," funeral brokers were less do-it-all service providers and more mediators who made all the necessary arrangements for the bereaved in funeral parlors, since funeral parlors' monopoly on death made them necessarily the dead body's primary stop. Therefore, Chinese funeral brokers are not similar to American funeral directors, who do provide one-stop services. Analogically, Chinese funeral brokers were more similar to American wedding planners—they coordinated between their clients and a venue and other associated businesses, such as caterers and flower shops.

As a funeral broker, Chen Yu's job was to deal with office and administrative affairs. I came to particularly admire her ability to engage in office organizational jobs once I realized that she had only had three years of elementary school education. Because her parents needed her help with farm work and household chores, she had to quit school early. When working in factories in Suzhou, her colleagues led her into the world of romance novels. It turned out that she loved romance so much that she eventually taught herself how to read through them. She was still reading romance novels when I met her. Whenever I visited her office, she'd have an Internet romance novel open on her computer desktop.

Chen Yu's current husband, Tang An, also worked for the same funeral agency. Tang An is a Shanghai local with a high school degree. His marriage to Chen Yu was also his second one. Tang An's first wife was also a rural migrant. Chen Yu felt that Tang An's family still did not like her or trust her partly because of the general discrimination against, and suspicion toward, rural migrants that was prevalent among Shanghai people. Tang An was an outspoken and humorous person. This suited his job well since he had to hold business meetings with the bereaved to help them make their funeral arrangements. In this kind of meeting, he sold products and services to the bereaved. Perhaps not so coincidentally, before joining the funeral industry, he sold life insurance. When Tang An spent time at the office between business meetings, he preferred to research stock trading on the Shanghai stock market. Twenty years since Ellen Hertz (1998) published her book, *The Trading Crowd: An Ethnography of the Shanghai Stock Market*, the Shanghai stock "fever" appeared to have been normalized as a part of everyday reality.

Funeral brokers, be they rural migrants or Shanghai locals, were just ordinary people who had struggled to achieve their moderate success in post-economic-reform Shanghai. Being ordinary in most dimensions, however, did not exempt them from systematic marginalization and stigmatization due to their occupation. For example, I attended the 2011 First and Recurrent Training for Legal Representatives of Funeral Agencies and Funeral Agents in Shanghai City along with several agents from Longevity Funeral Agency. The chair of FIS gave an opening presentation at this conference. In his presentation, he first reviewed and commented on the market conditions of the funeral industry in Shanghai and other parts of China. He then discussed funeral agents to his audience of funeral agents typifying them with an anecdote about stolen legs that I transcribed as follows:

> A man accidentally lost his two legs while working in a factory in Jiangsu Province. When his colleagues sent him to the hospital, they brought his legs as well, thinking the doctor might be able to reconnect them. Unfortunately, this man did not make it. He passed away in the surgery room. A funeral broker in the hospital saw what happened. When he found out that this man had died, the broker went to talk to

a hospital employee who was in charge of medical waste. He offered a couple of hundred RMB to the hospital worker in exchange for the man's two legs. Meanwhile, the family members of the man who lost his legs were devastated when they realized that the doctor could not save him. After they cried for a while and began to accept the reality of his passing, they decided that they should at least cremate the two legs together with his body so this man could still be whole in the other world. Thus, the bereaved asked the doctor to give the deceased's legs back to them. The doctor then told them to talk to the people who are in charge of medical waste. Because the employee had already sold the legs to someone else, he told the bereaved that the legs were missing for some reason, and he could not find them. The bereaved were very upset and quarreled with the doctors. Just as the situation seemed to be escalating out of control, the broker approached the bereaved through the chaos. He said to them, if you give me RMB 20,000, I can find this man's legs for you.

I asked Tang An a bit later what he thought of the story. He pushed back at the FIS director's implication of broker immorality, saying: "This story was more about an immoral man who tried to blackmail a bereaved family who only just happened to be a funeral broker. The story is not truly about funeral broker malpractice even though he meant it as such. If that man had told the bereaved something to the effect of 'if you hire me to arrange your funeral, I can guarantee you I will find your loved one's legs,' then the situation would have been about funeral broker malpractice."

While I agree with Tang An here, this style of immorality narrative was the most common representation of funeral brokers in public discourse. Ever since their emergence in contemporary China, funeral brokers have been represented as amoral if not outright immoral. Although part of this moral ambiguity was due to the nature of their job as death workers, this was not the only reason. If we compare state practitioners with funeral brokers, we found that while state practitioners sometimes were represented as morally problematic just like funeral brokers, they were also occasionally represented as selfless, dedicated heroes who served the people. This kind of positive representation, however, would never be associated with private funeral brokers in Chinese media (which was largely controlled by the state).

This chapter explores who funeral brokers were as persons, what funeral brokers did in their mundane everyday work, and what funeral brokers were as an occupation in relation to other occupations in the Shanghai funeral industry. Through examining the Shanghai funeral industry from the perspective and position of private funeral brokers, I show that if the ethnography of state practitioners in the last chapter tells a story of dissonance born out of the complicated articulation of the market governance of death with the reestablishment of civil governance, the ethnography of funeral brokers tells a story of resonance instead. Many funeral brokers were self-motivated and self-managing market subjects. Just as the formation of the working-class consciousness of state workers was an unintended consequence of the market governance of death, however, the cultivation of the entrepreneurship of funeral brokers was also an unintended consequence of state governance from the perspective of the state. In fact, funeral brokers became self-managing subjects despite the state attempting to limit their pursuit of self-managed entrepreneurship.

Through this ethnography of resonance and of funeral brokers, I identify fragility as the key condition of possibility for the construction of their market subjectivity. Fragility has two interrelated dimensions. The first refers to the ontological condition of being fragile. Many funeral brokers felt vulnerable, insecure, always at risk, and unjustly forced into marginality. The second refers to a structural condition of fragility. For funeral brokers in Shanghai, their fragility was created by their structural position at a micro level of being a rural migrant, in a transient form of employment, or of a lower social class (usually due to a lack of education) combined with being death workers. At a more macro level, their structural condition of fragility was caused by their unique middle position in the Shanghai funeral industry, especially related to the fact that the funeral industry was a state monopoly that has gone through rapid marketization.

However, despite this fragility entailing structural limitations, fragility is here also agentive in the sense that fragility transformed existing structures. At an individual level, being fragile motivated brokers into becoming self-managing entrepreneurs. At a societal level, funeral brokers' fragility has set the conditions for them to push the legal and moral boundaries of death so much that they modified contemporary urban Chinese funerals. They did so by creating a platform for religious ideas of persons to reenter Shanghai people's commemorative practices. In this sense, fragility was productive—it made structural change possible.

The concept of fragility developed in this chapter complements the concept of precarity—a term often discussed in relation to neoliberalism (Bulter 2004). Like precarity, fragility is both a generalized ontological condition (fragile or precarious) and a particular structurally changing position (fragility or precarity). As in Japan (Allison 2013), fragility recognizes the vulnerability as well as agency born out of such vulnerability. There are, however, some critical differences here. Unlike precarity, which is most often associated with neoliberalism and liberal democracy, I argue here that fragility is a distinctive product of authoritarianism, socialist economies in transition, or the combination of the two. These very different historical trajectories of political economy meant that fragile people shared different sets of ideas and imaginations about self, vulnerability, and hope. Moreover, unlike precarious people generally standing on a moral high ground in terms of the leftist values of liberal democracies, fragile people were rather more morally ambiguous. At times it can be hard to see the way fragile people push legal boundaries as righteous civil disobedience when they occupy such a morally ambiguous position all the while. As this case will show, it may be exactly in the cracks and at the edges of morality and legality where change is possible under authoritarian regimes. After all, moral discourses and the rule of law are often the authoritarian state's most powerful weapons to silence political opposition. Fragility, with its legal and moral ambiguity, is particularly productive under authoritarianism, where there are few alternatives for balancing powers or calling for change.

As such, while precarity is born out of the withering of the welfare state in pursuit of economic efficiencies in managing both the state and the self, fragility is born out of authoritarianism. Precarity and the precarious are, first and foremost, economic concepts with political consequences. Meanwhile, however, fragility and the fragile are, first and foremost, political concepts that come with economic consequences. By moving beyond the prominent simplistic and dichotomous representation of funeral brokers in China—good versus bad, the vulnerable bereaved versus profiteering funeral brokers, legal state practitioners versus semilegal funeral brokers—this chapter unpacks the twists and turns of the unintended consequences of the market governance of death to show how fragility emerged as a condition of possibility for the formation of market subjectivity under authoritarianism.

In the following section, I first delineate fragility from the individual and person-centered perspective of a funeral broker. I then explain the social position of funeral brokers to illustrate the structure of fragility. Finally, I discuss how these fragile funeral brokers pushed the moral and legal boundaries of the Shanghai funeral industry in ways that created structural changes in the commemoration of the dead.

Being Fragile

The funeral agency at which Chen Yu and Tang An worked belonged to Chen Yu's sister, Chen Ting, and her husband, Du Tu. Chen Ting called her company Longevity Ritual Service Company. This term, "ritual service company" (*liyi fuwu gongsi*), was relatively rare in China. Most funeral agencies did not name themselves as such, and the general public did not refer to funeral agencies as ritual service companies. Chen Ting told me that she got this idea from Taiwan as many funeral ritual providers are called ritual service companies in Taiwan. Chen Ting preferred this name instead of a more conventional one, such as *zhongjie* (agent), because she felt that the conventional name has been too closely associated with the dragon service label, which she strongly felt to be a derogatory term.

From conversations like this, we can see how articulate Chen Ting was. Because of this, combined with the fact Chen Ting ran a successful small company, we could also deduce that she had at least a basic level of literacy and math ability. Chen Ting was very vague about how many years of formal education she had had, however. In fact, if our conversation had not accidentally stumbled onto the topic of educational degree, nothing about my interactions with her would have led me to guess that Chen Ting (and Chen Yu, for that matter) had very little formal education. She always struck me as a smart, independent, and beautiful woman who knew her business very well. Yet underneath her entrepreneurial and sophisticated mask, she had a soft, warm, and vulnerable heart.

Chen Ting was the first of her family to move to Shanghai. Growing up as the second child of the family, Chen Ting carried more responsibility than other second-born children might have because her elder sister was mentally handicapped. About a decade ago, she left her home village, her parents, her mentally challenged older sister, Chen Yu, and two younger brothers in a rural part of northern Jiangsu, also known as Subei, to find work to help her family. Shanghai people have a long history of discriminating against Subei people—one often overlooked but prominent social inequality based on one's native place in (especially) urban China. Emily Honig (1989) described this prejudice against Subei people in Shanghai extending back to the nineteenth century. Shanghai people's association of Subei people with a backward, untrustworthy underclass has remained strong (and perhaps grown stronger in some ways) today as contemporary social conditions have perpetuated Subei people's previous social, economic, and legal positions as unskilled laborers and less-educated slum residents in Shanghai.

Chen Ting started out as a waitress in a noodle shop after she arrived in Shanghai. That was the only job she could find as a young, unskilled woman with little education and who did not speak Shanghainese. When working there, she became familiar with a frequent customer who was a local Shanghai man. He owned a photography and videography shop to which a funeral parlor outsourced part of its business. This older man grew to like the young, joyful, and diligent waitress enough that he eventually asked her to work for him, and this was how Chen Ting entered the Shanghai funeral industry. The older man taught Chen Ting how to operate a camera and film funerals. She very quickly learned photography, videography, and some basic computer-based video-editing techniques. More than just acquiring technical knowledge, she quickly found a talent for following, maintaining, and even creating the rhythm of the funeral.

The friendly relationship between the older man and Chen Ting, however, changed after she fell in love with his son. Being a diligent and good worker and being a proper daughter-in-law were not the same thing. The man liked Chen Ting enough to offer her a job and to train her to be a good funeral camera operator, but he refused to accept her as a daughter-in-law. Her rural background made her an "unsuitable" spouse for his precious only son. Love won out, however, and Chen Ting married the son. Since Chen Ting's father-in-law did not like this marriage, he followed the common Shanghai practice of only "tacitly" providing a place for the newlyweds to live. This meant that although he owned several pieces of property in Shanghai, the living space he provided to the young couple was located in a shantytown. Although neither of the Chen sisters lived in shantytowns when I knew them (they both owned modern apartments in downtown Shanghai), I visited several when I accompanied funeral brokers to business meetings at the homes of the bereaved. Shantytown housing generally did not have flush toilets or a gas supply for heating and cooking. Moreover, residents only had limited access to running water. The living conditions in the shantytowns were often worse than life in the countryside, even though most urban Shanghai people imagine rural life to be inferior.

Chen Ting knew that her father-in-law put them in shantytown housing to break up the marriage. However, she did not have much choice. In such an environment, Chen Ting lived through her first childbirth. The battle between "bread" (money) and "roses" (love) did not fall in Chen Ting's favor. Chen Ting's husband was used to having a relatively prosperous life and could not handle this change. He failed to be the breadwinner for their small family after they were forced to relocate to the shantytown. When Chen Ting's baby boy was four months old, she decided to send him back to the countryside to her natal home so that she could go to work. After all, one of them had to make money. Once the baby was sent to the countryside and she began to work outside the house, Chen Ting and her then husband lived separate lives. The long-term separation was eventually formalized as a divorce several years later.

During this time, Chen Ting worked as a waitress in a coffee shop owned by a Taiwanese man for a while. From him, she told me, she learned how to do a service job well: you had to talk to your customers in a soft and feminine voice to interact with them as if they were your boss. This kind of "emotional labor" in the service industry (Hochschild 1983) was something rather foreign to people who grew up in the countryside in China at that time. The coffee shop's business, however, was not very good. According to Chen Ting, at least this was in part because the Taiwanese boss was an incompetent manager. For example, he often allowed his acquaintances to eat and drink for free without caring about the shop's balance sheet. Chen Ting wanted to rescue the coffee shop because she felt that the shop's problem was a managerial one. She volunteered to be the manager. She told her boss that if he promoted her to be the manager and gave her the authority to run the business, she promised to generate a profit for him. The boss agreed, and Chen Ting did not disappoint. During this time, she learned the managerial skills needed to run her own business, including negotiating prices with suppliers, managing cash flows, and building supplier and customer networks.

One day, Chen Ting received a phone call from a friend she knew back from when she worked at the funeral photography and videography shop. This friend offered Chen Ting the opportunity to work as a full-time contracted funeral photographer and videographer at Huangpu Funeral Parlor. In the late 1990s and early 2000s, many Shanghai people liked to hire photographers and videographers for funerals. Chen Yu, who later learned funeral photography and videography from her sister, told me that filming and photographing funerals was new at that time. Many Shanghai people thought that having such things in funerals was modern, resulting in high demand for these services. Chen Ting accepted the job offer and began working in Huangpu. This spatial proximity was how she met her current husband, Du Tu, who was a state practitioner at Huangpu. Through herself and her husband, she built a solid network of connections with people at Huangpu. Later, these networks turned out to be extremely important. After Chen Ting and Du Tu were married, she left her job at Huangpu. While she was "between jobs," she started to help her friends, their acquaintances, and friends' friends' acquaintances arrange funerals because she knew the funeral process very well and had all the connections needed to make the arrangements smoothly. This act of "helping" eventually turned into a real business. Chen Ting and Du Tu, who had stayed in the parlor, decided to set up the Longevity Ritual Service Company.

Chen Ting's intelligence and perseverance led her into a new world of prosperity that was beyond anything her farming parents could ever have imagined. However, she was not happy overall, partly because at the time of my fieldwork her marriage with Du Tu was crumbling. He rarely spent time at home with Chen Ting and their baby girl. Instead, he went out most nights to drink, gamble, and carouse with his funeral broker friends at Prosperity, the restaurant that I previously described. While Du Tu was not involved in the company's daily business, this did not mean that he was hesitant about enjoying its profits. He came to the office mainly when he needed to collect money earned by the hardworking team that Chen Ting had assembled. Occasionally, after she had a serious fight with her husband, she would stand in front of an office window and let her tears fall quietly when other people were out doing their jobs. One of the few moments that I saw happiness on her face (rather than the friendly face that she put on for her customers) was when she was in the office and was holding her eight-month-old baby girl.

From Chen Ting's life trajectory of becoming a funeral broker, I want to highlight two characteristics. The first was her entrepreneurial skill. We can see this from her ability to learn funeral recording, specific tactics of emotion management in doing service jobs, and practical skills in running a small business through managing the coffee shop. In this process, she cultivated both a customer-oriented practicality and business sense. As I will elaborate on later, however, even though this kind of practicality and sensibility are necessary qualities, these are also what make people think of such petty capitalists as unprincipled and calculating. Moreover, these qualities were even more morally ambiguous in the context of a business that relies on the death of others. Secondly, being a young, rural, and female immigrant living in Shanghai was a Janus-faced position. On the one hand, it indicated a clear limit to her possible success. On the other, it also referenced the fact that she was not bound to the local moral and legal world as much as a Shanghai person might be. It would be relatively easier for her to break existing social norms. In her case, these two characteristics worked in tandem.

What led Chen Ting to fully embrace her entrepreneurial skills and to be able to work with (or to work out) her fragility, however, was living in a shantytown with a newborn baby and an unproductive and unsupportive husband. In that fragile moment of life, she decided to send the baby back home and go out and find a job. Her desire to escape was such that she "dared" to voluntarily take over the managerial job of the coffee shop. At that moment, we begin to see her transformed from a timid, obedient, and filial young woman to a self-disciplined and self-motivated entrepreneur. Chen Ting's life history showed that the ontological condition of being fragile was a form of affect that animated her to move from one condition to another. It motivated Chen Ting to act as a self-managing entrepreneur-subject—from leaving her rural home and migrating to Shanghai, from leaving her unskilled waitress job in a noodle shop to become a skilled funeral photographer and videographer, and from leaving her single life and entering an unblessed (and ultimately unsuccessful) marriage to becoming a single mother.

Fragility

This ontological condition of fragility was created and sustained by specific structural limitations. At the personal level, these structural limitations were often related to funeral brokers' migration status and the associated transience of their employment. In Shanghai, funeral brokers emerged in the early 1990s. In the beginning, the majority of them were rural migrants. Rural immigrants in urban China were known as the "floating population" (Zhang 2001), a term meant to convey their lack of "roots" in the city. They did not have access to many of the rights and privileges of urban residents because they did not have urban *hukou* (household registration). They were de facto second-class citizens in urban China. This status was in contrast to state practitioners who were either people who already had an urban Shanghai hukou or people who graduated from civil affairs schools in other provinces. These nonlocal civil affairs graduates usually received a Shanghai hukou after they started working in funeral parlors.

In conjunction with hukou status was the type of employment that funeral brokers had. Funeral agencies were small private businesses, also known as *getihu*—self-employed households or individuals. As a type of employment, getihu emerged rapidly after the beginning of the market reforms as the state-assigned lifelong employment opportunities disappeared (Bruun 1993). People who worked for getihu were people who "worked for hire" (*dagong*)—a transient form of employment that was highly unstable, risky, and volatile. In contrast, funeral parlors were proper work units (danwei). While work units were themselves by no means permanent anymore since the introduction of China's market economic reforms, working in state units was still highly desirable and relatively stable.

Moving from the micro to the macro level, the most critical factor in the structure of fragility of funeral brokers was the legality of their occupation. When I did my fieldwork in 2011, the existence of funeral brokers was not entirely legal in most parts of China despite their ubiquity throughout the country. Unlike other kinds of business, funeral-related businesses had to register with both the local-level Administration for Industry and Commerce and Civil Affairs Bureau. While the former, where all businesses were to register, was relatively easy to secure (and most did), it was much harder to get the latter's approval. Shanghai was the first municipality or province (and, when I did my fieldwork, one of only four) to have granted legal status to funeral brokers and their companies. Funeral brokers in Shanghai were legalized in 2006. The Shanghai Funeral and Interment Trade Association (hereafter, the trade association), rather than the Civil Affairs Bureau, was the authority that legalized funeral brokers (see figure 2.2 on its administrative position). The rule was that if funeral brokers registered as part of a funeral agency (that is, no freelancing) and attended the annual conferences organized by the trade association, then they could receive work permits (*shanggangzheng*) from the trade association. Full attendance was effectively the criteria for individual funeral brokers to gain work permits. In other words, the barrier for becoming a legal funeral broker was rather low. This policy was more or less aimed at legalizing all funeral brokers in Shanghai.[2]

I interviewed the secretary-general of the trade association about why they decided to legalize funeral brokers in Shanghai. He said that the existence of funeral brokers and their increased popularity showed "the demand of consumers." Moreover, "because Shanghai is more modern and progressive, funeral governing institutions are willing to recognize consumers' needs." By contrast, for Shanghai funeral brokers, legalization was the Shanghai Civil Affairs Bureau's way of ensuring that funeral parlors could continue to compete with funeral brokers and of reasserting the state's monopoly over the death industry. The issue here was that, from the perspective of funeral brokers, the legalization of brokers provided a legal framework that guaranteed the competitive advantages of funeral parlors. For example, the Shanghai Civil Affairs Bureau distinguished two categories of funeral products and services: "folk custom items" (*minsu xiangmu*) and "civil affairs items" (*minzheng xiangmu*). All services and products that were directly related to dead bodies were civil affairs items, and funeral parlors monopolized these. These included body transportation (hearse and driver), body handling (embalming, makeup, body dressing, and so on), and body display (from cremation coffins to memorial meeting halls). Any other products, such as cremains caskets ("urns" in English), flower baskets, banquet services, and religious goods belonged to the category of folk custom items. Folk custom items were open to market competition.

Since the bereaved could directly make funeral arrangements with a funeral parlor without hiring a broker, the bereaved were more likely to purchase all folk custom items from parlors when there were no brokers involved. This essentially means that while funeral brokers had to cooperate with funeral parlors, since all bodies went through them from funerals to cremation, they were also business competitors. As such, to compensate for some of the profit the parlors were losing in competition with the brokers over folk custom items, funeral parlors exerted unspoken rules that forced brokers to only introduce higher-end civil affairs items to the bereaved. For example, cremation coffins are coffin-like boxes made of paper or bamboo for the deceased to lie down in during the funeral. It was a civil affairs item. At Huangpu, the cheaper cremation coffins cost less than RMB 1,000 (USD 158). However, when brokers introduced this item to the bereaved, they could only introduce items costing RMB 1,380 (USD 219) or higher.

Of course, funeral brokers thought that competition with funeral parlors was unfair. According to Chen Yu:

> After people started to say that funeral parlors were profiteers, they [the parlors] decreased their prices on folk custom items. Funeral parlors' cheapest, low-end cremains caskets are now so cheap that they are losing money on them. However, funeral parlors then increased their prices

for civil affairs items! In other words, the funeral parlors lowered their prices for products that were open to market competition and increased their prices for the products they monopolized. And then they [funeral parlors] blamed the profiteering on us, that the creation of excessive profit was our [funeral brokers'] fault even though the portion of that [profiteering] money that we are making is based on competition while the portion they are making is based on their monopoly.

The legalization of funeral brokers not only granted state funeral parlors advantages in business competition but also turned the relationship between brokers and parlors into a quasi-governing one. We could see this clearly in the use of work permits. Once they were legalized, funeral brokers had to bring their work permits with them to arrange any services in funeral parlors. The permits contained the brokers' names, their companies' names, and their pictures. Without these papers, the parlors would refuse their business meeting requests. This work permit was originally a paper booklet. Several months into my fieldwork, in January 2011, the trade association changed the paperwork permit into a plastic card with an IC memory chip for storing data. The trade association stored the broker's so-called honest-and-trusted file (*chengxin dang'an*) on this ID card. This technological change allowed state practitioners to add notes to the IC card of each specific broker. A higher number of negative marks that a broker received would result in a weaker honest-and-trusted quality score for the broker. Funeral parlors could then refuse to serve brokers with a poor honest-and-trusted rating or could simply tell the bereaved directly that the broker they had hired had a bad record. Although this Orwellian surveillance later became everyday reality in China in 2019 and 2020 (and some might even argue that the outbreak of the COVID-19 pandemic in 2020 has further facilitated this surveillance system), the controversy in this specific case was that this entire set of information was collected and stored not by the government but in the computers of their partial business competitors—funeral parlors.

The third part of the structure of the fragility of brokers was a set of seemingly innocent and apolitical economic regulations that functioned to ensure political domination. One of the best examples was the Shanghai government's promotion of the Shanghai Standard Funeral Brokers' Service Contract (Shanghaishi binzang daili fuwu hetong). Early on in my fieldwork, the vice chair of the trade association told me that they were in the process of drafting this regulation. He said that signing such a standard contract was a way to protect both the brokers and the bereaved. Brokers could know for sure that the bereaved would pay them. The bereaved would gain a legal basis for making sure that brokers followed their business agreement. At that time, I did not give much thought to this issue. His statement seemed to make perfect sense. I only later began to realize how this practice would push brokers into an even more fragile position.

This standard contract was to be written in triplicate. One copy was to be given to the bereaved, one to the broker, and the other to the funeral parlor. The most controversial part of the policy was this last part. As Chen Yu pointed out, many brokers did not object to the idea itself. Rather, forcing them to give a third copy to the funeral parlor was ridiculous because they were business competitors. Once state funeral parlors had the third copy of standard contracts, the state could then control the broker in many more ways. Tang An said, "For example, if the parlor thinks you earn too much or you disobey their rules, they could bring a copy of all of your business transactions to the tax bureau." Alternatively, the parlor could also make the tax bureau check your suppliers' taxes. Most suppliers of funeral brokers manufactured their products in small workshops (*xiaozuofang*) run by mom-and-pop businesses who, like other such businesses in China, rarely paid full taxes. As Tang An said, the Shanghai government was "using the name of the market to exert political sovereignty" (*yi shichangzhiming xing zhengzhizhishi*).

In fact, brokers' concerns over the standard contract became a full-blown drama in the middle of the 2011 training conference I attended. On that day, one of the morning sections was a class given by a government official from the Shanghai Municipal Bureau of Quality and Technical Supervision. She presented their newly proposed policy, Procedures of the Shanghai Municipality on Funeral Brokers. She talked about the content of this policy with specific emphasis on why people needed standard contracts in general. She said that the standard contract was a way to civilize (*wenming*) business conduct and raise the quality (*suzhi*) of the industry—both phrases were commonly used to govern and discipline, especially rural, Chinese people (Kipnis 2007). With the speaker's Power-Point slideshow projected on the screen, for a moment I thought that I was in a lecture at a university law department. The speaker definitely made no effort to accommodate her audience, most of whom did not have college degrees (and many of whom had never graduated from or even gone to high school).

After the class finished, we went to lunch. Unlike the silence of the two lectures, everyone at the table (some were from Longevity, but there were many others as well) heatedly criticized the standard contract, asserting that this was the state's next attempt to "kill" funeral brokers' business. When the afternoon lecture started up again, however, the atmosphere was suddenly quiet and lifeless again. The speaker was another government official. He was from the Contract Supervision Division (Hetong jiandu guanlichu) in the Shanghai Administration for Industry and Commerce. He started his talk with (again) a legal presentation on a contract. For example, he said that a contract is the legal representation of an agreement between two parties. It details the rights and responsibilities, and duties and obligations, of each party to the other and so on. To further illustrate what a contract was, he used a cell phone as an example to explore the conditions under which his saying that he gave his cell phone to you constituted a contract. Although I found his explanation to be quite clear, I saw how this display of legal "expertise" was so completely detached from the brokers' concerns. Sitting down as one of the nine hundred or so people in the audience, I thought this lecture would pass in a similar way as the morning one—with brokers sitting and sleeping to make the time pass by faster.

However, about twenty minutes into the presentation talking about what constitutes a contract when someone gives you a phone, a man stood up and yelled:

> We don't give a fuck about your cell phone or my cell phone! Our concern is this Shanghai Standard Funeral Brokers' Service Contract! Why do you guys have to do this to us? Why can't you leave us a means of making a living? People say that rural migrants working in cities are pitiful, but at least they can go back to their hometown if they lose their jobs. Where can we go [the "we" referred to local Shanghai people working as brokers]? I guess we can only go to funeral parlors [meaning all they could do was die, with the added irony that even *dead* funeral brokers had to go through state funeral parlors].

This incident halted the conference for ten minutes. Although the drama was eventually resolved, it forced the speaker to give up on his original talk. The presenter then started to talk about the content of the contract and why it was "good" to have a standard contract for funeral brokers' own "self-interest." Although the audience sat through the talk in the end, their puzzled and worried expressions were not in any way resolved because their worries were about how these legal documents might be used, their potential forced disclosure to a competitor, and the fact that a legal form created a variety of outcomes that quickly spiraled beyond brokers' control. All of these factors went well beyond any "legal" understanding of why a contract might be good.

To sum up, their largely rural migrant status combined with brokers' temporary form of employment, the semilegal status of funeral brokers, the quasi ruler-subject relationships between funeral brokers and the funeral parlors they both competed with and were forced to cooperate with, and the seemingly purely economic measures that established political control all contributed to the fragility of funeral brokers both politically and economically. This structure of fragility is the infrastructure to their feelings of being fragile. Taken together, these revealed the extent to which funeral brokers were vulnerable under an authoritarian market economy where there were few meaningful methods for accountability, balance of power, and political change.

Playing Edge Ball: Crossing the Moral and Legal Boundaries

So far, I have laid out how funeral brokers were positioned in a structurally frag-ile middle position that is characterized by risk, vulnerability, and instability. While in liberal democracies people who are in a comparable position might have institutionalized social mechanisms to react against such a crisis, people who live under authoritarian rule have fewer existing means to tackle these issues. In their hope to not only survive but also to prosper as they navigated through their fragile middle position, funeral brokers conducted their business in cre-ative ways to deal with their structurally fragile position. While some of these practices were entirely legal and moral, some were not. This section tells stories of how funeral brokers did their business, how some of these business practices were at the edge of moral and legal boundaries, and how these not entirely legal or moral practices created a platform for the resurgence of popular religious practices and religious ideas of self in conceptualizing the dead in contemporary urban China.

When I did my preparatory fieldwork in 2009, I interviewed a scholar from a civil affairs school. When I asked him about a story on funeral brokers that I had seen in the news, he started his explanation by telling me that funeral bro-kers were "hitting edge balls" (*da cabianqiu*) in the death industry. Originally a sports term, an edge ball is played to touch the very edge of the sideline of the table tennis surface. For now, this phrase can be translated as "pushing the en-velope." The way this scholar used this term emphasized the semilegal and amoral aspect of funeral brokers. His usage was consistent with dictionary def-initions. For example, the *Contemporary Chinese Dictionary* explained that people use "hitting edge balls" figuratively to mean "conduct that is on the bor-derline of legality but not yet illegal" (Chao and Han 2005). The *New Age Chinese-English Dictionary* (Wu and Cheng 2001) explained this concept in English as "something almost, but not quite, illegal; circumventing the law or regulation by doing something quasi-legal."

Funeral brokers were seen as playing with edge balls for many reasons. Their legal status, registered with one but often unable to register with the other bu-reau, is one that I discussed earlier. Here, I would like to discuss their business practices and how these practices pushed the legal and moral boundaries of death management. The first was related to nominal affiliation (*guakao*). Although le-galization seemed to suggest that Shanghai funeral brokers were all legitimate, the reality was a little messier. For example, affiliation with a registered com-pany was part of the criteria for retaining work permits in Shanghai. However, not everyone wanted to work for an agency as this also required sharing profits

and a loss of independence. This led to the phenomenon of being nominally affiliated with a company but working more as a freelancer as a way to bend the
requirement for the actual employment relationships between brokers and their
companies. Such nominally affiliated funeral brokers did not need to directly
share profits with the shell company they "worked for," hence the "nominal" description. For example, Prosperity (the restaurant) established a funeral agency
and then allowed individual funeral brokers to be affiliated with it as their agency.
Prosperity was willing to go to all the trouble, work, and cost of establishing and
maintaining a company because these brokers then persuaded their customers
to host their funeral banquets at Prosperity.

While nominal affiliation seemed harmless enough even if this was an edge
ball play, funeral brokers also engaged in other actions that might evoke very
different moral judgments. Specifically, here I talk about the fundamental challenge of how funeral brokers found their business. Since the bereaved could just
as easily go directly through the parlors without hiring a broker at all, funeral
brokers had to find the dead (and thus their bereaved) before they arrived at the
funeral parlors. As such, every funeral broker I knew told me that their business was essentially built on "information sources" (*xunxi laiyuan*) about dead
bodies. Moreover, to sustain a business, the flow of information from these
sources had to be steady. There were several ways to cultivate steady information sources. The first way was to build a network of paid informants. Paid informants came in several forms in Shanghai. Generally, they were either full-time
or part-time. Full-time paid informants were best exemplified by "watchers"
(*dinggong*). Watchers hang out in a hospital all day to wait for someone to die,
and then they pass this information on to one of the funeral brokers who hired
them. A broker I knew started his career as a watcher. He then quickly learned
the necessary skills of arranging funerals and eventually became a funeral broker working on his own. Perhaps because he started his career as a watcher, when
I met him, he was still relying on hiring watchers as his information sources.
Although registered as a funeral agency, he was the only person working at his
company. He did not have office space and said that hospitals were his offices.

As for part-time paid informants, they existed in a variety of places with direct or indirect connections to dying, death, and dead bodies. One common type
of part-time paid informant was ambulance drivers. Several brokers told me that
the number of emergency line personnel who joined teams of part-time paid informants had increased since the Shanghai government outsourced its emergency
calling service. Other common locations for recruiting part-time paid informants
were nursing homes and morgues. Tang An became a funeral broker because his
father was a guard at a morgue. Tang An's father was a sent-down youth who spent
many years in rural Yunnan Province. Years later, after he retired there and with

some difficulty, he moved his household registration back to Shanghai. However, because living expenses were high in Shanghai and his retirement income was an amount meant to supplement a rural life, he wanted to continue working. The only job that he managed to find was as a security guard in a hospital morgue. Soon after Tang An's father started working in the morgue, he discovered the world of funeral brokers. He then asked a broker to train Tang An to be one.

Regardless of whether we were talking about full-time or part-time paid informants, funeral brokers generally paid their informants about RMB 500 (USD 82) for each case sent to them during my fieldwork. Most anyone who lived in China at the time of my fieldwork would know that receiving a cut for business transactions represented a much broader social phenomenon beyond the death industry. For example, when you walked out of a train station in China and a taxi driver picked you up and helped you find a hotel, you could assume that the driver received a cut from the hotel. Or when you took your friend to buy a car from the salesperson you just bought one from, you would expect to receive a cut from the car salesman. When there was a void in legal regulations, the line between commission and kickback was blurred. At the same time, I would be cautious to describe receiving a cut as "Chinese behavior" in some essentialized manner, however. When I bought a car in Boston in 2012, the American salesperson there told me that he would give me a small amount of cash if I brought in another customer for him.

In the Shanghai funeral industry, what made paid informants particularly controversial was not the payment per se. Rather, the controversial part was that sometimes a paid informant reported the same information to more than one broker. They did so because funeral brokers had to pay for the lead regardless of whether they closed the deal. One immediate problem with this double selling was that occasionally this led to two or more funeral brokers fighting outside hospitals or outside the deceased's home over the right to represent the bereaved—sometimes even without the bereaved knowing about the conflict. This kind of incident had decreased significantly by the time I did my fieldwork. The turning point for the industry to move away from such a frontier mode of doing business was Shanghai's hosting of the 2010 World Expo. This major international event gave the Shanghai government an excuse (and enough capital) to "clean up" funeral brokers' business operations. In fact, the brother of a funeral broker I know was one "victim" of exactly this cleanup operation. Her brother, who was also a funeral broker and had had previous fistfights over business competition, was arrested about a year before the 2010 World Expo without any trial or sentence. Approximately ten months after the 2010 World Expo finished—meaning that he was in jail for almost two years without any trial—her brother was released.

The second way to gain information was to control one of the portals for death-related information. Fortunate Funeral Agency was a funeral agency employing two full-time brokers (in addition to its boss), and it had real office space. Its owner told me that he gained access to information through an official contractual relationship with a telephone company. The Shanghai branch of a Chinese telecom company has a special information-providing hotline. Customers can call to ask for any kind of information. Although this hotline is similar to a Yellow Pages listing in the United States, information on only a few selected companies was provided in each case. As such, companies generally had to pay to be selected—very similar to one of Google Search's sponsored links. Fortunate paid to be one of the first three funeral broker companies mentioned if someone called the hotline and asked for information on arranging a funeral. A lower, second-tier payment would have gotten them a mention only if the caller—having heard the first three companies—asked to hear additional names. Needless to say, because only three companies were mentioned (or six including the additional choices), not everyone who could pay and was willing to pay could receive this spot. The owner of Fortunate Funeral Agency told me that "of course" he had a special under-the-table deal with the person in charge of the decision. He replied to my inquiry as if I had just asked one of the stupidest questions he had ever heard.

The third method to gain information was through "neighborhood community committees" (*juweihui*). These neighborhood community committees are parallel to the work unit's links through work in that both were grassroots governance associations that linked individuals directly to the party-state. These grassroots party organizations (and, in particular, work units) played a critical role in performing death rituals in contemporary Shanghai (I come back to this in chapter 5). All urban residents necessarily belonged to neighborhood community committees. Neighborhood community committees were good information sources because people had to report a death to them immediately after it happened. In fact, it was not uncommon for residents to ask representatives of their committee questions regarding funeral arrangements. People in neighborhood committees were also aware of who in the communities were terminally ill in the first place.

The fourth way for funeral brokers to secure steady information sources was through interpersonal networks. Early on in my fieldwork at Longevity, I often asked each broker there how they found the case they were working on. The answer was always the same: a friend (or a friend of a friend) introduced this customer. I was curious about how they managed to have so many friends (and friends of friends) who needed funeral arrangements. It turns out that Longevity's foundation for building up such a broad and steady interpersonal network was Chen Ting's connections to Huangpu Funeral Parlor. When relatives and friends of state practitioners at Huangpu needed to arrange funerals, they approached these state practitioners for guidance. However, many products sold in parlors were more expensive than comparable options sold via brokers. As such, as one state practitioner told me, "You should not introduce people you know to a bad deal." They thus took people to Longevity instead. The emphasis on preexisting social relationships was why funeral brokers at Longevity often told the bereaved at the end of their business that they would not charge a "service fee" (RMB 200, approximately USD 32), because their common friends had introduced them. Brokers at Longevity considered themselves morally superior to the ambulance-chasing kind of funeral broker who relied on paid informants to report random deaths. Liang Wan told me that Longevity's model (interpersonal networks) was a more decent (*zhengpai*) kind exactly because its primary information source was friends. Meanwhile, the ambulance chasers' model was a form of "walking through the side door" (*zoupianmen*, meaning "dishonest" or "indecent"). I heard this positive comment about Longevity from the Fortune Funeral Agency as well.

From these different information sources about dead bodies, it seems that while searching for dead bodies was morally problematic, as long as the acts were mediated through interpersonal relationships, it then became (relatively) moral. On the surface, this distinction was also consistent with the way funeral brokers told the story of the origins of their profession. I gathered four versions of this origin myth. The first version said that there had always existed a set of "good-hearted people" (*haoxinren*) who liked to help their friends and relatives organize funerals (or other rituals). They did not do so for a fee but still usually received a red envelope (with money in it) from the bereaved as a show of gratitude. In this sense, the kind of relationship between the bereaved and these good-hearted people was based on gift exchange; both sides entered into a social debt similar to how other social relations work in China. They were more similar to "friends" who helped each other with what they had experience with. The second version traced funeral brokers to the fact that, historically, well-off families often hired a "grand manager" (*dazongguan*) to organize funerals in Shanghai. These managers were known for their skill at organizing events and provided their services for a fee. In this case, regardless of whether or not these grand managers and the bereaved were friends in the first place, the kind of relationship between them was based primarily on market exchange through which one side provided labor and expertise while the other side gave money in return.

The third version traced the origins of funeral brokers to retired state practitioners or the close friends and relatives of state practitioners in Shanghai. These people often helped their acquaintances organize funerals because they had knowledge of and better access to funeral parlors and, thus, could manage to

pull off "special" funeral arrangements if needed. Finally, the fourth version was
that funeral brokers emerged when funeral parlors asked state practitioners to
go out to get more business at the very beginning of the market reforms in Shanghai. This was a part of the parlors' efforts to marketize and earn larger profits,
as described in chapter 2, but as a consequence, it also made an increasing number of people realize the potential of, and some methods of being, a private
broker in the funeral industry. Although both the third and the fourth traced
the origin of funeral brokers to state practitioners or their friends and relatives,
the third version emphasized helpful characteristics while the fourth stressed
entrepreneurial characteristics. The difference between the third and fourth versions thus also echoes the contrast between nice, altruistic people (the good-
hearted) and self-interested entrepreneurs (the grand managers).

These four origin stories reveal two different ways of conceptualizing the self of
funeral brokers and the role of exchange in creating social relationships. One envisioned brokers as a kind of relational person clearly (and necessarily) embedded in
reciprocal social networks. The other saw them as self-motivated and individualis-
tic entrepreneurs engaged in utilitarian transactional relationships with their customers. The former entered funerals through friendship and gift exchange (red
envelopes), and the latter entered customer relationships through market exchange
(service fees). D. J. Hatfield observed a similar kind of contrast for opera troupes
(actors and musicians) and matchmakers in Taiwan (Hatfield, email communication). Moreover, Hatfield noticed that professional actors and musicians of opera
troupes and matchmakers were (and still are) often considered "mean" (*jian*)
people in Taiwan. Meanwhile, amateur troupes (*zidi tuan*) and "friends" who engaged in the very same matchmaking or performing were considered good people.
The key here was that when the truth of these relationships was produced as
friendships, such as those between the amateurs and their friends, then the actions
fell into a moral realm. In contrast, when the truth of the relationship was produced through professionalization and professional interactions, the interactions
could more easily be viewed as immoral. The same actions (whether we are talking
about funeral brokers, opera troupes, or matchmakers) implicated different truths
based on how the truth of relationships is produced in the interaction (Foucault
2001).

However clear such contrasting views and the ethical judgments they supported were made in origin narratives, in practice, the truth of relationship was
a lot more ambiguous here. For one, in Shanghai, both the grand managers and
the good-hearted people could be ethical. One reason for such ambiguity was
because there was a tripartite relationship of brokers, introducers, and the bereaved involved. As such, both the good-hearted and the grand managers could
be ethical or unethical depending on the logics of interrelations in and the

specific perspective one takes on this tripartite relationship. For example, generally, when a friend introduced her or his friends and relatives to Longevity, this person received money for each case she or he introduced. At the time of my fieldwork, these "introducers" to Longevity received 50 percent of the profit of each transaction. While this general ratio varied over time (I was told that earlier, when the funeral broker business was less competitive, funeral brokers in general paid less to introducers) and it is more expensive than a paid informant, it is still economically worthwhile because bereaved who were brought in by an introducer were usually a done deal. Although the introducers, in theory, could decide to keep the money or give it (back) to the bereaved, funeral brokers had no choice but to give this money to the introducers to make sure they would be willing to introduce business to them again in the future. As for the bereaved, they might or might not know that their friends (introducers) received a cut from their business. From the perspective of the bereaved, the unethical one is more likely to be the friend who received a cut in this tripartite relationship.

Secondly, on extreme occasions, the same person could try to occupy two positions in this tripartite relationship. Such collation could cause deep ethical concerns. One night, Chen Ting invited her employees and me to a nice restaurant. During our dinner, Chen Ting left our table several times to talk on the phone. She said that a woman was arranging the business of her father's funeral and was quite a difficult customer. Chen Ting said that this woman was the only child of the deceased. Moreover, her father's work unit was a state institute—meaning that the daughter would already receive a hefty lump sum of money to cover her father's funeral. Despite all these factors that indicated that the daughter should be more likely to spend money for her father's final farewell, in reality, she engaged in a very harsh and drawn-out negotiation (and then renegotiation) of nearly every price.

On our way back from the dinner, as we all sat in Chen Ting's car, this bereaved called yet again. Chen Ting asked us all to be quiet because she wanted the phone call to go through the car's speaker system. All of us sitting in the car then heard the bereaved speak:

> THE BEREAVED: I just finished a phone call with some people in my father's work unit. They want to purchase ten flower baskets from you.
>
> CHEN TING: This is great. I will call the flower shop as soon as we hang up the phone. What else can I do for you now?
>
> THE BEREAVED: I introduced my father's work unit to buy flower baskets from you. What are you going to do?

At this moment, I was sort of in a state of shock. I exchanged eye contact with Chen Yu. At first, I was not sure if I had heard what I thought I had heard because what I had heard was so strange. It sounded like I had just witnessed a daughter asking to receive a cut on her own father's funeral costs.

> CHEN TING: I don't understand what you mean by this. Could you please be more specific?
>
> THE BEREAVED: Hmmm . . . I persuaded my father's work unit to buy flower baskets from you. Don't you think that you should show some gratitude?
>
> CHEN TING: Gratitude? I don't understand what you mean. I gave you the cheapest price for these flower baskets. The reason I suggested you buy flower baskets from me was because the meeting hall looks better when all the flower baskets are the same. Plus, I can arrange the baskets [bought through me] in advance so that when the guests arrive, all the baskets will already be lined up. If you think that I offered you a bad deal, you are welcome to buy flower baskets from someone else. I will still put these baskets together for you. If you think that this is not enough or my service is just not good enough, I am truly sorry I made you feel this way. You are, of course, welcome to walk away from our deal. However, I truly don't know what kind of "gratitude" you are expecting from me.

My intention in telling this story was not to say that this case was in any way representative or common. It was extremely rare to have a grieving family member also function as an introducer who is entitled to receive a cut. Rather, my intention was to show that the seemingly clear distinctions between unethical kinds of funeral brokers and ethical state practitioners or the vulnerable bereaved and the profiteering funeral brokers were a lot blurrier than is commonly assumed once you have a chance to see the complexity of positions and relations in managing death as a business. If anything, these examples all point to the moral ambiguity both of being a funeral broker and of their necessary relationships with different kinds of bereaved and with the relative morality of finding bodies via friends or relatives of the bereaved.

At the end of the day, part of these moral ambiguities stemmed from the fact that funeral brokers were somewhere between the good-hearted people and the grand masters. These types of complexes of ethical positions and moral ambiguities are especially prevalent in modern China—a place that has gone through a rapid change from authoritarian planned economy to authoritarian market economy (though not in any clear-cut, teleological way). Funeral brokers were not good-hearted people because they were not amateurs who just helped their friends. They were full-time professionals. Meanwhile, however, they were not the grand managers of the origin stories because they were indeed helping friends, and their friends who introduced the bereaved to them would also get a cut from whatever the funeral brokers earned. The boundary between the ethical and unethical was blurry because the truth of the relationships was ambiguous in the first place.

What legalization did, then, was to clarify and rationalize the ambiguous nature of being funeral brokers. Legalization meant that funeral brokers were asked to be individual entrepreneurs who were professionals (and could only be such) and who entered into a market exchange with the bereaved. This was particularly important for the state because the only way for the state to have legitimacy to govern funeral brokers was to define brokers solely as grand managers. It is then along this line that we can understand the implementation of training sessions, work permits (be it in a paper form or an IC card), and standard contracts.

While legalization might appear to be a path toward the moral and was presented as such in the state discourse of honest-and-trusted scores and standard contracts, here it pushed brokers toward ethical positions more likely to be seen as immoral—the anonymity inherent exchanges framed in such a way was a key reason earnings in the death industry were seen as immoral. Once the truth of the relationship was remade or clarified, then the relationship produced in this truth lost the ambiguity that gave individual brokers a degree of agency and became then either ethical or unethical. The critique of the American funeral industry for profiteering is built precisely on a narrative of a greedy funeral director taking advantage of a stranger at the latter's most vulnerable time (Mitford 1978). This was why many American funeral directors at the time of my fieldwork never called the bereaved "customers." Instead, they called the bereaved "family." One important task in running a funeral home in the New England area in the American Northeast, for instance, is to participate in local civic groups, such as by sponsoring children's football teams, to establish connections with people within the community "unrelated" to one's work (Jim McQuaid, personal communication, 2012). The assumption behind active participation in local civic groups was exactly based on thinking that as long as the relationship between a funeral director and the bereaved was no longer anonymous, somehow their transactions became moral.

To sum up, on the one hand, the state defined funeral brokers as market subjects by disambiguating the ethical ambiguity of being funeral brokers in the name of professionalization, marketization, and transparency. On the other hand, the state blamed funeral brokers for not serving the people by being grand managers. The contradictions in these two processes, paralleling the structural impossibilities posed by their need to work with, compete with, and be regulated by state funeral parlors, have left these brokers in an impossible position.

Edge Ball Play and Fragility as Affect

Even while occupying such an impossible position, it was these fragile and morally ambiguous funeral brokers who succeeded in reshaping funerals by reintroducing religious practices into secular civil funerals despite these being exactly what Funeral Reform intended to destroy. In this section, I explain the mechanisms involved in this process. Recalling the distinction between folk custom items and civil affairs items, funeral brokers at Longevity followed such a distinction when conducting their business meetings with the bereaved. They usually started their business meetings by introducing the civil affairs items on which the parlors had a monopoly first and relatively quickly. Then, they concentrated on the folk custom items by giving in-depth elaborations on why the bereaved might want a particular folk custom item because these were the things that brokers could make money from. For example, both Huangpu and Longevity sold coarse yellow paper (*huangzhi*) in squares. Shanghai people put this paper inside the cremation coffin and underneath the body. The squares were also used to rub the cremation coffin before it was ceremoniously nailed shut. The same paper was also used as spiritual money to burn to the deceased once it was rolled up like an egg roll. When state funeral practitioners sold coarse yellow paper, they simply asked the bereaved if they wanted some. In fact, these coarse yellow papers were not even displayed in one of the transparent, glass-door cabinets in funeral parlors.

However, when funeral brokers sold them, they often offered specific discursive explanations (*shuofa*) of their meaning and use. For example, in one business meeting, Liang Wan at Longevity said to the bereaved:

> Do you want to buy some coarse yellow paper? I don't know if you know that many people prefer to use yellow paper to rub the coffin. There are several explanations for having these. A more traditional, more superstitious[3] explanation is that symbolically rubbing the cremation coffin turns it into a golden casket. Additionally, people usually apply a thick layer of yellow paper underneath the body. This yellow bottom layer added to the layer of *xibo* [a different kind of spiritual money made of silver-colored tinfoil paper] placed on top of the body symbolize

"wearing gold with sliver" [*chuanjin daiyin*]. Of course, this practice reflects personal beliefs. If you don't believe these superstitions, there is another explanation that I have heard of. It was more of a scientific explanation. That is, if you put yellow papers in the coffin, it helps the body burn better.

During the process of offering explanations, Liang Wan observed how the bereaved responded to determine whether he should elaborate on one explanation more than the other. As far as Liang Wan was concerned, why the bereaved bought these yellow coarse papers was not important at all as long as they bought them. Yet, as a result of this process, funeral brokers transmitted religious practices to the bereaved, who might or might not have known about them before. On a larger, cumulative scale, offering explanations eventually became a platform for religious revival in Shanghai's deathscape. Outside Baoxin Funeral Parlor is the famous "Funeral Avenue" (Binzang yitiaojie). All of these shops were either owned by funeral brokers or, at least, kept operating by funeral brokers. Many people who worked on the state side told me that this Funeral Avenue was one of the centers of "superstition."[4] Once certain items gained in popularity, however, then state funeral parlors, too, started to sell them because, as one state practitioner put it, the bereaved would buy these things just because "it is better to believe in its efficacy than not" (*ningke xinqiyou*). Consequently, a state practitioner told me, "Much of the stuff we [parlors] have is now all 'the result of [funeral brokers] messing around' [*luangao de jieguo*]." Whether or to what degree these religious explanations and practices were traditional or invented is truly not important here. What is key is that people in the funeral industry themselves also recognized and attributed the rise of popular religious rituals in funerals to funeral brokers, even if such attribution was cast in a negative light.

With this possibility for structural change in mind, one can start to see the moral ambiguity of funeral brokers in a different light. What role do fragility and amorality (or even immorality) play in our thinking about what resistance and civil disobedience mean? For example, recall the technique of nominal affiliation mentioned before; funeral brokers used this as a work-around for the legal registration requirement. This technique, however, was by no means an exclusive tactic used in the funeral industry. Rather, it was a commonly observed phenomenon in China for all social organizations, from environmental NGOs to religious organizations, as a way to deal with registration issues and to negotiate state control (cf. Chan 2005; Howell 2004; Kipnis, Tomba, and Unger 2009). As such, the concept of playing edge ball suddenly might take on a whole different set of moral implications. In fact, reading hitting edge balls as righteous resistance is not such a stretch if we look into the origin story of the edge ball metaphor. Here, let me tell the story of Qin Benli.

Qin Benli was the founder of the *World Economic Herald* (*Shijie jingji daobao*). Founded in 1980, Qin's weekly newspaper quickly developed a reputation for advocating for reform policies. This short-lived newspaper played a key role in the lead-up to the 1989 June Fourth Movement, which ended with the CCP killing many students protesting in Tiananmen Square in Beijing (Jernow 1994). Qin specifically used the hitting-edge-balls expression to illustrate his idea of running an ideal newspaper. In an interview with a *New York Times* reporter, Qin said, "If you hit the ball and miss the end of the table, you lose. If you hit near the end of the table, it's too easy. So, you want to aim to just nick the end of the table. That's our policy" (Kristof 1989). To hit an edge ball in news reporting meant to "push our coverage to the limits of the tolerance of the government while reducing the political risks for the paper to the lowest level" (Pei 1998, 175). Qin's ultimate goal was to expand the "table" itself by constantly attacking the boundary (Shen 1991). In this context, a linguistic scholar, Li Anxing (2008), criticized the dictionary translations and definitions of *edge ball*. Li explained that edge-ball conduct in sports could be completely legal, not to mention that skill at edge-ball play might be a trait of champions in their sport. As a result, Li (2008, 155) proposed to translate "playing edge ball" as "playing by the rules even if one bends (distends or stretches) the rules to a breaking point; to push the envelope; to play by rules that are open to interpretation."

With this reading of hitting edge balls in mind, we can then observe a very different genre of edge-ball play in China—something closer to Qin's notion of running his newspaper. For example, a Kong lineage temple in northern China was rebuilt with two halls and two sets of ritual performances to allow it to claim to have moved from being a potentially suspicious ancestor worship site to a public "cultural education" site of Confucius tradition (Jun 1996). Similarly, making a popular religious temple—the Dragon Temple—to instead be seen as a more orthodox Daoist temple enabled it to be legible to the eyes of a state that views popular religion not as a religion but as dangerous "superstition" (Chau 2006). In this case, temple leadership also associated it with an international environmental nongovernmental organization, which legitimized its existence not only as a site of religion but also as a site for nature conservation. Both of these plays can be described as clever edge-ball plays that could serve to expand "the table" of religious possibilities. In fact, some people consciously use this edge-ball phrase in such a positive manner. For example, when Robert Weller (personal communication) conducted fieldwork in Jiangsu in 2014, temple managers constantly used the term "playing edge ball" when describing what they had to do to manage their temple.

This righteous, morally grounded, and politically loaded concept with clearly stated rebellious intentions for press freedom goes hand in hand with a mostly derogatory term describing loophole conduct since hitting edge balls can be downright nasty at times and in some extreme cases lethal (the adulterated baby formula cases in China around 2005 that led to several deaths is a relevant example here). Edge-ball plays could be entirely legal but immoral; illegal but moral; or, regardless of the legality, simply ambiguously amoral. Yet, in certain specific contexts, hitting an edge ball was and could still be the sort of "righteous" resistance—similar to Qin's newspaper model—that anthropologists would have very little difficulty embracing. I argue that it is exactly this inherent ambiguity that gives the edge ball power to push back against authoritarian regimes when there is little institutionalized space for demanding social change.

It is also important to point out that hitting edge balls was neither clearly resistance nor "corruption." Rather, doing so was more of a tango dance that required both the state and the public (assuming we can somehow separate the two in the first place) to coordinate keeping the boundaries ambiguous. A step forward on the public side meant that the state was willing not to push back and vice versa. The state deciding not to push back did not necessarily mean the triumph of the public but, simply, that the state decided not to govern that particular thing at that particular moment; it could always do so later (thus the fragility of structure). Most important of all, fragile people hit edge balls because they were fragile, not because they were rebellious.

The technique of hitting an edge ball, as opposed to heroic individual acts, is particularly effective in authoritarian states. Heroism as a form of resistance or a way to create social change has only very rarely worked in China; heroes have been too easy put down. Qin Benli and his ideal of running a newspaper is probably the best example. When the edge-ball players were part of an anonymous mass, it worked best. This kind of collaborative and cumulative effort by nameless funeral brokers at hitting edge balls effectively carved out an institutional space for their businesses within the Shanghai funeral industry despite the industry still remaining (to a large degree) a state monopoly and their business practices threatening a portion of Funeral Reform's tenets. The best example for how this anonymous mass of fragile individuals created real structural change is the inclusion of religious morality within secular socialist commemorative rites that I describe in detail in later chapters of this book.

As a result, a single narrative of state despotism or either people's obedience or rebellion does not help us to understand authoritarian governance and the possibilities for reacting against such governance. Rather, I suggest treating the metaphor of hitting edge balls as a key concept to explore how an authoritarian regime maintains and re-creates the conditions of its power: the regime needs to be both autocratic and restrained as well as responsive and expansive. Only by focusing on the intricacies of edge-ball play as a form of governance and a power play from the edges of that governance do we get greater clarity on how authoritarian governance works beyond the often assumed simple distinction between domination and resistance. "Resistance" of this edge-ball type might entail a push toward justice or freedom based on liberal democratic values, but it might just as easily be amoral or even immoral pushes in other directions. Expanding the boundaries of state limitations in some cases meant increasing personal freedom and the availability of public goods, but this certainly was not always the case. "The public" (or what a "public good" is) is never a concept without ambiguity or contradiction.

Conclusion

To conclude, fragility motivated funeral brokers to act in certain ways in response to their fragile middle positions. As I have shown in my story of Chen Ting, her fragility animated her to be a self-motivated entrepreneur even though it simultaneously conditioned her. Fragility created, conditioned, and sustained a market subjectivity in China. Consequently, whereas a market economy might least benefit such fragile people, these people might be exactly the group most likely to become market subjects. As state practitioners came to live in dissonance with the state's desire to render them market subjects, funeral brokers highly resonated with the state's desire to focus on economic efficiency, professionalization, and self-motivation even though, in its regulation of them, this was not the goal of the market governance of death. Both this chapter and chapter 2 show that the market governance of death does not necessarily entail market subjectivity.

Meanwhile, however, fragility not only pushed funeral parlors to change but also opened up a space for the possible return (or reinvention and even creation) of popular religious and other folk death rituals within state institutions. Despite the fact that most brokers were simply trying to make money and have a better life at a time when they were otherwise being left behind in the growing gap between those with and without better incomes, education, and social connections with the state in urban Shanghai, their edge-ball plays nonetheless expanded the table itself by constantly attacking its border. It is the same ambiguous amorality inherent in edge-ball politics that both makes it difficult to cheer for and produced significant change.

Moving away from funeral professionals, the next question then is whether the state attempted to also make the bereaved and the dead into market subjects, as China moved from a planned to a market economy. If so, how did they do this? What were the consequences of these governing attempts? Did we see a rise of individualized selves in commemorating the dead? In the next chapter, I illustrate how the state attempted to transform both the bereaved and the dead into market subjects by promoting personalized funerals.

Part 2
DEATH RITUAL AND PLURALIST SUBJECTIVITY

INDIVIDUALISM, INTERRUPTED

Zhou Enlai, the first premier of the PRC, once said that Chinese people needed two revolutions to change traditional (read "feudalist") Chinese funeral and interment customs. The goal of the first revolution was "not keeping corpses" (*bubaocun yiti*), and the second was "not keeping cremains" (*bubaocun guhui*). Zhou was probably the best exemplar for the CCP of both revolutions. When Zhou died in 1976, his body was cremated ("not keeping corpses") and then scattered into the water ("not keeping cremains").[1]

From the perspective of the people who implement funeral governance (including government officials, scholars, and funeral professionals who work in various state funeral institutions), Shanghai accomplished the first revolution of not keeping corpses in less than thirty years.[2] Shanghai is now officially striving to complete the second revolution.[3] Not keeping cremains entailed at least two distinct policy orientations in practice. The first was to develop alternative methods for the disposal of cremains, which meant that, instead of burying or storing cremains in cemeteries or columbaria, Shanghai residents were encouraged to embrace sea burials (*haizang*), tree burials (*shuzang*), and grassland burials (*caopingzang*), among others. These alternative methods return cremains unboxed to the natural environment without, ideally, leaving a trace of the identity and ownership of the cremains. The theory was that human flesh and bones become an unidentifiable part of the ecosystem that sustains all life.

Along these lines, I once attended a funeral industry conference in Shanghai, and one of the speakers introduced the latest and the most "environmentally friendly" body disposal method developed in Germany—"water burial" (*shuizang*)—as a future potential alternative for China. The original term for this burial is *resomation*. The resomator, itself, resembles an airport baggage-screener device that can transform dead bodies into a coffee-colored liquid that is ready to "flush down the drain into the sewerage system" (Ayres 2010). The point of this presentation (in fact, of the entire conference) was to show that the human world is supposed to be for the living and not for the dead. The dead should leave the living world without a trace (or with as little trace as possible). Whereas the speaker who presented this latest technology was well aware of the impossibility of implementing water burials in Shanghai, his presentation nevertheless indicated the type of inspiration that higher-up officials and industrial leaders had in mind when imagining the most "modern" ways of interment.

The second policy orientation in thinking about not keeping cremains was to find a way to "preserve a culture of life" (*baocun shengming wenhua*). The concept behind this slogan was that the cremains had no meaning in themselves—what was important was to preserve the meaning of the life that the cremains once embodied. In practice, preserving a culture of life involves developing techniques of representing the deceased in "authentic" ways such that the deceased's life culture is "preserved," as if taking a picture of the deceased. The representation and its consequent preservation could last a long or short period depending on the person. In fact, one interviewee went as far as to say that preservation depended on the social worthiness of the person. From his perspective, funerals should be occasions for the celebration of life (or of particularly worthy lives) instead of ritual, which was viewed as conventional, prescribed, formalized, and repetitive, if not outright empty and meaningless.

As a result, people in the Shanghai funeral industry—specifically those involved on the governing side—have been hoping to promote "personalized rituals" (*gexinghua yishi*). Many interviewees told me that personalized funerals are (and should be) the way of the future. They also said that the biggest problem with contemporary Shanghai funerals is that they are too programmed (*chengshihua*) and lack personal characteristics (*geren tese*). Some stated directly that modern funerals should reflect individuality. For them, modernity entailed a linear development from programmed ritual to personalized commemoration. Given this assumption, the pursuit of personalization in funerals was not only worth striving for to carry out the second funeral revolution (not keeping cremains) but also was the believed destiny of modernizing funerals. Therefore, personalized funerals were both the means and the end in funeral governance under a market economy.

This chapter recounts the story of the state's attempt to transform dead bodies into individualized subjects and the unexpected consequences of such governance. I do so by first describing state funeral parlors' promotion of personalized funerals and then by explaining how state funeral practitioners and the bereaved arranged funerals. To do the former, I use a specific example to analyze the thought processes behind the promotion of personalized funerals by exploring proposed techniques for preserving a culture of life and how such techniques constructed dead bodies as individualized subjects. For the latter, the second half of the chapter tackles what happened on the ground in the mundane interactions between the state (via state practitioners) and the public (the bereaved) in funeral parlors as they made funeral arrangements. To foreshadow my findings, I found that, in practice, Shanghai people primarily conceptualized the dead through collectively shared social conventions based on socialist, religious, Confucian, and relational ethical ideas of person and death. Market-driven ideas of person and of death, including authenticity and individualism, were of only marginal importance (if not entirely absent) despite the fact this was what state funeral parlors had been promoting. The gap between the state's imagination and promotion of personalized funerals and people's actual ways of death shows that the state's initiation of a top-down effort to promote personalized funerals had failed. Taking this a step further, I describe how the very process of the market governance of death has hindered the development of market subjectivity at the end of life.

Constructing Individuals

In June 2011, I attended a national conference called the Modern Funeral Ritual Demonstration and Learning Conference (Xiandai binzang liyi guanmo jiaoliuhui) in Changsha, Hunan Province. During the conference, funeral professionals from all over China went to learn what a modern funeral might look like. I estimate that several hundred representatives from funeral parlors and cemeteries were in attendance. Conference speakers included people from Japan (representing a flower altar design company), Taiwan (representing a large funeral service company), Sichuan Province (representing a private funeral agency run by people from Taiwan), and Shanghai (representing a famous private cemetery). These speakers either presented or demonstrated their respective versions (and visions) of modern funerals. That two out of the five presenting institutions came from (or were associated with) Taiwan was not accidental. (This number may have been closer to three because the famous private Shanghai cemetery was started by people from Taiwan as well.) Taiwan has been one of the most important sources of inspiration for the Chinese death industry and for rites of commemoration.

In any case, at the conference, the Taiwanese speaker gave a thirty-minute presentation in which she shared her experiences designing personalized funerals in Taiwan. The following is a partial transcription of her talk:

> We should imagine a personalized funeral as a graduation ceremony for the deceased. This graduation is the deceased's last show. Therefore, he or she should be the main character [*zhujiao*], the protagonist, of their life graduation. The bereaved are the actors and actresses who perform this show. Funeral professionals are the directors, scriptwriters, and people who move the stage settings during the show. We are not the stars. So, as much as possible, we allow the bereaved to perform the front stage activities, such as hosting. We step back to let the spotlight fall on the deceased and performers [the bereaved]. Funeral professionals should remain behind the scenes even if they are directing the show. . . .
>
> A truly personalized funeral places the deceased as the center of attention and storytelling. A personal funeral also shows the entirety of the deceased's life, whether we are talking about moments that are happy and glorious or frustrating and sad. A personalized funeral is the representation of the deceased's life on a stage.

In these opening remarks on personalized funerals, the speaker presented a particular view of conceptualizing the dead. First, the deceased was foremost a unique and standalone subject merely by dint of having once existed on earth. This uniqueness gives the dead a natural right to be the main character of their "life graduation" (a funeral). Furthermore, this distinctiveness is unable to be reproduced or substituted for—therefore, although the bereaved might be the actors and actresses of a funeral, they never become the main characters (nor could the funeral professionals take center stage). No one can be a full replica of another person, regardless of their biological connections. Consequently, this fact gives the (dead) subject a clear boundary that distinguishes self from other. This bounded sense of self assumes that the dead is an individualized person whose existence is prior to and independent from the social relationships around him or her. In other words, to begin with, this type of self is not a socially embedded person but an individual person who meets and interacts with other people along his or her way. Finally, the deceased is also envisioned as an agent who is the locomotive of his or her life journey. Agency and free will are conceptualized as inherent and innate characteristics of such a person. As a result, the mere existence of an individual being is enough to be the basis for a personalized commemoration, whether the deceased was a housewife, a small business owner, or an architect. Personalized funerals were based on (and operated through) these ways of constructing the self of the dead.

The speaker then presented three examples of personalized funerals that she had organized in Taiwan. While the first case was a housewife's funeral and the second was an ordinary businessman's funeral, I have omitted both here to focus on the third case.

> Now I discuss the third personalized funeral that I designed. This one was also my favorite. However, it is worth noting that, although all three cases I share today are personalized, this last one only works when the deceased's life is full of stories. The main character of my third case, Zhang Xifan, was an architect and professor. He also owned an architectural company and was a part of the team that designed the World Trade Center. In addition to his profession, he also liked painting, calligraphy, and drawing, among other things. He even enjoyed cooking and often baked cakes for his granddaughters.
>
> In his old age, he called himself "an old naughty boy" [laowantong]. He hoped his funeral represented his talents, artistic characteristics, and humor. He wanted his funeral to show who he was. He also did not want people to shed tears for him at his funeral. He wanted people to enjoy themselves and have fun. Zhang hoped that all of his friends who came to accompany his last journey might get to know each other just as they all knew Zhang himself. In accordance with his wishes, I designed a personalized funeral that suited him.
>
> First, we rented an old warehouse for his funeral. We divided this warehouse into several sections. At the entrance where people could sign in and offer gifts, a staff member took a Polaroid of every guest. We set up the "Connecting Plaza" [Lianyi guangchang] in the middle of the warehouse. Light food and drinks were provided in this section. Zhang felt that, in modern life, people were too busy to connect with each other. He hoped that his funeral might be a place where people connect and reconnect and where people paused for a moment in an otherwise incredibly busy life. Whether Zhang's friends wanted to visit him or simply visit with each other, they were all welcome.
>
> On the other side of Connecting Plaza, we set up the "Time Axis" [Shijianzhou], printed on a twenty-meter-long piece of paper that hung on a wall. This Time Axis was a detailed timeline of Zhang's life journey from birth to death. Guests then fixed the Polaroids that we took of them to the Time Axis to mark the intersection of their lives with Zhang's life. For example, if you were Zhang's student in 1978, then you put the Polaroid you received at the entrance at the 1978 mark. By the end of the day, Zhang's children could see the numerous people

who had accompanied their father throughout his life. This Time Axis provided an exemplar to Zhang's children for being a proper person and was a transcript that testified to Wang's life achievements.

Behind the Connecting Plaza and Time Axis was a space called the "*fanjian.*" *Fan* was the third character of Zhang's name, and *fanjian* sounds similar to *fangjian* [rooms]. In the fanjian, we displayed eight different tables that Zhang used when he was alive. They included a blueprint-drawing table, a computer table, a poker table, a calligraphy table, a painting table, and so on. We even had the kitchen table that he used to bake cakes and cookies for his granddaughters. Of course, the most important one—the mahjong table—was there as well. Zhang was always very proud of his mahjong skills—his most glorious moments were at the mahjong table! Everything on these tables were articles that he actually used when alive. The guests saw Zhang's preferences and tastes through these items.

Then, an exhibition area was on the left. We exhibited Zhang's architectural works, blueprints, paintings, and calligraphy and notes and drawings that he made for his family, especially his granddaughters. People who only knew his architectural side could learn about his other sides and vice versa.

Additionally, notice the logo and its design. We thought of this logo, "knickknacks under rulers and compass" [*juguixia de wanyier*]. Rulers and compasses are tools used to make blueprints in architecture. Each of the seven characters in this logo was, in fact, Zhang's [calligraphic] work. We found and copied an example of each character from his work and then put them together. . . .

Then, we had a farewell room. We set up a wooden table in the middle of the room. On that table was a wine cup on the right and a teacup on the left. Guests went in to say good-bye to Zhang by having a last cup of tea or wine together. Where is Professor Zhang? He was on the large screen! We created a PowerPoint slideshow of his life. We made sure that we selected at least one picture of him for every five to ten years throughout his life. We put several chairs and sofas in front of the screen to allow people to enjoy watching this slideshow [when drinking].

We also set up a table where female guests could give Zhang a yellow rose [that we supplied] if they felt like doing so. Roses were Zhang's favorite flower. However, he did not like red or pink ones because he thought that they were too feminine. He liked yellow roses. You could also give something else. Zhang's granddaughters made an origami bird from copies of the notes that their grandfather left to them.

This funeral was a whole-day event. We started at ten a.m. I was the emcee for a small memorial service for Zhang at three p.m. Zhang wanted people to say good-bye to him in ways that reflected his interactions with friends. He wanted everyone to feel relaxed and free and to be friends with each other. If you noticed [from my PowerPoint], you did not see many of our staff at this funeral. In fact, among the three personalized funerals that I introduced today, this one used the least amount of staff and had a very good profit margin.

Zhang's funeral first visualized this idea of a unique, bounded, and coherent self in his Time Axis. Allowing every guest to mark the point in time at which their respective timelines intersected with Zhang's Time Axis assumed that Zhang's timeline had its beginning and (now) end and that it is different from yours and mine. Although different timelines might cross each other, everyone is essentially a loner with his or her distinct destiny. In this construction, whether or not the abstract "universe" has its timeline (that is supposed to be total and inclusive), Zhang's personal timeline put him at the center of his "universe." This idiosyncratic version was what mattered. As a result, instead of imagining a human being born into a universe in which people might come and go but the impersonal universe remains, the Time Axis emphasizes the creation and disappearance of many individual universes. It is about an individual journey and the intersections of many individual journeys. Once they passed the intersection, they were already moving on in their respective ways. The Time Axis represents an ego-centered view of self, time, and existential meaning.

Moreover, Zhang's funeral constructed him as a bounded self by emphasizing the totality of his life. By working on representing various aspects of Zhang's life, from the professional (his architectural works) to the personal (his artwork and cooking) and from his serious achievements (being involved in building the World Trade Center) to his more frivolous achievements (mahjong skills), all of these differences could be merged into a single unity. This merging was possible because a core was assumed underneath the diversity. In Zhang's funeral, this dynamic was also articulated through space. This spatially structured self was materialized through tables in designing the fanjian, which was probably because Zhang was an architect. From the table he worked on to the table he used to entertain, together these tables were coherent because Zhang's "true" self was moving from one space to the other and, thus, unified the differences. Each represented a segment of Zhang's true self. In other words, not just time but also space was conceptualized through an ego-centered view.

However, this unique and bounded self that is on its journey to somewhere did not mean that Zhang was constructed as an isolated atomic subject. To the contrary, this unique, coherent, and bounded self was situated in a wide network of relationships. The Taiwanese speaker described the Time Axis as an exemplar for Zhang's children because it showed that there were so many people whose life journeys intersected with that of their father. She did not describe Zhang's architectural and artistic works as his life achievement. In other words, whether or not the Taiwanese speaker was conscious of it, she described his accumulated social capital as the life achievement of the deceased. She associated this achievement with a preexisting cultural concept of being a proper person. In Sinophone studies, scholars have long identified the link between being a proper person and her or his ability to maintain interpersonal and reciprocal relationships. These relationships are created and maintained through gift exchanges (which are viewed less as events and more as proper etiquette). As a result, to also see food and drink being provided and given in the Connection Plaza was not surprising—banquets were one of the most common ways to engage in a gift exchange. The Connection Plaza provided a node to facilitate interactions between individuals who might be too independent and, thus, fall into anomie today.

Beyond constructing the subjectivity of Zhang in a particular fashion, the second important theme that emerged in this imagination of a personalized funeral was the pursuit of authenticity. At the beginning of the presentation, the Taiwanese speaker pointed out that personalized funerals aim to faithfully represent the true totality of the deceased, whether about glory or sorrow. We observe the attempts to authentically represent Zhang in the Exhibition Area and the fanjian. They needed to display eight different tables in the fanjian and both architectural works and other artistic and nonartistic works to cover his professional and private lives. To just display Zhang's achievements as an architect and artist but fail to show his "old naughty boy" side would be hypocritical and, thus, morally wrong. Idealized representations of Zhang (such as the attempt to disguise his naughty side) are more embarrassing than showing the naughty side of him. Just as Zhang was perceived as unashamed of telling other people that he was naughty and good at mahjong, his funeral should not be ashamed to show these aspects as well. In this personalized funeral, authenticity was one of the highest moralities, if not the only morality, in constructing the self. This pursuit of authenticity was further articulated through the Taiwanese speaker's emphasis that all tables and items displayed in the fanjian were the actual possessions of Zhang in their original condition. They were not replicas or the results of picking and choosing. This obsession with faithful representation exemplifies this strong moral idea of valuing authenticity.

The third theme that emerged in this presentation of personalized funerals was the desire to reject social convention. People should be able to do things because they want to and not because they have to. As a result, a guest who went to Zhang's funeral to see his old friends instead of going to see Zhang was legitimate. Pretending you were not doing so would be worse. People should not go to a funeral because they were obligated to go. By the same token, if you are happy because you see old friends, then you should not feel obligated to cry even if you are at a funeral. We see this same rejection of rules and formality in the description of the ways to say good-bye to the deceased. The guests were welcome to come and go as they pleased. When they were at the funeral, they could stay in the Connection Plaza and socialize with other guests. They could have a final cup of tea or wine with Zhang. They could offer yellow flowers. They could enjoy reading through Zhang's Time Axis. They could watch the PowerPoint slideshow of Zhang's life. What mattered was the spirit and the heart instead of the formality and the gesture. Ritualized acts were not needed. Based on these assumptions, everyone at Zhang's funeral, including Zhang himself, was constructed as autonomous individuals who had free will and should act as such instead of being constrained by formality.

Zhang's personalized funeral was an exceptional case in many ways. As the presenter said at the start, the deceased himself was an unusual character to begin with. However, the purely epistemological justification that everyone is an individual and should, thus, be commemorated as such is not enough to justify going through the trouble of designing a personalized funeral. As the Taiwanese speaker told funeral professionals attending her presentation, she "used the fewest staff" for this funeral, and it had "a very good profit margin." Indeed, the capitalist logic of cost and benefit also played a crucial role in China in general and in Shanghai in particular even though, as we have seen with other encounters between this logic and Funeral Reform, this is not the only factor. Part of the reason for Shanghai funeral parlors themselves to promote personalized funerals was precisely because they needed to increase profits without fostering religious practices that were too often standing at the boundary between customs and "superstitions" in China.

State Experiments with Personalized Funerals

Since the 1990s, Shanghai funeral parlors have been experimenting with new services and products to facilitate personalizing funerals. For example, Huangpu Funeral Parlor started a new service item called "A Little Movie of Life" (*rensheng xiaodianying*) several years ago. For this service item, the bereaved could choose up to twenty pictures of the deceased that were supposed to provide a narrative of his or her life. Huangpu put these pictures together into a PowerPoint slideshow and played it during the memorial meeting. My friends told me that this technique was already commonly used in weddings in Shanghai. Another example, also a new service item, was a "personalized meeting hall" (*gexinhua liting*). This service allowed the bereaved to decorate the meeting hall to match the unique personality of the deceased. One example that Huangpu constantly advertised was a music professor's funeral. At his funeral, the meeting hall was decorated with flowers arranged in the shape of musical notes. This type of personalized decoration of the meeting hall could generate significantly higher profits than simply selling generic flower baskets to the bereaved. One of the most ambitious attempts at personalization was probably the idea of "flower basket literature" (*hualan wenxue*) or "cultured flower baskets" (*wenhua hualan*). The intention here was to create a new literature genre specifically for couplets on flower baskets. Instead of using generic content for couplets, people could use individualized content with various literary genres (such as poems or short essays) to commemorate the deceased. In this way, they would be able to memorialize the deceased as an individual and cultivate a personalized memorial for the deceased's funeral.

Despite these efforts, however, personalized funerals and their related service items had not succeeded in Shanghai by the end of my fieldwork in 2012. I remember the first Little Movie of Life that I watched at Huangpu. This slideshow was just a collection of family gatherings and travel pictures of the deceased. The deceased spent a large part of her life during the years of high socialism, and this may well be why not many pictures showed her early life. All the pictures obviously concentrated on the postreform era. No effort was made to represent a coherent (not to mention to find "the authentic") narrative of the totality of the deceased's life. Moreover, I later learned that the bereaved only used this service item because it was free. This family happened to choose a so-called special memorial meeting hall (*tese liting*) based on its size and scheduled availability. This meeting hall was "special" because, unlike other meeting halls that have flower decorations arranged in a rectangular shape surrounding the dead body, this meeting hall had flowers in a heart shape. Therefore, the price of this hall was slightly higher than that of other halls, but it came with a free deal for the Little Movie of Life, and, most importantly for the bereaved, it fit the scheduled time slot they wanted for the funeral. However, despite being free, when I subsequently went to other memorial meetings in the same meeting hall, I noticed that many families did not have this PowerPoint slideshow. For whatever reason, some people even gave up a free service item that accompanied their meeting hall choice.

Overall, during my time in Huangpu, I only heard about two large, personalized funerals (none of the seventy-five funerals that I attended in full was personalized). One of the deceased was a famous radio host. This funeral had many guests from the entertainment business. The other was an ordinary young woman who died in the 1115 Fire Incident. This fire happened in one of the wealthiest districts in Shanghai and claimed fifty-eight lives, eventually causing government officials to resign. Instead of making a statistical claim about the ratio of having personalized funerals in Shanghai, what you can see here (and what practitioners echoed to me) is that personalized funerals that address individuality were limited to artists or to a specific type of person or abnormal deaths (meaning dying young). They did not happen often, and they were not the norm. Moreover, after sitting through countless business meetings between state funeral practitioners and the bereaved, I did not see the bereaved express much desire for personalized funerals.

This absence of personalized funerals could also be observed in state funeral practitioners' job arrangements. A young woman I knew at Huangpu, who has a college degree, was hired specifically to assist a senior funeral practitioner to design personalized funerals. This senior was the only one in charge of personalized funerals for the entire parlor. However, when I met her—the supposed assistant to the senior state funeral practitioner—she was working at the reception desk. Personalized funerals had not been a success, and she could not do much on a daily basis. I later asked the senior funeral practitioner in charge of personalized funerals about what he did to operationalize personalized funerals. He told me that personalized funerals are "special" funerals, and, thus, his job was to make special arrangements. I then probed into what "special" funerals meant. It turned out that most of his work involved arranging government officials' or other important people's funerals. Political ranking and social prestige defined "personalization" here. The most important part of his job was to make sure that he correctly handled the politics of the memorial meetings. Specifically, he had to think through the correct hierarchical relationships between bureaucratic units and individuals. This task was made all the more complex and ambiguous when referring to parallel units, ranks, and high-level people retiring from one unit to another. From this senior practitioner's perspective, everyone's funeral is and should be personalized because each person occupied a specific hierarchical position. This specific position then linked them to a set of hierarchical relationships surrounding the deceased. Personal temperament, individual preference, and authenticity were unimportant, if not outright irrelevant, in his imagination and the operation of such personalized funerals. If we compare the Taiwanese case that I heard about at the conference with what personalized funerals were in actual practice in Huangpu Funeral Parlor, we can see how radically different they were. The latter constructed the "individuality" of the deceased in terms of hierarchical rank while the former did so in terms of personal autonomy, personality, relationships with other individuals, and uniqueness of life experiences.

If personalized funerals and their associated types of self were not what were being produced inside Shanghai funeral parlors, then what types of self of the deceased were created in the mundane interactions between funeral practitioners on the ground and the public as bereaved? In the next section, I first provide a detailed account of how a funeral was arranged in Shanghai between state funeral practitioners and the bereaved. I consider these business meetings as a "backstage" (Goffman 1956) of sorts and analyze the kind of self of the deceased that was imagined and constructed in this setting. What I find is that Shanghai residents conceptualized the dead in this process first as religious and relational subjects and then second as socialist citizen subjects.

Arranging Funerals: Business Meetings in Funeral Parlors

The Ding family just lost their father last night.[4] Ding Wen and Ding Jia are the brother and sister children of the deceased and are both in their forties. They are both married, have their respective nuclear families, and live separately from their parents. After the father died in the hospital, Ding Wen and Ding Jia accompanied their mother back to her apartment to decide what they should do next. Shanghai people had less than three days to arrange the funeral—a daunting task for the many people who had never done it before. Ding Jia made some phone calls to her friends and searched the web to determine what they should do next. She found a 962840 phone number to contact a funeral parlor—a newly established "white event hotline" (baishirenxian) that gives callers direct access to any of the three Shanghai city funeral parlors twenty-four hours a day. This hotline was initiated in August 2010, two months after I started my fieldwork. FIS used to have 6464-4444 as its main telephone line. This older phone number played with Chinese people's common association of the number four with death given the similarity between the two words' pronunciation.[5]

It was late at night. A funeral practitioner, Li Shan, answered the hotline that night. He told Ding Jia that the parlor would send a hearse to pick up her father's body from the hospital: "What type of hearse do you want to be used to take your father from the hospital to the parlor? Do you want a RMB 240, RMB 600, or RMB 1,000 [USD 39, 97, 161, respectively] kind? The first one is a minivan, the second one is a Buick, and the third one is a Cadillac." Ding Jia paused for a second as if she was thinking. Li Shan continued, "I don't think we need to have a really nice car for this trip. A minivan will do just fine. If you want to let your father enjoy a nice last ride, you can rent a nicer hearse for his departure from Huangpu Parlor to the crematorium [rather than from the hospital to the Huangpu]." Ding Jia then decided to go with a minivan.

Li Shan continued, "It is late night already. Our salespeople have left work now. If you want us to provide house service [shangmen fuwu], you will have to wait until tomorrow morning. You can also come to Huangpu yourself. It all depends on you. Our newly initiated door service is free of charge. The salespeople can conduct their business meeting with you at your place to make arrangements for your father's memorial meeting. However, the disadvantage is that you will not be able to see our funerary products in person. Our salespeople carry only computers and catalogs with them to let you see the products." Ding Jia talked to Ding Wen for a while and then decided they would go to Huangpu Funeral Parlor in person the next day.

The next morning, Ding Wen, Ding Jia, and their spouses got in a cab to go to Huangpu. I happened to see them get out of the cab and walk across the eight-lane street as I entered Huangpu to start my fieldwork for the day. After the Dings got out of the cab, they saw a large drivable entrance on the other side of the eight-lane road. A large security guard's booth is on the left side of the entrance, and a grand-looking granite stone engraved with the name of Huangpu Funeral Parlor is on the right. After walking in, the Dings saw a gray and white, modernist-style building, approximately six floors tall, on the right. Some other buildings were on the left, and some were farther down. Between the buildings are well-paved and maintained driving and pedestrian ways surrounded by nicely trimmed trees, flowers, and shrubs. I later realized that this was the first time that the Dings had been to a funeral parlor. In fact, they were a bit surprised to see how nice this place of death was. The generally held the stereotype of a crematorium (huozangchang)—as all funeral parlors used to be called—as a dark, scary, ugly, and cold place.

Following a security guard's directions, the Dings turned right into the first large building. Another guard in a blue uniform standing outside the automatic glass doors waved his hand in front of the sensor to open the door for the Dings when he saw them approaching, as if they were customers entering a five-star hotel. When they walked through the automatic doors, they found themselves in a large, bright space with vaulted ceilings six stories up. This grand lobby had a very open feel to it and was interrupted only by two rows of four large marble columns setting off a central area from the sides of the room. They could see from the first floor directly up to the sixth. The marble-looking tile floor of the lobby was so clean that it shone, even though it required much effort to stop the buildup of grimy dust from Shanghai's streets and skies. At the other end of the lobby (opposite the entrance) was a large reception counter. Behind this counter was an approximately four-floor-tall painting that showed a person's life cycle from birth through marriage, children, and death. At the five o'clock position, the Dings saw a baby. Then, the baby became older and moved from being single to becoming a parent and grandparent, following a clockwise direction around the painting. The painting was full of color and formed a dramatic contrast to the bright but gray and white stone color of the rest of the lobby. Four small offices flanked each side of the lobby on the first floor. These offices looked similar to the private consulting rooms commonly seen in banks in American cities. A digital LED screen was displayed next to each office door, showing the number of the customer being consulted inside.

Four people were standing behind the reception desk. They all looked to be in their twenties. All of them wore uniforms resembling those of flight attendants. The female receptionists were even wearing silk scarves as part of their uniform. The Dings soon found out that all funeral practitioners wore these uniforms.[6] The Dings approached one of the receptionists and told him that they wanted to arrange a funeral for their father. Ding Jia told him that she had called the night before to arrange for her father to be picked up from the hospital. The receptionist checked his computer and found the record. He told Ding Jia that her father was already in the parlor. The receptionist then took a number from an automatic number machine on the counter and handed it to her. He told the Dings that they could sit on one of the benches in the lobby to wait. When it was their turn, the digital number display screen on the wall behind the counter would show the office number they should go to. The screen outside each office also showed the customer's number, and there was a voice announcement as well.

During their wait, the Dings talked to each other occasionally, but most of the time they remained silent. After twenty minutes or so, a mechanical female voice announced, "Number fifty-six, number fifty-six, please go to office room three." The Dings walked straight to room 3. "Please sit down," Xiao Lin said, standing up as they walked in. Xiao Lin was in her midthirties. When she spoke, she used many softening words, such as "please" and "thank you"—a relatively rare habit among Chinese living in mainland China. Xiao Lin gave each of the Dings a glass of water as they sat. She told me that she believed offering water immediately would relax the bereaved, and, instead of worrying about how the funeral practitioners might overcharge them, they would be more likely to take any advice from them regardless of whether that advice added to the funeral costs.

Xiao Lin's office was equipped with a large desk, a desktop computer, and a couple of filing cabinets—similar to all the other offices in the lobby. A sign, approximately half a letter-sized piece of paper, was displayed on her desk and described the standard process of arranging funerals. It stated as follows:

1. Fill out an application form for funerary [*bin*] rites.
2. Present the death certificate.
3. Make a reservation for body transportation.
4. Book a memorial meeting hall.
5. Order funerary service items.
6. Hand in the deceased's clothes for the memorial meeting at the Clothing Collection Station.
7. Pay the bill.

This sign was mainly for decoration. Most bereaved did not seem to notice it, and the Dings were no exception.

Xiao Lin gave the Dings an application. Ding Wen told Ding Jia to fill out this form because she had better handwriting. The form requested basic information, such as the deceased's name, sex, where he had died, and the chief mourner's contact phone number and address. After Ding Jia returned the form to Xiao Lin, the latter started to key the data into her computer. Xiao Lin's computer showed more information categories than were present on the application form, such as "confidentiality level" (*baomidengji*) and ethnicity (*minzu*). Salespeople usually also left these categories blank on their computers. Whenever Xiao Lin found a few illegible characters on the application form, she would stop typing to verify something with the Dings. Things as simple as data typing needed to be done very meticulously in funeral parlors. After all, no one would be happy if funeral parlors misspelled the deceased's name or were unable to reach the bereaved because they had the wrong contact information. During this process, Xiao Lin also asked to see the death certificate of the deceased.

Xiao Lin asked the Dings when they wanted to have their father's memorial meeting. "We want to have it the day after tomorrow," the Dings said. Xiao Lin then asked how many guests they expected, and Ding Wen suggested approximately seventy or eighty. Ding Jia added that there might be fewer. Xiao Lin reassured them that the exact number did not matter. Once you had more than fifty people, you had to book a medium-sized meeting hall. Xiao Lin then checked on which medium-sized halls were still open. She asked the Dings if they wanted to have the meeting in the morning or the afternoon. Ding Jia said the afternoon would be better, especially close to dinnertime, but that morning could also work if any time slots ended around lunch. Holding funerals right before mealtimes was the ideal for Shanghai people. On her computer, Xiao Lin checked the availability of all the medium-sized halls and told the Dings that all the morning time slots were booked. All 3:05–4:05 p.m. time slots were booked as well, and they had to book an earlier time. Ding Jia and Ding Wen exchanged a glance. They were not too happy with this situation.

"The parlor has an 'overtime' time slot between 4:25 and 5:25 p.m.," Xiao Lin offered. "But you need to add RMB 100 (USD 16) more for renting that hall. Also, you are only allowed to book the overtime time slot if you purchase the funeral banquet from Huangpu's restaurant." "How much does the banquet cost?" Ding Wen asked. Xiao Lin took out a menu from her folder and explained the prices. At the parlor's restaurant, each table accommodates ten people. Per table cost options included RMB 680, 880, 1,180, and 1,580 (USD 109, 141, 190, and 255) depending on the choice of different meal packages. The Dings decided to book an RMB 1,180 (USD 190) per table banquet for five tables. Xiao Lin told the Dings they would prepare two extra tables for them just in case they needed them on the day. Although the banquet prices at state funeral parlors were not too different from those outside, state funeral parlors often used tactics like having an "overtime time slot" to maximize their profit in competition with private business providers.

Once the Dings confirmed their intention to purchase a funeral banquet from the parlor, Xiao Lin started to look at her computer to find medium halls that had the overtime time slot available. The Dings had several choices. They could choose a Chinese-, Western-, or modern-style meeting hall. Ding Jia asked about the differences, and Xiao Lin showed them several pictures of each hall. At this point, Xiao Lin realized that this business meeting would take a while. The Dings were more meticulous than many of her customers. Xiao Lin (and I, in this regard) saw plenty of Shanghai people book their memorial meeting halls without bothering to ask what the hall looked like even though its decoration is one key to personalization.

In the end, the Dings chose the Evergreen Hall. Xiao Lin explained that the basic charge for that room was RMB 1,600 (USD 258). The fake green plant decorations and the flower decorations that surrounded the plastic cover where the deceased would be displayed cost RMB 300 (USD 48) and RMB 200 (USD 32), respectively. "Do we have to use both of these sets of decorations?" Ding Jia asked. "I am sorry, but I'm afraid that they all come together when you rent a meeting hall." At the end of my fieldwork, FIS canceled these extra charges and just increased the basic charge to cover the difference. People in FIS told me that when you charged for these items separately, you told the bereaved that they still had to buy them in a package deal, and the bereaved felt this was profiteering. However, if you offered them a single price that included the same things for the same overall cost, they were less likely to feel they were being forced to purchase additional items.

Xiao Lin paused briefly before beginning again. "Now that we have a meeting hall reserved, we can talk about the details of the memorial meeting. How do you want to address your father on the horizontal banner? This banner will hang in the center of the meeting hall toward the front during the memorial meeting. The deceased is usually addressed in either kinship terms or as a comrade—either 'Father' [*fuqin daren*] or 'Comrade' [*tongzhi*] in this case."

"Which is more common?" Ding Jia asked.

"Will you invite your father's work unit to attend the memorial meeting?"

The Dings replied, almost in unison, "Yes, of course!"

Xiao Lin said that memorial meetings without the presence of any work unit representatives typically used kinship terms. However, for those meetings with work unit representatives in attendance, both forms of address are common. Xiao Lin emphasized that it all depends on what you want. The Dings talked among themselves for a while and decided to address their father as "Comrade" because not only would their father's last work unit send someone to attend the memorial meeting, but Ding Wen's work unit was also sending someone to attend his father's funeral.

"So the horizontal banner will read, 'Deeply Mourning Comrade Ding Daozhong' [*chentongdaonian dingdazhong tongzhi*], unless you want to write your own version."

"Oh, no, we don't need to write our own. Let's just stick to the generic one," Ding Wen replied.

Xiao Lin then asked the Dings about the couplets they would choose for their father's vertical banners. They could choose from the list provided by Huangpu or write their own. Either way, the parlor's calligrapher would handwrite whatever they wanted.

Ding Wen looked at Ding Jia and said, "I don't think we need to write our couplets." Ding Jia agreed, "There's no need to write our own." Xiao Lin then passed a piece of paper to the Dings that listed the following couplets:[7]

1. Kindly father, your kindness is as heavy as a mountain.
   We sons and daughters are tearful to show grief and remembrance.
   [*cifu enqing rushanzhong // ernu huilei jixiangsi*]
2. Cry for my kind father who spared no effort to devote his whole life.
   Mourn a decent person whose merits of simplicity and purity will
     last eternally
   [*kucifu xinlaoyisheng jugongjincui // daohaoren shanliangchunpu
     gongdeyongcun*]
3. My kind mother whose affection in raising us is as deep as the ocean.
   We sons and daughters are tearful to show our grief and
     remembrance.
   [*cimu yangyu qingsihai // ernu huilei jixiangsi*]

4. She labored all her life. Her affection in raising us is as deep as the ocean.
   She is tender, kind, and frugal. The bond between my kindly mother and us is strong.
   [*xinlaoyisheng yangyuenzhong // wenhoujiejian cimuqingshen*]

5. Being peaceful, being kind, being sincere to people.
   Being industrious, being frugal, being hardworking for their whole life.
   [*yiheyiai zhenchengdairen // keqinkejian xinlaoyisheng*]

6. Being kind, being respectable. So much affection in raising us.
   Being diligent, being busy. Working so hard for the whole of life.
   [*cixiangkejing yangyuenzhong // qinkenmanglu xinlaoyisheng*]

7. Dying so young that we haven't had enough household warmth.
   A one-day farewell becomes painful grief for eternity.
   [*yingnianzaoshi tianlunweijin // yichaoyongbie tongsizhangyuan*]

8. An exemplar of teachers that shines on future generations.
   Devoted to education and contributing merit to eternity.
   [*weirenshibiao guangzhaohoushi // xianshenjiaoyu gongzaiqianqiu*]

9. Being eighty-something with a smile up in the heavens.
   Your longevity is like a mountain that blesses your descendants.
   [*baxungaoling hanxiaoxianjing // shoubinanshan fuzhaozisun*]

10. A life long with hardships keeps the spirits true.
    A lifelong simplicity keeps moral standards high.
    [*yishixinlao benseyongbao // yishengchunpu pindechonggao*]

11. Pure and clean-handed throughout life.
    Diligent and industrious throughout life.
    [*qingqingbaibai weirenzhongsheng // qinqinkenken xinlaoyisheng*]

12. Open, candid, and righteous throughout life.
    Being diligent and law-abiding keeps clean hands uncorrupted.
    [*guangmingleiluo yishengzhengqi // keqinfenggong liangxiuqingfeng*]

→ 13. Believe in Jesus to gain eternal life.
    Enter heaven to enjoy eternal prosperity.
    [*xinyesudeyongsheng // jintiantangxiangyongfu*]

Xiao Lin explained, "Numbers 1 through 6 and 9 through 11 would all work for your father. Number 7 is for people who die at approximately fifty years or younger. Number 8 is for any deceased people who were educators. Number 12 is usually for people who work in the government. Finally, number 13 is for Christians. You can substitute 'father' for 'mother' in number 3 and number 4. You can also substitute 'nineties' for 'eighties' for number 9." The Dings stared at the list and could not decide which one to choose. They asked Xiao Lin if she had any suggestions. Xiao Lin told the Dings that her personal suggestion was one of numbers 3, 4, 5, or 6. "However," Xiao Lin said, "I don't know your father, so it is really hard for me to make a suggestion. They are all very common. It really depends on the kind of person your father was. You choose one that represents your father best."

Ding Wen commented that number 9 seemed better. He asked Xiao Lin if that one was popular. Xiao Lin said that it was also very common, especially for more traditional families. Ding Jia was still staring at the list. Xiao Lin sensed that the Dings might not be able to make a decision immediately. She suggested the Dings take the list home and discuss it with their mother. "Your mother knows your father the best. Maybe she can help you make the decision. You can always confirm the couplets later by phone." The Dings decided to follow her advice.

"Now we can talk about coffins and other funerary merchandise." Xiao Lin suggested moving to the display room, so they could see the samples in person. All of us stood up and walked across the lobby to the display room located in a set of rooms in the back half of the building behind the reception desk. Xiao Lin led them first to the coffin display area. "These coffins are cremation coffins [huohuaguan]. This means that the coffins will be cremated along with the deceased. Since they are for cremation, they are made of paper or bamboo. These coffins are more environmentally friendly [huanbao]."

The Dings were quite surprised. "Can't we get one that is made of wood?" Ding Wen asked.

"There are wood coffins here, but they are all for body burial [tuzang] instead of cremation. Only Muslims, Macanese, Hong Kong residents, Taiwanese, or foreigners who have been legally authorized to have body burial here or whose body will be transported internationally may buy wood coffins."[8]

The Dings continued to look around at the coffins. Ding Wen asked about the difference between the ten or so coffins displayed there. Xiao Lin said that if they wanted to nail down the coffin to ritually seal it (fengguanding), they would have to buy a coffin that cost RMB 980 (USD 159) or more. The Dings looked at the coffins not suitable for the nailing ritual and decided they wanted the more expensive type. Ding Jia asked about the more common coffins purchased in this category. Xiao Lin pointed at the coffins that fell in the price range between RMB 1,000 (USD 161) to more than RMB 2,000 (USD 322). Xiao Lin suggested to the Dings that if they wanted to enable their (deceased) father to "live" better, they might in fact spend their money buying a more expensive cremains caskets instead (coffin-like urns). They did not need to spend too much money on cremation coffins that would just be burned. A little more than RMB 1,000 (USD 161) was just fine. Ding Jia then asked her brother if he liked the RMB 1,320 (USD 213) one, and they settled on that one.

Xiao Lin jotted down "1,320" in her notes and then led the Dings to the cremains casket section. She said that they had a very wide range of prices, from two hundred to several thousand yuan. Xiao Lin pointed out a few that cost around RMB 300, 1,000, and 2,000 (USD 48, 161, and 322).

"What price point do most people choose?" Ding Jia asked.

"People usually spend about a thousand or two thousand something."

Each cremains casket had a tag that explained the type of wood that it was made of and its price. The types of wood included sandalwood, rosewood, blackwood, and so on. They were all decorated differently. Some had evergreen tree carvings, Buddhist texts, or red-crowned cranes (*xianhe*, a bird that symbolized prosperity and longevity). Some looked like mini coffins, and others resembled the architecture of traditional Chinese palaces. Some were wood inlaid with jade flowers or other patterns. In the end, the Dings chose one costing RMB 2,288 (USD 369) because they liked the symbolic meaning of the red-crowned crane.

Xiao Lin then led the Dings over to the other part of the display room, where a variety of funeral outfits for the deceased were displayed. She asked the Dings to first decide whether they wanted Chinese- or Western-style outfits. The latter was a black suit, and the former was a set of garments that contained "five tops and three bottoms" (*wuling sanyao*) to resemble imperial-style dress. The five tops included four shirts and one cloak, whereas the three bottoms referred to three different types of pants. Xiao Lin explained that the idea behind the five tops and three bottoms was to make sure that the deceased had enough different types of clothes to help him go through seasonal changes. Depending on the material (cotton or silk), Xiao Lin explained, funeral outfits could cost anywhere from several hundred to several thousand RMB. The materials were also of different colors and patterns, such as red (and several shades of red for that matter), yellow, pink, white, purple, blue, and brown. The Dings, almost without hesitation, chose the Chinese style even though this seemingly archaic style of dress did not at all resemble the types of clothes that people wore in their daily lives.

After deciding the style, then they needed to decide on a specific one. Ding Wen was interested in a red outfit, but Xiao Lin said, "People usually buy red only if the deceased died at approximately eighty years, since this kind of death counts as a 'happy death' [*xisang*]. Your father might be a little bit too young for the red color. But, of course, this is all just custom [*fengsu xiguan*]. You don't have to follow it." Meanwhile, a staff member brought out several bedding sets for them to consider as well. Xiao Lin explained that there were Chinese and Western bedding styles. The main difference was the pillow. The Chinese-style pillow looked like an ingot and came with another ingot-like pillow for the deceased's feet as well. Worth noting is that the current residents of Shanghai have long since stopped using this type of bedding. Again, these bedding selections were meant to present an archaic aura for taking care of the dead. When waiting for the Dings to make up their minds, Xiao Lin brought out a set of one handkerchief, one fan, and one wooden comb (in a single package), several pairs of shoes, and some pairs of socks (that would match the funeral outfits) for the Dings to consider. Xiao Lin said that the handkerchief and fan were to make sure their father had something to hold in his hands and that the wooden comb was for them to comb their father's hair one last time at the funeral.

Ding Jia asked Xiao Lin if they had to buy these things from Huangpu. Xiao Lin said, "No, you can buy these things outside. You just need to bring the clothing and bedding to us the day before the memorial meeting, so the funeral practitioners have enough time to dress the deceased and make his bed for him." Ding Jia thought it might be a good idea to go somewhere outside the parlor because of the general impression that state stores had higher prices. However, Ding Wen felt that going out to a different place to buy the things was too much trouble. In the end, they bought what they needed at the parlor to save time and trouble.

Before they headed back to the consulting room, Xiao Lin asked the Dings if they were thinking of buying flower baskets at the parlor and if they were interested in seeing any samples. The Dings said yes, so they walked to the flower shop located in a different building, where most of the memorial meeting halls were. Xiao Lin introduced some basic flower baskets and told the Dings their respective prices. She told them that they did not have to make this decision right then if they were not ready. Ding Jia asked if it was acceptable to purchase flower baskets outside. Xiao Lin said of course, but said to them that if they were to buy flower baskets at the parlor, they could be arranged in the hall in advance to save time. The Dings decided to defer the flower basket decision.

They then walked back to Xiao Lin's office. Xiao Lin entered into her computer the data on the types of merchandise that the Dings had chosen. She then explained the procedure of a memorial meeting from the beginning to the end. By the end of her explanation, Xiao Lin asked the Dings about the type of car they wanted to use to send the deceased from Huangpu to the crematorium. She explained the price differences, similar to how Li Shan did the night before when they arranged a minivan to take their father from the hospital to the parlor. Xiao Lin said that a minivan was more economical (*shihui*) unless they wanted something nicer. Ding Wen said that this would be his father's last ride, so he wanted to give him something better. In the end, the Dings decided to book a Buick.

"Huangpu Funeral Parlor's rule is to allow only one passenger in the hearse with the deceased on the way to the crematorium. However, this person is responsible for finding their way back, and there is no subway stop at the crematorium."

"So what do people normally do?" Ding Jia asked.

"Most people don't go to the crematorium because it is too hard to see their beloved being burned."

The Dings agreed with Xiao Lin's point and decided not to go. Xiao Lin explained that, in this case, all they needed to do was to pick up the cremains on the third day after the memorial meeting.

Finally, Xiao Lin explained, "There are two different ways of sending the deceased from a meeting hall to the hearse parked in the parking lot. People used to call this the funeral procession. One is to have coffin carriers—a group of six men in black suits—pick up the coffin and put it in the hearse. The other is to have special coffin carriers who wear white marine-like uniforms to carry the coffin on top of their shoulders (this higher position is more prestigious) while doing their goose-step march. The first costs RMB 300 [USD 48] and the second costs RMB 900 [USD 145]. This latter service item is known as a 'ceremonial funeral procession' [liyi chubin]. Either can be combined with a marching band playing music for an additional RMB 200 [USD 32]. If you want the band to stay throughout the memorial meeting, it will cost RMB 400 [USD 64]." Ding Wen said that because this funeral procession would be their father's last journey, special coffin carriers would give him more face (mianzi). Ding Jia added that hiring a band in that case might also be good, which would make the entire event more "hot and noisy" (renao). In the end, the Dings bought the ceremonial funeral procession and the band service.

Xiao Lin then printed out a receipt for their total cost of RMB 13,648 (USD 2,199) and verified each item with the Dings. When the verification was complete, Xiao Lin took out a customer satisfaction questionnaire and asked the Dings to fill it out. Because this questionnaire was written in front of Xiao Lin, not surprisingly, Ding Jia's answers were all positive. After filling out the questionnaire, Xiao Lin first led the Dings to the parlor's cash register to pay their bills and then to the reception desk to pick up a cremation license. Before the Dings left, Xiao Lin reminded them about the documents and receipts they needed to bring with them on the day of the memorial meeting, as well as other pending items. Xiao Lin wished the Dings a safe trip home and walked back to her office. The entire business meeting at the parlor from entrance to exit took about an hour.

Social Conventional Ideas of Self

Let me start my analysis by pointing out a few absences. The type of perception of the dead constructed in the mundane interaction between state funeral practitioners and the bereaved is anything but individualized. One of the best places to see this phenomenon is in the discussion over the vertical couplets. Recall that Xiao Lin said that she could not help the Dings choose vertical couplets because she did not know their father. She was clearly indicating a connection between who the deceased was and the chosen couplets. To be clear, having custom-made couplets does not mean that the entire funeral was personalized. However, throughout the entirety of any business meeting, this is the most obvious place, if not the only place, where state funeral practitioners actively identify for the bereaved a chance to show individuality in a typically generic funeral. During my fieldwork, however, I was surprised at the consistent lack of interest on the bereaved's side in doing so. The most common response from the bereaved was that "it is not necessary" (*bubiyao*) or "there is no need" (*buxuyao*). Similar to the Dings, the question that most of the bereaved asked was not what would fit their deceased relatives but, rather, what "most people did" or what was "most popular." This lack of interest in personalizing couplets' content is even more ironic considering that my field notes recorded more bereaved inquiring about the couplets' font style (though still unusual) than about the appropriateness of the words.

Overall, although funeral practitioners often introduce couplets as something that would represent who the deceased was in life, the majority of Shanghai people made decisions on couplets during business meetings without giving them too much thought. The vast majority of people chose couplets from the set lists provided by the parlors, apparently encouraged by the knowledge that these couplets were "popular." This process showed that the bereaved did not consider vertical couplets as somehow representing the deceased as an individualized subject except in the most generalized way—by ethics, relations, age, gender, and religion.

Taking the couplet list previously translated as an example, numbers 1, 3, and 4 concern the relationship between parent and child. They show that the deceased is understood as a person embedded in family relationships instead of assuming that an individual existed before the occurrence of social relationships. Moreover, the specific parent-to-child relationship is described in terms of debt. This feeling of indebtedness is the foundation of Chinese notions of filial piety. Numbers 2, 5, 6, 10, 11, and 12 emphasize the moral character of the deceased. Specifically, all stress a lifelong endurance of hardship. Although being frugal, devoted, diligent, and so on were by no means new moral values in China, they reflected the type of ethics that the Chinese Communist Party has praised (a topic on which I elaborate in the next chapter). The difference among these is that the first three couplets (2, 5, and 6) are still more or less conceptualized in terms of parent-child relationships, whereas the last three (10–12) have transcended family relationships, which means that regardless of the relationship between the deceased and the people who choose (or read) their couplet, these moral categorizations make sense because they represent absolute values that are beyond relational difference. In other words, if we imagine that Confucian morality and Chinese Communist Party morality are at the two ends of a spectrum that describes the embodied morality of the deceased, then numbers 1, 3, and 4 are at the Confucian end, numbers 2, 5, and 6 are in the middle, and numbers 10, 11, and 12 are at the socialist end. In fact, Xiao Lin once told me that "the Old Revolutionists" (*laogeming*) like to use numbers 10–12. This comment shows that she clearly saw strong socialism in numbers 10–12.

Number 7 is specifically for people who die young. Of course, the age that counts as "young" is rather subjective. I remember a business meeting in which the bereaved said that she wanted to choose number 7 for her mother. The salesperson told her that her mother died when she was sixty-four. He said, "Of course, you can use this [no. 7] if you want to. But this is usually for people who die in their fifties or even younger. Dying in her sixties usually does not count as 'dying young.'" This woman then decided to choose number 3 to stress her "debt" to her mother by raising her. From this conversation, we can see that she clearly felt that her mother died young. Choosing number 7 would represent her sincere feeling of loss. However, instead of choosing a couplet that represented her sincere feelings about her mother's death, she chose to follow the practitioner's suggestion to follow convention.

Numbers 9 and 13 are the only two that are obviously religious in nature. The former refers to popular religion whereas the latter is about Christianity. For the former, two important concepts are at play. The first is the notion of a happy death (xisang). In Chinese folk beliefs, someone dying at an old age is a good thing because, even though death is unavoidable, the deceased has shown his or her good fate by living for a long time. In Shanghai, funeral professionals generally defined this as older than eighty years of age. A second related concept is that this longevity can be transformed into prosperity for the living and contribute to the living's own potential for longevity—why the second half of the number 9 couplet is "your longevity is like a mountain that blesses your descendants." A happy death presents the deceased as having a magical efficacy to bring blessings to the living.

During my fieldwork, if the deceased qualified for the number 9 couplet, funeral professionals often asked the bereaved if they wanted to buy "longevity bowls"—rice bowls that have the Chinese character for "longevity" (*shou*) printed in red. The bereaved will then give away these bowls (along with other small gifts, including a towel, and often a Dove chocolate bar or something else sweet) to every guest who attends the funeral. People believe that if they use this bowl to eat their rice, they might gain a piece of the long-lived deceased's blessing and longevity.[9] My explanations of these related concepts are meant to illustrate some ways that ideas and practices of popular religion and reciprocity conceptualize the dead and death, as packed into couplet number 9.

Finally, the last religious couplet, number 13, is obviously for Christians because it mentions Jesus. Although not all Christians chose number 13, the majority did, and for non-Christians to choose this would make no sense. This logic also applies to number 8, which is specifically for educators. Although not all educators were commemorated with this couplet, to memorialize someone who was not involved in education with number 8 made no sense culturally. Overall, instead of searching for individualized ways to represent the deceased, Shanghai people preferred these poetic narratives of the deceased based on conventional understandings of generically proper persons as provided on the lists. Whether about kinship roles, gender roles, social relations, religion, or socialist morality, these couplets provided different framings of social convention. The descriptive content is more secondary than the category of person or the form of social convention itself.

The one meeting in which I happened to see a representative of the bereaved wanting to write an individualized set of couplets was the funeral of someone who died on duty at a relatively young age. This deceased was a schoolteacher in her late forties. When representing her school on a visit to Taiwan, she had a bike accident. After the accident, she fell into a coma for several weeks before finally passing away. Her son, who was only a teenager, went to Taiwan to take care of his mother and eventually brought her cremains back to Shanghai. During my fieldwork, most funerals were organized by the family of the deceased. One major exception to this, however, was for people who had died on duty. As such, it was one of the deceased's fellow schoolteachers who asked whether they could use a personalized couplet. In fact, this person asked even before the state practitioner said anything about couplets.

At this funeral, the vertical couplets used to commemorate her were as follows:

Right Couplet:

The red cloud suddenly disappeared, but we could not stop thinking about you. This is because you are the eternal exemplar of the educational world.

[*tongxiahuxiao sinanting kancheng taoyuan shifan qianqiu*]

Left Couplet:

The red candle [dawn] is suddenly blown out, but the light is still on.
   This is because of your heartfelt loyalty to education.
   [*jiangzhu congba guangbumie zhiyin xingtan danxin yipian*]

The color red and dawn were not random choices. The deceased's first name literally meant "red dawn." Both this name and its echoes in the couplets also referred directly to a patriotic connection to CCP China that was not uncommon in mainland Chinese names at that time. Overall, this funeral was not personalized as a whole. Nevertheless, even though the funeral followed standard funeral procedures, her former colleagues at least gave her personalized vertical couplets. My intention to provide a few details about her death is meant to point out the uniqueness of this death and how it explains the existence of the personalized couplets. This unfortunate death has the three common ingredients that established a higher likelihood of having a personalized funeral in Shanghai: she died young, she died in an accident, and she was someone from the category of artists/intellectuals/celebrities.

Moving from the absence of the individual to the most significant way to conceptualize the deceased, I find that religious ideas of person and death were the dominant framework for conceptualizing the dead in these mundane funeral arrangement meetings. For example, from the beginning, when Li Shan and the Dings discussed the hearse, Li Shan suggested a cheaper first ride because he thought, "If you [the Dings] want to let your father enjoy a nice last ride, you can rent a nicer hearse for his departure from Huangpu to the crematorium." The idea of treating the dead as if they are still living is one of the most important principles in handling death in traditional Han Chinese funerals. In fact, the entire discussions of choosing cremains caskets, funeral outfits, funeral processions, and hearse rides were based on an ongoing dialogic imagination of the deceased as one who could still live, behave, and feel just as the living could but in the other world. Therefore, the deceased resided in cremains caskets, funerary outfits were clothes for him in the next world—one that also experiences seasonal changes such that the Dings provided their father with five tops and three bottoms—and a ride in a Buick with a "hot and noisy" ritualized funeral procession would give their father "face" as he left this world (as well as giving face to the living Dings). These points were aimed not just at being proper but also making the deceased happy.

Other than constructing the dead as religious subjects, another prominent perception of the dead as observed through business meetings is based on Confucian hierarchical differentiations. Hierarchy in traditional funerals is understood as a relational difference but is often articulated through numerical differences. For example, in imperial times, if the deceased was an ordinary person, 4, 8, 12, or 16 people would carry his coffin depending on how much his descendants could afford. Sixteen carriers, also called "dragon head carriers" (*longtougang*), represented the highest level of treatment that an ordinary deceased (meaning someone without official title) could enjoy. People with official titles could have 32, 48, or 64 carriers depending on their rank. Only the emperor could have 128 carriers (Shanghai Funeral Museum 2010).

Recall Li Shen's introduction of the hearse options to the Dings. Li Shen asked the Dings if they wanted the RMB 240, 600, or 1,000 (USD 39, 97, or 161) kind. The same thing happened with Xiao Lin's introduction of the cremains caskets. She asked if they wanted the several hundred or several thousand type. In fact, all funeral professionals with whom I worked (whether they were state funeral practitioners or private funeral brokers) framed their introduction of products first in terms of prices. The content differences (about the types of cars or caskets, for instance) only came in as a secondary explanation. In many cases, the bereaved made decisions even before they found out how one product was different from the other. For the bereaved to decide they wanted to hire an RMB 1,000 (USD 161) hearse instead of an RMB 240 (USD 39) type hearse (or vice versa) was not uncommon, even before they knew that one was a Cadillac and the other was a minivan. This heightened interest in hierarchies articulated through numerical differences that disregard the content always amazed me. I saw many people making decisions about which meeting hall to use without even asking to see the differences among the Chinese, Western, or modern styles of meeting hall. This tendency indicates that content does not matter as much as the message about face, social status, and hierarchy.

The third and last way to conceptualize the deceased in these business meetings is based on socialist ideas of a person. Within the process of arranging funerals, the first and probably the most obvious part that constructs the deceased as a socialist subject is the discussion of the horizontal couplet in addressing the deceased. Recall that Xiao Lin asked the Dings how they wanted to address their father. Did they want to address him as "Father" or "Comrade"? Over the course of my fieldwork, I estimate that half of the people I saw chose kinship terms and half chose "Comrade" when selecting a horizontal couplet. Comrade was used as a general title to refer to anyone without regard to sex, age, or political hierarchy in the PRC. Comrade indicated a way of conceptualizing the dead as an equal, nondifferentiated person whose identification was directly connected to citizenship. This conceptualization contrasted with conceptualizing the deceased as embedded in kinship or other horizontal networks.

Some subtler places where we can see the dead being perceived as citizen subjects in business meetings was in the discussion over cremation coffins, citizenship, and minzu (state-determined ethnicity) categories. When Xiao Lin introduced the cremation coffins, she explained that cremation coffins were made of paper or bamboo. When the Dings asked if there were any wooden coffins, Xiao Lin said that only Muslims, Hong Kong residents, Macanese, Taiwanese, and foreigners who were allowed to perform body burial were allowed to use wooden coffins. This categorization marked ideas of citizenship and minzu categories in the PRC and showed how these identity categories related to the materiality of the coffins and, therefore, to the applicability of the law forcing cremation. Finally, we see the idea of citizen subjects in the category of "degree of confidentiality." Degree of confidentiality was related to political reliability. During the era of high socialism, counterrevolutionaries often died and were cremated without their family members even knowing about it. Today, a similar situation might involve the cremation of executed criminals or, on the other end of the spectrum, the funeral of an elite politician that required additional attention. Filling in this category would trigger an entirely different set of assumptions and actions by state practitioners. Although the current form that the bereaved had to fill out did not contain minzu and confidentiality categories, their presence in the funeral parlors' computer system (for funeral practitioners' use) reminds us that the deceased were nevertheless (also) conceptualized in terms of state-authorized ethnic categories and political implications.

To summarize, in a business meeting for making funeral arrangements, the deceased was primarily conceptualized within a Confucian hierarchical and popular religious framework. Then, secondarily, he or she was conceptualized according to conventional categories of age, sex, and so on and finally as a socialist citizen subject. The relatively minor role of socialist identity would be reversed in memorial meetings themselves—a topic that I explore in depth in the next chapter. Whereas the ratio of these different social conventions changed from business meetings to the backstage arrangement of funerals to memorial meetings as the funeral's front stage, one thing remained consistent: the absence of individualized subjects conceived of as based on unique, autonomous, bounded, independent, and coherent selves. This despite funeral officials and industry leaders attempting to promote personalized funerals. The next logical question is then: Why was this the case? Why did Shanghai people not want to commemorate their dead as individuals?

Marketization without Market Subjects

I asked many people why these attempts to personalize commemorations had failed. Many pointed to the way a variety of technical limitations limited the likelihood of having personalized funerals. For example, I had conversations with some officials from Beijing and with Shanghai industry leaders right after the presentation of the Taiwanese architect's funeral described at the beginning of this chapter. I asked them whether the same kind of funeral could be held in China. They all said no. One of them said that the Taiwanese architect's funeral was held several months after he passed away. In Shanghai, however, even though the law gives people fourteen days to have their funerals, people prefer to have memorial meetings on the third day after death. The amount of time between death and funeral matters because personalized funerals tend not to be held nearly as quickly. Time is needed to reflect, to gather materials, to design, and to organize. The pursuit of authenticity takes more time and deliberation than following social convention.

The second factor is that the type of labor needed in organizing personalized funerals is different from conventional styles of memorialization. Ritualized funerals relied heavily on experts to perform the rituals or to guide the bereaved in their performance. Personalized funerals, however, do not need ritual experts to tell them what to do at each step because acts and feelings should be spontaneous, original, and authentic. Once the ritualized performance is given up, the idea that, as the Taiwanese presenter said, funeral professionals stay behind the scenes as much as possible makes perfect sense. The experts simply set the stage and allow spontaneity to flow. Of course, being behind the scenes does not mean that funeral professionals have no role. In contrast, they are there to be "directors." People who design personalized funerals work more as an event planner, who needs to do everything and all of it creatively (and relatively invisibly). This type of work requires staff who can think beyond the norms instead of following a set pattern.

However, the reality in Shanghai was that funeral parlors operated more in line with Taylorism. Each funeral practitioner oversaw a small part of handling the dead bodies that passed through the parlor each day. People in the same unit were doing more or less the same jobs. Although they were experts in their units, generally, anyone in the same unit could be easily replaced with another. As an attempt to solve this issue, Shanghai funeral parlors recently worked to recruit college graduates into their ranks as mentioned earlier. However, these graduates were still assigned jobs more or less based on a Taylorist style. The key factor behind this work arrangement was the considerable number of bodies that funeral parlors must handle each day. For example, Huangpu Funeral Parlor was deluged each day with 60–80 bodies in the summer and 100–120 bodies in the winter. The mass production characteristics and highly industrialized operation made individualization very difficult to achieve in Shanghai funeral parlors. These characteristics, of course, also have everything to do with Funeral Reform's emphasis on mandatory cremation, the history of the nationalization of funeral parlors, and the state's desire to maintain its monopoly over dead bodies.

There are also significant cultural assumptions about proper funerals in Shanghai that have prevented the take-up of personalized funerals as well. For example, Shanghai people prefer to have open-casket funerals. This preference limits the possibility of using different types of spaces in which to hold funerals because dead bodies cannot be moved outside the parlors. This preference for open-casket funerals contrasted with the Taiwanese architect's funeral discussed above. Recall the Taiwanese speaker's presentation on personalized funerals—she did not mention whether the architect's body was present. The actual physical, corporal dead body did not matter because what mattered was the "life culture" he left behind, which was represented in the funeral and not the material remains—a point that is consistent with the idea of personalized commemoration.

Finally, the very market logics of maximizing benefits themselves have prevented Shanghai people from accepting personalized funerals. As the funeral industry became more market driven, Shanghai people have become more suspicious about profiteering and overcharging, and the bereaved's distrust of funeral professionals grew. As such, the whole point of a business meeting (and the key to having a successful business meeting) was to build trust out of distrust. For funeral professionals, this approach meant they avoided suggestions that might make the bereaved think they were just trying to sell them something. This avoidance included any suggestions of "unconventional" services and products, which was why most salespeople in state funerals parlors did not even mention to the bereaved the possibility of a personalized funeral when making funeral arrangements. Many grassroots state practitioners told me that if the bereaved truly wanted a personalized funeral, they would say so without needing a salesperson to suggest it. They told me that if a salesperson was stupid enough to ask the bereaved if they wanted a personalized funeral, then this person was on her or his way to ruining the deal.

In fact, smart funeral professionals knew that the trick to selling more was to start off selling less. My description of the Dings' business meeting showed that both Li Shan and Xiao Lin had to be very tactful in talking to the Dings when arranging their funeral. For Xiao Lin (and all the salespeople working in funeral parlors), the only way to make a sale go smoothly was to make the bereaved believe that the salesperson was on their side. One of the easiest ways to do so was to suggest only necessary funeral goods and services. Better, successful salespeople played down or recommended lower-priced options for the early service items (such as the hearse from the hospital to the parlor) as a way of gaining trust: "Clearly, this practitioner is not simply trying to sell me the most expensive option." This, in turn, would allow them to then make more money by selling bigger ticket items, such as the cremains caskets or the procession/band options introduced at the end of the sales pitch.

Recall the previous discussion on funeral parlors since marketization in chapter 2. One of the most important methods of marketizing state funeral parlors was to transform funeral practitioners from being responsible for funeral governance (civil governance) into service providers who were responsible for making a profit both for themselves and, therefore, for the funeral parlors (market governance). As a result, the imperative for funeral professionals was to meet and then exceed by as much as possible their monthly quotas to get higher bonuses. When funeral practitioners viewed their primary task as doing business, they were unwilling to carry out changes if they could not see how they could earn a profit from such changes. As a result, regardless of how people higher up envisioned the future of funeral governance or how personalized funerals might bring long-term profits (in terms of both larger earned incomes and lower costs of governing) for the state, practitioners on the ground had very few incentives to offer such service items and were not sure that they could (or sure they could not) sell these. After all, the state (in this case, the state funeral parlors) has never been a homogeneous unit, and we should not assume that what might benefit funeral parlors as an institution would also benefit the state as a group of actual people who are assigned to different jobs. What created profits on the funeral parlor's balance sheet did not necessarily also create profits on an individual funeral practitioner's balance sheet.

Finally, what did the bereaved want in commemorating the dead if not personalized funerals? Before moving into the last chapters of the book, I hope the following anecdote will provide a hint. One day, I went with Chen Ting for a business meeting at the apartment of an elderly man who had died at home. His body was still in the apartment when we arrived because his oldest daughter was a devout Buddhist. She insisted on having *zhunian*, meaning "assisted recitation of the Buddha's name," for twenty-four hours before moving her father to a funeral parlor. Chen Ting conducted the business meeting with the deceased's other daughters and sons in the hallway (and I was standing with them), while the eldest daughter (with her friends) recited the Buddha's name next to the deceased in the master bedroom. As the people in the business meeting were talking about couplets, the eldest daughter walked past me because another friend of hers had just bought some live fish so that she could have a *fangsheng* (meaning "free the captive animals") ritual later that day. Many Buddhists believed that performing fangsheng on behalf of the deceased could create merit (*gongde*) for the deceased and, thus, smooth their transition to the other world and perhaps even enhance their chances for a better eventual reincarnation. Since the son and other daughters had different opinions about the couplets, when the eldest sister passed us again the second time on her way back to the bedroom (with a bucket full of fish in her hands), they asked her opinion. The eldest daughter glanced at the couplet list while listening to her brother's explanation of their discussion over the couplets so far. She abruptly interrupted the explanation and said, "This [couplet] does not matter. They are all just formalities [*xingshi*]. They don't mean anything."

Considering the fact that she was in the middle of conducting Buddhist rituals that are no less formal than couplets, this comment only makes sense if we can reason through how she viewed rituals. For her, choosing a couplet that represented her father—even if one represented him more truthfully than another—was meaningless because it did nothing for him. In contrast, Buddhist rituals of reciting the Buddha's name or freeing an animal caught or raised for that purpose were meaningful because these rituals had efficacy to help her father in the afterlife. These rituals did something instead of just saying something, making her Buddhist ritual more than a mere formality. This was despite the fact that the eldest daughter's ritual acts themselves were formalized, prescribed, and repetitive Buddhist rituals. As a result, instead of treating all rituals (religious rituals no less) as just formalities (a view that is particularly promoted by state ideology), what made ritual empty and meaningless for this devout Buddhist eldest daughter was when a ritual was representative and descriptive, such as the ideals associated with personalized funerals. I explore these issues further in the next three chapters.

Conclusion

As death evolved from being a project of civil governance to one of market governance, the imagination of a particular type of self who is autonomous, bounded, and independent; the search for a modality of ritual that is meant to authentically represent this type of self; and the capitalist effort to provide a funeral service that is profitable have together contributed to the promotion of and desire for personalized funerals in state funeral parlors. However, although managers in the funeral industry wanted to have more personalized funerals that would commemorate the deceased as unique and autonomous individuals, ordinary people consistently preferred conventional memorials. From the business meetings between state funeral practitioners and the bereaved, we can see that they constructed perceptions of the dead based on social conventions associated with relationality, status, and gender, as well as religious and socialist morality. The type of subjects created at the end of life in the interaction between the state (via state funeral practitioners) and the public (via the bereaved) was anything but individual.

The reasons for the absence of market subjects at the end of life were many. First, certain assumptions about proper death and death rituals limited the possibility of having personalized funerals. More importantly, from the perspective of the bereaved, as people came to see the funeral industry through the lens of profiteering, any hint at unconventional services and products further increased the public's suspicion that death was being used as an opportunity for profiteering. Meanwhile, from the perspective of state funeral practitioners, the relationship between Shanghai funeral parlors and Shanghai citizens had clearly changed from one of rulers and subjects to one of companies and customers. As such, marketization meant that their primary goal was to earn their commission, which led them to cater to the beliefs and desires of their customers. It was no wonder that grassroots state funeral practitioners had little incentive to carry out such policies from above when neither efficiencies nor profits existed in cultivating the bereaved and the dead as individual, free, and self-responsible citizen subjects. If anything, promoting personalized funerals increased the distrust between grassroots state practitioners and the bereaved over the commemoration of death and therefore harmed the practitioner profits. Simply working with the bereaved to construct the dead as a Confucian or religious subject meant faster business meetings and more willing customers. In other words, as we can see from this chapter, the continued development of the market governance of death hindered the development of market subjectivity for both the bereaved and the dead. As a result, the goal of Funeral and Interment Reforms to "preserve a culture of life" through the development of personalized funerals only exists on paper and in the minds of senior government officials.

DYING SOCIALIST IN "CAPITALIST" SHANGHAI

> From now on, when anyone in our ranks who has done some useful work dies, be he soldier or cook, we should have a funeral ceremony and a memorial meeting [*zhuidaohui*] in his honor. This should become the rule. And it should be introduced among the people as well. When someone dies in a village, let a memorial meeting be held. In this way we express our mourning for the dead and unite all the people.

An excerpt from Serve the People, Mao Zedong

On September 5, 1944, a man died at the age of twenty-nine in Yan'an, Shaanxi Province—the sacred refuge and site of the rebirth of the CCP. This young veteran was Zhang Side. He was an ordinary peasant soldier. The official narrative describes Zhang as a dedicated Communist who was injured for the revolution at least three times before his death. What took his last breath, however, was not combat but an accident. Zhang was working in an earthen shelter called a *yaodong*, or a cave dwelling commonly found in the Yan'an area, when a charcoal-producing kiln collapsed on him. Such a seemingly humble death did not go without notice—not when the CCP depended on peasants' support and when they were in the middle of their proselytizing expansion after their near extinction during the Long March. The Central Committee of the CCP organized a commemoration with approximately one thousand mourners for this young man on September 8, 1944. On this occasion, the then chair of the Politburo of the CCP, Mao Zedong, gave a "memorial speech" (*daoci*). This speech, known as Serve the People (Wei renmin fuwu), later became one of the most famous speeches in the history of the CCP.

Recall the restaurant Prosperity I described in the introduction. That first time that I stepped into it, while I missed Mao's shrine, I did not miss what appeared to be the text of a political speech printed in large black calligraphy on a wall in its main hall. At that time, I did not know what I had seen was the full text of Mao Zedong's Serve the People speech. Although I had seen its title as a slogan many times, I had never read the speech itself before. As far as I could tell at the time, the wallpaper had no title, only content. I was carefully reading the text to figure out what it was and why it occupied such a conspicuous position at Prosperity. Chen Ting noticed that I was reading it. She told me it was Mao's Serve the People speech. She said this in a matter-of-fact manner, and I was embarrassed at not recognizing it. Nevertheless, I still had no idea why anyone would have printed the entirety of Serve the People on a wall in a funeral restaurant as a centerpiece. As any other anthropologist might, all of whom have had to overcome this kind of embarrassing moment in fieldwork, I asked Chen Ting to explain the existence of this speech in a funeral banquet restaurant to me.

Her eyes opened wide, and she replied, "Don't you know that Serve the People is a memorial speech written by Chairman Mao?" I explained, feeling even more embarrassed, "I knew that Mao wrote Serve the People, but I've never read it, and I didn't know that it was a memorial speech." Chen Ting then told me that this speech was also the first time that the Chinese people were asked to have memorial meetings instead of traditional funerals. As Chen Ting and I talked, one of the bereaved came to her to complain that his table did not have watermelon seed snacks even though all of the other tables had them. Thus, we had to abruptly end our conversation.

When we finally went back to Longevity's office, Chen Ting could not wait to tell Liang Wan, the first person she saw in her office, that I—someone on the road to getting a PhD—did not know that Serve the People was a memorial speech. Liang Wan was kind enough to save my face by reminding her that I am Taiwanese and told her that, because the KMT did not want their people to know about Mao's writings, I would not know this. Liang Wan then turned to me and explained that Serve the People was to modern Chinese funerals "as the Bible is to Christianity." "It is the sacred text for the contemporary Chinese funeral industry," he said. Liang Wan's Bible analogy reveals a deep, if not also somewhat sacred, link between memorial meetings and the idealized world that the CCP was supposed to lead the people to.

This chapter shows how contemporary Shanghai people performed memorial meetings and explains how these were based on modernist and socialist ethics, ideas of person, and understandings of death. Memorial meetings are highly stylized, composed of both prescribed bodily movements showing respect and expressing emotions as well as prescribed narratives in the form of musical sounds and verbal utterances. After analyzing each of these, I then describe how memorial meetings became the default funeral in Shanghai. To foreshadow my findings, memorial meetings were popularized because they were political rehabilitation rituals during the Cultural Revolution. The power of memorial meetings to exonerate meant that they became an efficacious means of transforming dead bodies into socialist citizens posthumously. These ethnographic findings address a set of issues in theorizing rituals and subjectivity that form the analytical framework of this chapter as well as of the next two chapters.

Specifically, I found that memorial meetings provided a cognitive frame that allowed ritual participants to conceptualize words and behaviors performed within the ritual in specific ways that are different from the world outside of the ritual. When performing memorial meetings, people in effect momentarily act as if they were all model socialist citizens living in an idealist Communist utopia. Ritual temporarily reframes perceptions and behaviors in a way that is parallel to what Bateson has argued in his analysis of play ([1955] 2000). This framing endowed memorial meetings with a sense of "formalism, traditionalism, invariance, rule-governance, sacral symbolism, and performance"—what Catherine Bell (1997, 138) has termed "characteristics of ritual-like activities." This was despite the fact that memorial meetings were invented in the early twentieth century and had only been popularized during the Cultural Revolution in Shanghai.

The concept of ritual framing is important because it indicates that ritual is always metacommunicative (Bateson [1955] 2000). The metacommunicative message in performing memorial meetings was a public commitment to accepting social convention that existed before and beyond those individuals (Rappaport 1999). As I show, what performing memorial meetings emphasized was the recognition of socialist ethics in the general sense of shared public life rather than in denoting who the deceased was or who the bereaved believed the deceased was. What was being communicated was the frame of the ritual and not the content (Goffman 1974). As such, memorial meetings are the sites where individual commitment and social convention converge whether or not participants "believe" the content of memorial meetings. It was this public recognition of the form of memorial meetings that constructed socialist citizenship posthumously, both during the Cultural Revolution and during my fieldwork. I call these ideas of self and person constructed in memorial meetings "ritually constructed subjectivity."

The concept of ritually constructed subjectivity allows us to see how self-reflexivity is an inherent component of convention-based, normative structures like ritual. Since ritual forms a contrast between the idealized world revealed in rituals and the world of reality outside of the ritual, the moment of entering a memorial meeting and "pretending" to only be idealized socialist citizens then also becomes a moment that people realize that they are not living in an idealized socialist world. Performing seemingly archaic rituals denaturalizes social reality as people move between the inside and outside of the frame of ritual. Ritual thus strikes a moment of dissonance in everyday life by requiring participants to cross its boundaries. In the following sections, I first explain what memorial meetings were by describing one memorial meeting I attended. This provides an anchor for explaining how this ritual was popularized in Shanghai, how we might interpret the meaning of having such ritual now, in the context of economic reform in China, and how we might understand its implications for ideas of self.

Memorial Meetings: Contemporary Urban Chinese Funerals

At the time of my fieldwork, memorial meetings in Shanghai were composed of five ritual acts. The standard procedure, with an emcee facilitating and explicitly directing participants to move from one step to the next, was as follows:

> Step 1: The master of ceremonies (MC) verbally announces the beginning of the memorial meeting.
> Step 2: All commemorate the deceased in silence while playing a funeral dirge [aiyue].
> Step 3: The work unit representative gives a memorial speech.
> Step 4: The representative of the bereaved gives a thank-you speech [daxieci].
> Step 5: All collectively bow three times to the deceased.
> Step 6: All participate in a farewell ceremony [gaobie yishi].

This procedure was posted on the wall at memorial meeting halls and displayed on the desks of the salespeople at all Shanghai funeral parlors. It was also printed on the pamphlets published by FIS. In fact, this text was found throughout China during my fieldwork. If you bought a Chinese-language how-to book that teaches people how to organize modern rituals, you would see this same procedure there as well (e.g., see Lu and Zheng 2011). All funerals held in Shanghai funeral parlors followed this procedure whether or not they also contained popular religious, Buddhist, Protestant, or Catholic rituals.

To better describe memorial meetings, I illustrate in depth here one meeting organized for Wang Dashan. Wang Dashan's memorial meeting was one of Longevity's cases. Tang An conducted the business meeting with the Wang family, but Chen Ting was the MC of the memorial meeting. Chen Ting often added her own "extra touch." When they appear in my description, I point out these extra touches. To a certain extent, differences between memorial meetings were to be expected; no funeral MC could repeat the exact ritual just as—as Heraclitus has told us—you can never step into the same river twice. Ritual is always characterized by simultaneity, multifocality, contingency, and indeterminacy once you see ritual participants as actors (Drewal 1992). However, this did not change the fact that a good portion of the river, as we understand it, indeed remained despite or in fact because of its water's flow. Whereas every funeral MC had her or his own idiosyncratic variations, these remained quite small, and all followed the basic steps of the standard procedure. As such, unlike the story of the Taiwanese architect's funeral described in the last chapter—meant to be an extreme case along a spectrum of possible personalized funerals—Wang Dashan's memorial meeting was very generic. Nothing in particular stood out that made this funeral somehow identifiably different from the rest of the memorial meetings that I observed in full.

Wang Dashan's Memorial Meeting

Wang Dashan had a daughter and a son, Wang Meifang and Wang Shaoquan. Both were married and had two children. On the day of Wang Dashan's memorial meeting, Chen Ting, Chen Yu, and I arrived in the meeting hall before the Wangs, as we usually did. The state practitioner assigned to be in charge of the meeting hall for Wang Dashan's funeral was Lu Yang. Lu Yang was in his early twenties, an age similar to the majority of the state practitioners who worked in the meeting hall section. I was helping Chen Yu arrange flower baskets, and Chen Ting went through the logistical details with Lu Yang. About twenty minutes before the scheduled starting time, Shaoquan walked into the meeting hall holding his father's portrait photograph (*yixiang*) in his arms. All the other family members walked in behind him. Shaoquan was first in the line because his father, Wang Dashan, would himself materialize in the meeting hall via the portrait photograph that was right in front of Shaoquan. The deceased had to arrive first to his funeral.

As soon as Chen Ting saw the Wangs getting close to the hall, she went out and waited in the entrance and told Shaoquan, "Let's first invite your father in." Chen Ting accompanied Shaoquan on his walk to the other end of the meeting hall and directed him to hang the picture on the wall. After the picture was properly hung, Chen Ting told Shaoquan to bow three times to his father—one of her unique touches. I do not remember seeing other funeral professionals asking the bereaved to bow to the deceased after hanging the picture. Then, Chen Ting took Shaoquan to see Lu Yang to verify and sign the necessary documents. Once Wang Shaoquan finished signing all the documents, Chen Ting, Wang Shaoquan, and Lu Yang again briefly talked through the procedure of the memorial meeting. When they were finished, Lu Yang led Wang Meifang, Wang Shaoquan, Chen Ting, and me to the body preparation room at the back of the meeting hall to verify the identity of the body. Meanwhile, the other funeral participants had arrived and were socializing with each other in the meeting hall.

When the meeting was about to start, Chen Ting urged people to line up in rows. Chen Ting asked Wang Dashan's wife to stand in the middle of the first row, with her two children—Meifang and Shaoquan—and their spouses next to her, one couple on each side. Then, Meifang's two children and Shaoquan's two children stood in the second row right behind their parents, making sure that a nuclear family member of the deceased's children was on each side of the deceased's spouse. Chen Ting separated the grandchildren from the children into two different rows because she liked to articulate generational differences when possible.

Chen Ting then asked the work unit representative to stand at the leftmost spot (from the deceased's perspective) in the first row because the left was the "superior position" (*shangshou*). Chen Ting then told the rest of the participants to stand behind the bereaved family in order of being closer or more distant relatives, friends, colleagues, and neighbors. These participants simply found a spot for themselves anywhere toward the back, however—as long as they stood in a row since the exact lines between these categories sometimes were not clear.

When everyone was lined up, Chen Ting announced, "We are now going to start the memorial meeting. We are here today at Huangpu Funeral Parlor to deeply commemorate Mr. Wang Dashan. First, allow me to represent the bereaved family members of Wang Dashan to thank you for your participation." After she finished, she stepped out from behind the podium and bowed once to the participants. Bowing at this moment was something that funeral brokers were more likely to do than state practitioners. Then, Chen Ting walked back to the podium and said, "Our dear and kind Wang Dashan has left us. He has gone to the Western Heaven to bless his children from afar. Now I announce that we are officially beginning the memorial meeting of Mr. Wang Dashan. Let's commemorate Wang Dashan in silence. Please play the dirge."

Lu Yang then pressed the play key on the CD player to play a mourning song called "The Dirge" (*Aiyue*). During this time, everyone looked down at the floor and remained silent, including the funeral professionals and me. Less than thirty seconds into "The Dirge," Lu Yang stopped the music, people lifted their heads, and looked again to the front. Chen Ting continued, "We now invite the work unit representative to give a memorial speech." Meanwhile, after playing the mourning song, Lu Yang slipped out of the meeting hall without attracting any attention.

The work unit representative then walked to the front and center of the meeting hall. He first bowed three times to the deceased and then turned around to face the participants and bowed once. Then, the work unit representative took a piece of paper from his pocket and started to read the speech in a flat, emotionless tone. In my transcription of his speech that follows, I have italicized those turns of phrase that have particular meaning as drawn from classic socialist narratives, slogans, history, or practice, and I subsequently analyze them. Note that these italicized words were spoken in the same monotone voice as the rest of the speech, not with additional emphasis.

> Dear *Comrade* [*tongzhi*] Guests:
>
> We are here today with extreme feelings of grief to deeply commemorate the retired employee, *Comrade* Wang Dashan. *Comrade* Wang Dashan, due to the failure of medical treatment of a heart attack, passed away at 10:38 p.m. on December 12, 2011, in the Fifth People's Hospital. He lived for seventy-one years.
>
> Comrade Wang Dashan was born on August 8, 1941, in Shaoxing, Zhejiang Province, in an ordinary *peasant family* [*nongmin jiating*]. He was born into the *Old Society* [Jiushehui]. He *suffered* and was greatly *oppressed*. When *New China* [Xinzhongguo] was born, he was *liberated* [*jiefang*], as were thousands of other fellow Chinese. Comrade Wang Dashan *joined the revolution* [*canjia geming gongzuo*] in June 1959 when he began to work for the Shanghai Textile Company. From June 1959 to May 1972, he worked in the Maintenance Department, and from June 1972 to May 1990, he worked in the Warehouse Department. From June 1991, he worked in the mailroom until he retired in May 1996. Throughout his work on *revolution*, he passionately loved the *homeland*, *socialism*, and the *Communist Party*.[1] He made great contributions to the Chinese *socialist* textile industry!
>
> Comrade Wang Dashan was *diligent* and *hardworking*. Regardless of the posts at which he worked, he was always concentrating on working. He loved his job and was good at it. He was dedicated to his job with his full heart. *Comrade* Wang Dashan was *an honest and frank* man. He was *humble and cautious*, as well as friendly and kind. He was *frugal and simple* and had *endured hardships and bitterness*. He was very strict in educating his children, and they were *law-abiding* and *studious* people.
>
> The death of Comrade Wang Dashan made us lose a good *comrade*. Although he has passed away, his spirit of *selfless dedication* to work, his *bitterness*, *hardness*, and *diligence*, as well as his *frugal* lifestyle, and his *decency*, *honesty*, and *frank* morality are examples for us all. Although human beings cannot return to life once they have died, we can transform our grief into a powerful force. Having this model, we can comfort the spirit of Comrade Wang Dashan by having even more passion to *devote* ourselves to the work of *socialism*.
>
> Comrade Wang Dashan, please rest in peace!

After he finished reading this, the work unit representative turned around and bowed three times to the deceased and then turned around again to bow once to the participants. When he walked back to his position, Chen Ting announced, "Now let's invite the bereaved to give a thank-you speech." Shaoquan then walked to the same spot where the work unit representative had stood earlier to give his speech. Before he started his speech, Shaoquan also bowed three times to his father and then bowed once to the participants. Shaoquan used the template that Tang An had given him after their business meeting as the basis of his thank-you speech. With this template, the bereaved only needed to fill in the blanks in the underlined places. Here, I translate Shaoquan's thank-you speech with the underline marks to show what the template looked like. As with the italicization, the underlined phrases were not spoken any differently than the rest of the speech.

Dear Relatives and Friends, Seniors, Leaders, and Guests:

First, I am representing my whole family to express our sincere gratitude to all of you who came to join our <u>father</u>'s memorial meeting. Today, with our painful sorrow, we are here to deeply commemorate our <u>father</u>. Our <u>father</u> had a <u>heart attack</u>. Even with the emergency treatment provided by the <u>Fifth People's</u> Hospital, he continued to deteriorate so much that no medical treatment could save him. On <u>December 12</u>, 20<u>11</u>, he passed away. He lived for <u>seventy-one</u> years.

On <u>August 8</u>, 19<u>41</u>, our <u>father</u> was born into a <u>peasant</u> family. When he was young, he was <u>filial to his parents and took care of his siblings</u>. After our <u>father</u> married our <u>mother</u> and started his own family, he educated us to be people who are responsible and compassionate.

<u>Father</u> endured a life long with hardship. He worked very hard and was frugal and simple. He loved his job and was very responsible. He was kind to his neighbors. He was the exemplar for us all as his children. When <u>Father</u> was sick, many relatives and friends as well as leaders came to visit him. After <u>Father</u> passed away, all of these relatives and friends, as well as leaders, came to show their condolences even though they were so busy, especially leaders from our <u>father</u>'s work unit, the <u>Shanghai Textile Company</u>. They valued our <u>father</u> and gave him a high evaluation. Here, I am representing my family. I want to thank you all and express my sincere gratitude.

<u>Father</u>, you have left us. No matter how hard we cry, we can never wake you up again. Yet your voice, face, laugh, and appearance will stay in our heart forever.

<u>Father</u>, please go away peacefully. Our family will exist in harmony. We will take care of our aged <u>mother</u> to make sure that she can enjoy her

old age. We will educate our children to make sure that they will become useful people in our society as our way to repay the debt of you
raising us.

Please rest in peace, <u>Father</u>. Please rest in peace.

Although Shaoquan started his speech sounding similar to a work representative with a flat and emotionless tone, by the end of his speech, his voice started
to break down. After Shaoquan finished reading the thank-you speech, he turned
around to face the deceased. He bowed three times and then turned around again
to face the participants and bowed once. Then, he walked back to his spot in the
first row. Chen Ting announced, "Now it is time for us all to bow three times to
the deceased." After saying this, she turned around, faced the deceased, and
started her three bows. All of the participants followed her moves, including
Chen Yu and me (Lu Yang was still in the back room, out of sight).

When all of us finished our three bows (in unison) to the deceased, Chen Ting
said, "We are now going to have our farewell ceremony to say good-bye to
Mr. Wang Dashan." After making the announcement, Chen Ting stepped to the
side. She used her hand to gesture and told Shaoquan to bring forward his mother
and his nuclear family. They then stood on the left side of the coffin, facing it
while standing in a diagonal line, and Chen Ting stood next to them. After everyone was situated, Chen Ting said, "First bow, second bow, third bow," to direct
Shaoquan's group to bow as she spoke the words. Chen Ting also bowed with
them. While verbally announcing the three bows for the bereaved is not exclusive to Chen Ting, her bowing along with the bereaved was again one of her extra touches.

When they finished bowing, they put the yellow flowers they had been holding the entire time on top of the plastic cover that enveloped the coffin. This act
of placing yellow flowers on top of coffins was relatively new and emerged only
after the marketization of the Shanghai funeral industry. Shaoquan's group
walked to the right side of the deceased after they performed their farewell to
form a receiving line that enabled others to express their condolences to the bereaved. Meifang's nuclear family then repeated the same acts and eventually
joined Shaoquan's group to stand on the right in the receiving line. After both
Shaoquan's and Meifang's families performed their farewell ceremonies, Chen
Ting then directed the work unit representative to give his three bows by himself. Again, having the work unit representative bow alone and right after the
immediate family members was Chen Ting's extra touch.

For the rest of the funeral participants, Chen Ting had seven people at a time
stand in a row to perform their farewells even if more than seven people were in
the original rows to begin with. The number seven was used because, first, odd

numbers are the proper numbers for funerals in Shanghai. The use of exactly seven was Chen Ting's arbitrary choice. Wang Dashan's memorial meeting was officially finished when the last group of funeral participants finished their farewell ceremony. This memorial meeting took about twenty minutes, similar to the majority of meetings that I observed.

Memorial Meetings as a Site of Subject Formation

I want to pull out the two most important characteristics that run throughout memorial meetings. The first characteristic was the modernist bodily movements performed in memorial meetings, particularly expressed through the expressions of grief and mourning and the act of bowing. The second characteristic was socialist rhetoric. These narratives were articulated through two different formats: musical sounds and verbal utterances. The former refers to the particular dirge that was used. The latter refers to the lexicon used in memorial and thank-you speeches. I analyze them in turn next.

Modernist Bodily Movements

Memorial meetings forced grieving bodies to move in a way that was calm, solemn, and restrained. I call this Puritan-like way of expressing emotion "modernist" because the two modernist Chinese states—the Nationalists and the Communists—both promoted this self-restrained style at funerals (although the former was not very effective) and consciously linked this style of mourning to modernity. This way of grieving and mourning is the work of "emotional regime" (Reddy 2001)—the modes of emotional expression and thought that were dominant in a particular time and space. In memorial meetings, crying was tolerated only as long as people could not hear you. This was in contrast to emotional expression at traditional funeral rituals where people were supposed to weep, pull their hair, stomp, and perform a variety of externalized bodily expressions of mourning in a cacophony of sound and chaos. The harder you cried, the more filial you were. In fact, if you could not do these things on cue, you could hire someone to do them for you (or to amplify your performance). Ritualized wailing and professional weepers were prominent parts of traditional Han Chinese funerals and remain prominent in some rural areas today (e.g., Stafford 2000; Standaert 2008).

Of course, the bereaved can cry tears and sob softly during memorial meetings and often did—they just did it in a controlled manner. There was definitely no space for ritualized weeping or uncontrolled bodily expressions of emotion in memorial meetings. In fact, uncontrolled crying, blubbering, and wailing were viewed as disruptive and inappropriate. If the bereaved began to display strong outward expressions of emotion, funeral professionals always spoke out to stop them. At one memorial meeting I attended, the wife of the deceased began wailing before the meeting had even started. Chen Ting pulled her and her son aside after she realized that this lady did not seem to want to stop. She told them, "It is OK if you want to cry now. I understand. But later, when we actually start the memorial meeting, you have to control yourself. Both of you want this memorial meeting to go on, right? If this is the case, then we have to control ourselves no matter how sad we are."

To be clear, I am not claiming that a teleological transformation from the traditional emotional regime of "the more you cry, the better" to a modernist model of "the less you cry, the better" happened in China. Historical critiques have long existed in China against crying too much (mainly because doing so was viewed as being vulgar). Nevertheless, Shanghai funeral professionals clearly saw a direct link between highly constrained emotional expressions and modernity. For example, Chen Ting and I had the following conversation:

> HUWY-MIN LUCIA LIU: This memorial meeting was really calm.
> CHEN TING: That's because we're in Huangpu.
> H. L. L.: What do you mean by that?
> C. T.: Well, Huangpu is like a five-star hotel. It is a five-star parlor compared with other parlors. Thus, people who have funerals here generally have more "culture" and suzhi. Have you ever been to other funeral parlors? If you have, you would see many more memorial meetings with people crying loudly and making noise.
> H. L. L.: Do you mean that crying is bad for a proper funeral?
> C. T.: Yes, of course. Crying ruins the solemn atmosphere of a memorial meeting.

In China, suzhi is a ubiquitous discourse about a person's level of "civilization," which generally hinged on class discrimination against rural residents who were often less educated (Kipnis 2007). Chen Ting's comments associating Huangpu with a five-star hotel and usage of suzhi revealed exactly how they connected being calm to being modern, educated, and urban.

Moving from the bodily expression of grief and mourning to showing respect, one of the most frequent bodily movements described in Wang Dashan's memorial meeting was the act of bowing. Recall how Chen Ting bowed once to the participants as she opened the ritual. Then, both the work unit representative and Shaoquan bowed three times to the deceased and one time to the bereaved immediately before and right after they gave their respective speeches. Later, everyone bowed three times in unison to Wang Dashan. Finally, when people performed the farewell ceremony in small groups, they also bowed to the deceased (also three times). According to Chen Ting, "three bows to the deceased and one bow to the mourners" was because "the deceased was the most important" (*sizhe weida*) at his or her funeral. Therefore, the three bows should be reserved for the deceased. Chen Ting even felt that, if any of the representatives accidentally bowed three times to the participants, it might upset those few who understood the rule because people might interpret this act as a sort of curse.

Whether one or three bows, without a doubt, during my fieldwork, everyone bowed when attending memorial meetings unless the meeting was a Protestant version (and I discuss Protestantism-related issues in chapter 7). Bowing, however, was not performed in traditional Han Chinese death rituals. Traditionally, prostration, also known as kowtowing, was the proper bodily movement to show respect in funerals. Just as common people prostrated themselves to the emperor, sons and daughters had to prostrate themselves to their parents, not only at funerals but also at a variety of rituals. Prostration was a bodily representation of a hierarchical relationship. However, as early as 1912, the republican government announced its reforms to replace prostration with bows as the proper way to interact among the living and between the living and the dead. The Communist Party's own attempt to replace prostrations with bowing was meant to transform this embodied hierarchy into a reinforcement of equality. In fact, Andrew Kipnis (1997) has further argued that kowtowing and the rules for who kowtows to whom produce membership in social groups and relationships among members. In this sense, the CCP's removal of kowtowing was not only the abolishment of a "feudal" practice that honored hierarchical relationships but also the elimination of an emphasis on the social relationships themselves.

Finally, one memorial meeting I attended illustrates the work of modernity and its assumed incompatibility with both the outward expressions of mourning and prostration as well as how the state made sure it actively maintained such incompatibility. The deceased of this memorial meeting was a man who died in his fifties—a rather young age in Shanghai. This family was originally from Heilongjiang, a province in northeast China. The direct descendants wore a full set of traditional white mourning dress. They were the first (and the last) people I saw wearing traditional mourning dress at Huangpu. In general, everyone else wore normal clothes plus a black armband as their mourning garment.[2] As such, the outward expression of mourning in full-body attire made them very noticeable. I happened to walk next to this group on their way to the meeting hall from the main entrance. When walking, I saw many people (who came to join other memorial meetings) blatantly turn their heads around to stare at this family even after they had passed us. At some point, I overheard three women passing by make comments in Shanghainese. One said, "Oh, no wonder. These people speak Mandarin." Referring to this family as speaking Mandarin, what this lady indicated was that these were not Shanghainese. Shanghai people had a tendency to see all non-Shanghai people as either backward or rural. By singling out the fact that these mourners spoke Mandarin, these three Shanghai ladies meant to explain why this family wore the full-body traditional mourning dress: they were outsiders and, thus, less modern and sophisticated, and therefore they expressed grief in this way.

Later, after this group lined up to start the memorial meeting, Chen Ting went to the back room to bring the deceased in as usual. However, as soon as Chen Ting and the deceased entered the meeting hall from the back, the people who stood in the first three rows suddenly knelt and started prostrating and weeping loudly. Having witnessed emotional control and bowing throughout my fieldwork, I did not expect to see such an outburst at Huangpu. However, equally fast was Lu Yang's reaction. As the state funeral practitioner on duty at that meeting hall, he ran to the front center of the hall and almost yelled at the bereaved, "All of you, stand up! Don't kneel. This looks really inappropriate. Stop crying! This looks really bad. How can we have a memorial meeting when you [chief mourners] act like this. Control yourself. We are at a funeral parlor."

Socialist Sounds and Words

If my analysis of mourning and bowing illustrate how memorial meetings were modernist, then my analysis of the funeral music and speeches below shows how memorial meetings were socialist. As stated in the introduction, the term *socialist* in this book refers to specific ethics and their related ideas of self, person, and death rather than a mode of production even though the two are linked. In the following sections, I discuss the commonly used music and speeches in memorial meetings in turn to illustrate how these sounds and words describe socialist citizenship.

In Shanghai, all funeral parlors used the same song as their mourning song. During my fieldwork, if the bereaved hired a band, then the band played "The Dirge." Otherwise, it was usually played on a CD player. However, no rule existed to force the bereaved to use this particular song. FIS has published a pamphlet, *Funeral Guide (Baishitong)*, that specifically states that bands could perform whatever mourning song the bereaved chose. Several state practitioners also told me that if the bereaved wanted to use their own music, they only needed to prepare a CD. However, the reality was that very few family members demanded that their choice of music be used. All of this is consistent with my discussion of the failure of personalized funerals in the last chapter.

"The Dirge" describes socialist citizenship because it is intimately tied to the birth of Communist China as a new nation-state. "The Dirge" was first played for the ground-breaking ceremony of the Monument of the People's Hero at Tiananmen Square on September 30, 1949—the day before the CCP officially announced the establishment of the People's Republic of China. As Mao Zedong threw soil to the ground, the PLA marching band of more than forty players performed "The Dirge." Years later, the same song was played at the funerals of Mao Zedong, Deng Xiaoping, and Zhou Enlai, in addition to millions of ordinary deceased citizens in China since 1949.

There were several versions of an origin story for this song that sought to explain how it came to be linked to the party. Some said that Yan'an-based musicians encountered a piece of folk music and then later reworked the folk song they had collected into a dirge for the memorial meeting of Liu Zhidan. Liu Zhidan was an early CCP member, a primary organizer of the CCP's rural-based guerrilla attacks against the Japanese, and the founder of the Chinese Red Army. He was killed in battle in 1936. The party later named him a martyr. In 1942, the Central Committee of the CCP decided to move his coffin back to his hometown. There, the party organized a large memorial meeting for him. Yu Ge (1998) believes that a song titled "Publicly Commemorating Liu Zhidan" was the first version of what later became "The Dirge." However, Luo Lang (1920–2015), a longtime leader of the PLA marching band, offered a completely different narrative. Luo was a composer of many famous "Red Songs" (Chen and Liao 2015). Luo claimed that the song was initially collected by him and his colleagues based at Jinchaji Base, the first guerrilla base for the CCP. When Yu Ge confronted Luo Lang about why there were such different narratives of the initial collectors of "The Dirge," Luo said that, in some ways, it was because the song was from "the People."

To some degree, which version was correct does not matter much here. What's important for the purpose of this book is that each story shows that the way "The Dirge" came to be played at memorial meetings was deeply intertwined with the construction of the party's desire to commemorate martyrs. Moreover, each version links the song to the sacred sites of the CCP whether discussing Yan'an (recall Zhang Side in the Serve the People speech) or Jinchaji Base. Beyond this, the consensus on how "The Dirge" emerged described it as originating from rural folk music, the People's music. Such an emphasis echoed the CCP's own narrative of how the party came to depend on a peasant revolution to carry out a socialist revolution and, thus, "liberate" the Chinese people. As a result, having no lyrics did not mean that this mourning song was devoid of meaning. Even though "The Dirge" today is a slow and solemn melody played by orchestra instruments without human voices, for participants in the moment, it told a recognizably socialist narrative in its musical expression of sounds that filled the public space of memorial meetings.

The second type of socialist narrative in memorial meetings was linguistic. It was specifically expressed through verbal utterances of the socialist lexicon. By analyzing both the memorial speech and the thank-you speech, we can see at least two types of vocabulary deployed in memorial meetings to evoke distinct conceptualizations of the dead. The first related to socialist ideas of the time, especially referring to Old China, New China, and Liberation. These temporal terms held within them the CCP's promises of a radical temporal disjuncture between the new and the old through rupture, a process that was known as "Liberation." The process was a rupturing because, once China was "liberated," all of the old vices were gone. However, to have this disjuncture, the CCP needed to first create a specific interpretation of what China was like before the revolution: Old China. To do so, the CCP developed a whole set of discourse and publicly performed testimonials to extract, essentialize, and reconceptualize certain characteristics of the past. Much of the CCP's early governance, as reflected in chapters 1 and 2, involved designating which ongoing practices counted as "old" and therefore needed to be revolutionized. Once the concept of Old China was created, a rupturing process (the Liberation) was needed that separated the Old China from the New China. The CCP's legitimacy was built on such an imagined temporal shift. This type of reiteration of a temporal shift froze the deceased within a socialist idea of time regardless of how she or he may have lived during the last several decades. For example, Comrade Wang Dashan was described as having been born into a peasant family of the Old Society and then "liberated." This liberation occurred despite the fact that Wang Dashan was not a farmer for most of his life and that his children did not call him "comrade" in real life.

Moreover, this universal temporal shift also indicated that working in New China meant that you were joining the revolution or contributing to the revolution whether or not your labor was directly linked to political work. A person could contribute to the revolution by sweeping the streets as long as the act was conscientiously carried out in New China. For this reason, Wang Dashan's humble work history was delineated as contributing to the Chinese socialist textile industry. In fact, I realized this personally from a conversation with a woman who was a charismatic leader in a lay Buddhist group in her late fifties. We spent a night in a temple outside Shanghai because her friend's relative was going to have a Buddhist salvation ritual performed early in the morning the next day. The night was quite surreal—I felt as if I was at a slumber party with six elderly ladies whose ages ranged from fifty to eighty years. Before we turned off the lights and proceeded to talk in the dark for the next three hours, this charismatic leader showed me her "Retirement Certificate"—a red booklet-like document. One column on the certificate indicated her "date of joining the revolution" (*canjia geming gongzuo nianyue*). When I saw this, I asked her, "Were you in the army, or are you a party member?" I asked this question because I assumed that phrases such as "join the revolution" must indicate some type of involvement in the party or military apparatus. She needed time to understand my question since my question made no sense to her. Once she figured out what I was asking, she explained that the date reflected her first day working in a factory in Shanghai after she had graduated from junior high school. The date on which she first joined the workforce was the first date on which she joined the revolution.

The second set of socialist lexicon used in memorial meetings related to the CCP's specific ideas of person. These ideas of person had at least two dimensions: status categories and personally embodied ethics. The former is best exemplified by the terms *comrade* and *peasant*. As I already explained the use of *comrade* in the last chapter, here I focus on the word *"peasants"* to explain why this, too, is a socialist status category rather than individual descriptor. While there was significant exploitation of farmers, the political and economic relations of prerevolutionary farmers in China did not remotely resemble the feudal relations of European peasants "tied to the land" and had not at least since the Song dynasty (Cohen 1993). However, to create a class-based understanding of Chinese society where the exploited majority that socialism was supposed to work for were farmers rather than workers, such farmers needed to be categorized as "peasants." In this cultural imagination, peasants contrasted with businesspeople ("landlords" or "capitalists") who built their wealth using their cleverness and calculation, thus implying they were somewhat dishonest (Hinton 1966). This category of peasants then became a part of official class classifications during the CCP's land reform in the early 1950s. Under such class classifications, each household was assigned a class category of landlord or rich, middle, or poor peasant. Once a class label was assigned, these categories became hereditary and largely remained with descendants of the household until the beginning of the reform period. In memorial meetings today, while no one would emphasize belonging to landlord or capitalist status categories, people still stressed the symbolically prestigious categories of workers and peasants as if these, too, were items of conspicuous consumption— something perhaps particularly important when the families had few other means to show off their status under a market economy.

The third aspect of narrating a socialist person was to talk about personally embodied moral character. In the memorial speech previously quoted, we can see that the third and fourth paragraphs narrate the idealized (if not outright imagined) merits of the deceased. These ethics included being diligent, hardworking, dedicated, honest, frank, humble, cautious, frugal, simple, law-abiding, and studious, as well as having endured hardships and bitterness and having suffered oppression. The same type of ethics was also repeated in the template-based thank-you speech. To understand why the recitation of these ethics narrate a socialist person, we can see their echoes elsewhere as well. For instance, a famous early CCP leader, Liu Shaoqi (1952, 31), in his article, *How to Be a Good Communist*, said as follows:

> He will worry long before the rest of the world begins to worry and he will rejoice only after the rest of the world has rejoiced. . . . Both in the Party and among the people he will be the first to suffer hardship and the last to enjoy himself. He never minds whether his conditions are better or worse than others, but he does mind as to whether he has done more revolutionary work than others or whether he has fought harder. . . . He is capable of possessing the greatest firmness and moral courage to resist corruption by riches or honors, to resist tendencies to vacillate in spite of poverty and lowly status and to refuse to yield in spite of threats of force.

This quote shows striking parallels between the narratives that appeared to be a description of the ethics of Wang Dashan and those present in Lin Shaoqi's propaganda work. All of these commonly evoked ethics in memorial meetings were not new: they were desired characteristics in the CCP's official ideology because these characteristics were said to be related to peasant virtues. These socialist ethics entered the public discourse at the mass level with the rise of the CCP and over the course of the continued recitation of such texts in school and during the high socialist period. Such narrations of socialist time and morality were even transformed into concrete ritualized activities, such as in *yiku sitian*, translated as "remembering the bitterness of the past and appreciating the sweetness of the present." This form of public gatherings brought people who were born before and after the liberation together (X. Liu 2004). In such meetings, frequent and well attended at various points prior to the Reform and Opening, people who were born before the Liberation rehearsed and (re)experienced the bitterness of the past by (re)constructing past memories for the younger generation who were born after the "Liberation." By artificially injecting an imagined past into the present, the current reality was fictionalized as real and happy.

To be clear, by pointing out how memorial speeches were based on socialist verbal utterances and canonical texts, I do not mean in any way to indicate that stylized speeches were something exclusive to the CCP. There has been a long history of a wide variety of literary genres associated with funeral speeches in Sinophone cultures. What I mean to point out here is that the specifically socialist ideas of time and person developed in these speeches are not seen outside the sovereignty of the PRC. While it may seem uncontroversial to describe memorial meetings as a socialist ritual based on the prominence of ethics, music, and bodily comportment with clear origins alongside the CCP, some PRC citizens I have spoken with rejected this description. Some told me that memorial meetings are simply something "Chinese" and therefore have no specific connection to the CCP. For these people, I had to remind them that Mandarin-speaking people outside the PRC did not use the same kinds of narrative devices even though they also used stylized narratives. Others rejected the label of *socialist* because they felt that this term is (and should only be) about a particular mode of production. While I agree that mode of production is one possible way to use the term *socialist*, I hope that my definition and analysis here has shown clearly that memorial meetings were built on the CCP's specific moral discourses of proper persons and citizens.

Political Rehabilitation and the Construction of Socialist Citizens

When work units received memorial meeting requests, they often simply took out the deceased's dossier (*dang'an*) and filled in the blanks based on their templates. Perhaps a bit more surprising, as we saw above, this fill-in-the-blank process even occurred in thank-you speeches given by close family members. Thank-you speeches serve three functions: (1) to thank people, especially the work unit leaders who come to the memorial meeting (or who could not come in person but sent their condolences); (2) to introduce the deceased to funeral participants; and (3) to express grief and mourning. Although the last two points, combined with the fact that the one who wrote and read the speech was a family member, seemed to suggest the thank-you speeches would be less stylized, they were often just as stylized as memorial speeches. Not only were there relatively few blanks to fill in, but also the space provided for improvisation was miniscule, and most blanks had easy, generic "answers." As a result, if neither speech was descriptive of the deceased, then what were they about or for?

To answer this question, I suggest examining how memorial meetings came to be the dominant form of commemoration in Shanghai. During the Funeral Reform campaigns in the 1950s and 1960s, the primary goal of state practitioners was to persuade the bereaved to accept five rules that were summarized in a campaign slogan called the "Five Replacements" (Wuyi wudai): using cremation to replace body burial, using flowers and wax fruit to replace the burning of spirit money and offerings of candles and incense, wearing black armbands and yellow flowers to replace traditional whole-body mourning garments, using three bows to replace kowtowing, and using memorial meetings to replace old funerary rites.[3]

State practitioners called the type of memorial meetings promoted during the promotion of the Five Replacements "public sacrifices" (*gongji yishi*). According to an internal document of the Shanghai Funeral and Interment Administration (1987), the specific procedures of a public sacrifice ceremony performed in a Shanghai funeral parlor in 1959 were as follows:

> Step 1: The bereaved family members (and later relatives and friends) offer wreaths and flowers.
>
> Step 2: The bereaved family members and then relatives and friends bow three times to the deceased and then stand to the side (the deceased's immediate family members stand next to the body).
>
> Step 3: Everyone stands up to face the deceased and commemorates him or her in silence for three minutes while the funeral dirge is played.
>
> Step 4: The bereaved family members then introduce the life history of the deceased to the participants.
>
> Step 5: Relatives and friends may give speeches.
>
> Step 6: Everyone then walks around the body once to say good-bye to the deceased.

A comparison of memorial meetings during my fieldwork in 2011 and 2012 with the public sacrifice ceremony of 1959 shows that they were quite similar. The most obvious similarity was the overall ritual procedure. Other continuities included bowing three times to the deceased, commemorating them in silence while playing a dirge, and family members giving speeches to introduce the life history of the deceased to the participants. Moreover, step 6 in the public sacrifice that describes everyone walking around the body to say good-bye to the deceased was also step 6 in memorial meetings, now known as the farewell ceremony. Overall, bodily performances in public sacrifice and memorial meetings were also parallel.

Looking more closely, however, there were also significant differences. The most significant change that emerges when comparing these two formal procedural outlines was the presence of work units and their reading of a memorial speech.[4] There was no mention of work units giving speeches in public sacrifice in the previous description. Instead, step 5 said that "relatives and friends may give a speech." This difference was crucial because, during my fieldwork, the memorial speech was the most important step in memorial meetings. In fact, Shanghai funeral professionals maintained that funerals without memorial speeches were not memorial meetings at all. What makes a speech a "memorial speech" was exactly determined by the speakers' identities. These speakers had to represent the work unit of the deceased. If the deceased did not have a work unit, but the bereaved still wanted to have a memorial meeting, then a representative from the deceased's "residential committee" (juweihui) could give a memorial speech. During my fieldwork, funeral professionals called those funerals that followed the format and narrative styles of memorial meetings but did not have a work unit reading memorial speeches "memorial services" (zhuisihui) or merely "farewell ceremonies." In other words, more than what was being said (since in theory anyone could verbalize these socialist narratives of time, ethics, and person), what was even more important was who said it.

What happened to memorial meetings that made work units and their memorial speeches so essential that their absence could render a funeral in its most important sense not a proper funeral, not a memorial meeting? To answer this question, I quote a long interview I conducted with Master Gao below. Master Gao entered the Shanghai funeral industry in 1959 at the age of fourteen. He first worked in one of only five funeral homes remaining after the nationalization of all funeral homes in the early 1950s. When the Red Guards shut down all funeral homes and cemeteries at the end of December 1966, Gao was transferred to one of only two funeral facilities open in Shanghai at that time.

> MASTER GAO: No, no, the kind of funeral in 1965 was different from the current kind [in 2011]. In 1965, when I was still at Peace Funeral Home, we still did superstitions. . . .
>
> H. L. L.: Do you mean that there was no work unit giving memorial speeches in 1965?
>
> M. G.: No. No work unit gave memorial speeches in 1965. . . . Our current ritual, the memorial meeting kind of ritual, originated from pingfan zhaoxue ["righting the wrongs and rehabilitating the disgraced"] during the Cultural Revolution. That was the Cultural Revolution. There were many injustices. So many people needed pingfan zhaoxue. This is how memorial meetings actually started. . . .
>
> When the Cultural Revolution began, you could not do the old stuff anymore. So, in the beginning [of the Cultural Revolution], people who came [to Huangpu Crematorium] for funerals simply "took a look and had a cry." Some may have bowed once. Then, they pushed the bodies into the cremation units to burn them. We did not know what to do after we could not do the old stuff anymore. . . . There was no coffin. Coffins were superstition. You put dead bodies in bags and then burned them. . . .
>
> Nothing really. No ritual. Only "taking a look and having a cry." Everything was simple. Then, some work units did rehabilitation here

[at Huangpu Crematorium]. We [state practitioners] soon learned
that this way of doing ritual was how you could do [it, then]. So later
when the bereaved came to ask us how to do a funeral, we told them
about this kind. I would say that memorial meetings [with memorial
speeches] started to show up in Huangpu in the second half of 1968.

From Master Gao's words, we clearly see that the turning point was when
there was the need for political rehabilitation. Prior to the Cultural Revolution,
as he said, "we still did superstitions." Starting from December 1966 though,
in the aftermath of the first Red Guard movement, suddenly no elements of traditional death rituals were allowed in crematoria. Shanghai people were left with
no rituals in funeral parlors except "taking a look and having a cry" until "some
work units did rehabilitation." This was confirmed for me in a separate interview I conducted with someone high up in the Shanghai Funeral Culture Institute. He also told me that although Mao called for memorial meetings as early
as the 1940s, these meetings did not emerge in Shanghai as the default ritual until
the need for political rehabilitation.

To understand how memorial meetings could rehabilitate the dead, we need
to know the type of people who qualified to have memorial meetings in the first
place. Recalling Serve the People, Mao said that whether the deceased was a soldier or a cook, as long as he is "in our ranks" and "has done some useful work,"
he deserved "a funeral ceremony and a memorial meeting in his honor." Mao
aimed to create a disjuncture between locating the deceased in hierarchical relationships and locating him in a new equal comradeship. This equality-based
commemoration was, hopefully, to eventually become a standard practice not
only among people in "our ranks" (i.e., the party) but also among "the people"
in general. As such, the only distinction allowed was to separate the people from
those who were not the people.

This distinction was determined by whether you worked for the people or for
"the fascists, exploiters, and oppressors." If you worked for the people, even if
you died in a politically insignificant event or served in a menial job, your death
was worthy and meaningful. Therefore, dying in an accident as unremarkable
and undistinguished as getting caught off-duty under a falling kiln could still
count as "dying for the people." However, if you worked for fascists, exploiters,
and oppressors, even if you died in the middle of political duty, you died for nothing and did not deserve a memorial meeting. Consequently, to be a part of the
people meant to be socialist and vice versa. Being a nonsocialist rendered you
neither "of" the people nor "for" the people. Personhood and citizenship here
coalesced; the denial of the latter also denied you the former, which is why the

word *comrade* was used so frequently in memorial speeches. Comrade, citizen, and person were merged into a single concept in memorial meetings.

As a result, politically problematic people—often labeled "ox demons and snake spirits" (*niugui sheshen*)—could not have funerals; their identities were obliterated.[5] They were not (the) people. As nonpeople, their deaths did not deserve funerals, and they need not (read "could not") be mourned because the death of the people's enemy should be celebrated. At this time, many people died without any recognition at all. They were cremated under pseudonyms, and their families did not know until years later. One senior state practitioner told me that, every once in a while, she and her colleagues went to a beach outside Shanghai to collectively "deep bury" (*shenmai*) unclaimed cremated remains at that time. Those cremains often were cremated under a fake identity and then buried in a mixture of undifferentiated ashes whose identities were completely scattered similar to the sand around them.

For those who were wrongfully accused, as political tides swung back the other way, memorial meetings were then their final chance to regain personhood regardless of whether they were newly dead or were long gone from the living world. The mere fact of having a memorial meeting with a work unit agreeing to deliver a memorial speech already indicated that the deceased was rehabilitated. Therefore, what was said in the memorial meeting was less important than the fact that the memorial meeting was being held. By the same token, if your work unit did not give you a memorial speech even if you were a part of the people when you were alive, this refusal effectively removed you from humanity. This postmortem evaluation had the power to officially override whatever you had accomplished when you were alive. As Catherine Bell (1997, 166) states, we see here "the simple imperative to do something in such a way that the doing itself gives the acts a special or privileged status." What had been more of a family ritual became a party-state–centered ritual as this secular commemoration transformed from being public sacrifice in 1959 to a memorial meeting in Shanghai during the Cultural Revolution. Performing memorial meetings in this context thus created that direct link the CCP had long sought between atomized individuals and the state without any intermediate links, such as lineages, religious affiliations, or native-place associations.

In this sense, memorial meetings are performative in that they do something rather than say something. What they did during the Cultural Revolution was to construct socialist citizenship for already dead bodies by carrying out an act of public commitment that allowed dead bodies to reenter, remain, or be excluded from the social world of proper persons—socialist citizen subjects. Whether the deceased had ever lived as the socialist narratives describe or whether the bereaved believed the content of socialism did not matter. Regardless of who the deceased truly were and what the bereaved believed about who the deceased were, the act of performing such ritualized, externalized, formalized, and convention-based socialist rituals effectively constructed socialist citizenship in the public domain.

Constructing dead bodies' socialist citizenship in memorial meetings was not merely symbolic. It had a real social impact on the living because bad status categories (landlord, counterrevolutionary, or capitalist) were largely inherited at that time. This means that if you were a counterrevolutionary, all of your nuclear family members would be classified as such, and their children could be so classified. Consequently, once a dead nonperson was rehabilitated, all of his or her living family members would be rehabilitated as well. This was why there were many memorial meetings for people who were already long gone. This "magical" power was needed particularly when the posthumous construction of citizenship was just as important (if not more) and when the construction of dead bodies' citizenship had a direct impact on the material well-being of the living. In a truly satirical and ironic twist, rehabilitation through the memorial meeting turned out to be much more immediately effective in bringing prosperity to the deceased's descendants than the traditional death ritual's creation of benevolent ancestors had ever been!

As a result, modernist bodily movements (bowing instead of prostration, solemn and calm expressions of grief and mourning) and socialist verbal utterances ("The Dirge," stylized memorial speeches, and thank-you speeches) evoked in memorial meetings were not meant to be authentic representations of the deceased or indications of the bereaved's beliefs about the deceased. These modernist bodily actions and socialist narratives did not contain denotative meanings that anchor the words to the person they addressed. Performing memorial meetings did not somehow magically turn the deceased somehow into "authentic" socialist citizens (no matter what we mean by authenticity) or mean that the bereaved somehow "sincerely" came to believe their beloved had been good socialists. What it did was to construct socialist citizenship for the dead posthumously *in public* by having individuals committing to social convention. The final "magical act" that granted memorial meetings the power to construct socialist citizen subjects was the power to rehabilitate dead bodies.

Social Convention as Dissonance

Surprisingly, after China adopted market economic principles, the politically correct position became not to have memorial meetings, despite their popular-

ity. At the national level, the CCP issued several documents to discourage memorial meetings following the end of the Cultural Revolution, especially with
regard to high-ranking cadres. In a real sense, these are a part of the ongoing
relevance of civil governance demands even in an era where the market governance of funerals appears dominant. In 1980, the General Office of the Chinese
Communist Party Central Committee released a statement, *Regarding Avoiding
Propaganda for Individuals*. This statement prohibited party members from having a memorial speech. Point 5 of the statement even said, "In the last few years,
to rehabilitate those old comrades who were wrongfully accused, we had many
grand memorial meetings. This situation should be close to ending. We should
not spend so much labor and money on it."

The CCP's objection to memorial meetings after the Cultural Revolution
ended can be understood at two levels. At the rhetorical level, the CCP's official
ideology has always been about simplifying ritual. Investment of both time and
money in any ritual was viewed as a type of waste. It not only failed to contribute to production and to the material well-being of the people but also took away
the fruits of production and wasted money. At a level of governance, however, the
state's intention to move away from memorial meetings was more related to
the political consequences of organizing memorial meetings. Death in China has
always been a powerful mobilizing symbol for protest. For example, the two relatively recent large political movements in China—the Tiananmen Incident in
1976 and the Tiananmen Democracy Protests in 1989—both started with people
mourning recently deceased CCP leaders: Zhou Enlai and Hu Yaobang, respectively. The general mobilizing power of death, combined with the specific power
to rehabilitate, made (and perhaps still makes) memorial meetings particularly
dangerous from the state's perspective because memorial meetings were when
mourners were allowed to witness an authoritarian regime admitting its mistakes
in public.

While the national government decided to discourage memorial meetings,
Shanghai government bureaus and funeral parlors decided to (re)interpret the
central government's effort to ban memorial meetings as merely a means of regulating high-ranking cadres. An internal document of the Shanghai Funeral
and Interment Administration in 1984 titled *Stepping forward to the Reform*
stated,

> Regarding the No. 75 Document, it asks people not to keep cremains nor
> have memorial meetings. [However,] we should correctly understand the
> No. 75 Document. This document was meant to solve internal Party is-
> sues and correct the Party line. The intention was to criticize the phe-
> nomenon of "there are no good people in criticism meetings and there

are no bad people in memorial meetings" [*pipinghuishang wuhaoren zhuidaohuishang wuhuairen*]. Regarding ordinary people's funeral and interment issues, we cannot fix these in any short-term period. Having memorial meetings is better than having feudalist superstitions.

Meanwhile, however, the right to and responsibility for organizing funerals has been returned from work units to families. During my fieldwork, the bereaved no longer needed permission from work units to organize funerals. Work unit representatives no longer showed up at memorial meetings unless invited because most work units did not even know about such deaths if the deceased's families did not notify them. Moreover, as described in the previous chapter, Shanghai funeral parlors have also shifted to promote personalized funerals, in part as a means of threading the needle between the demands of civil and market governance. Yet, when funeral professionals asked the bereaved if they would invite a representative of the deceased's work unit to give a memorial speech, grieving family members often made a face as if the question was silly. They responded as quickly as possible, "Yes, of course." Most bereaved still bothered to invite work units to deliver memorial speeches even though it might take the bereaved a bit of effort to track down what and where the work unit of the newly departed was, as people are living longer into their retirements and work units have been merged and restructured constantly since the Reform and Opening.

How do we interpret the resilience of memorial meetings when it was clear that neither the national nor the local state wanted its citizens to have such a form of commemoration (no matter what their respective motivations were)? Here, I propose to focus on the dissonance between ritually constructed subjectivity and the ambiguity and plurality in everyday life. As the market economy took root in Shanghai, everyday reality in Shanghai has become anything but an idealized socialist utopia of comradeship and equality (and perhaps it never was). Shanghai at the time of my fieldwork was a cosmopolitan city with residents who spoke with great pride about hosting the 2010 World Expo. This sense of cosmopolitan nationalism was in conjunction with the sense of fragility that migrant workers and other fragile people toiled through to find prosperity, if not merely to survive. The relationships between socialist ethics and other ethical ideas of person and death have been constantly reordered and contested in daily life. As such, performing ritual denaturalizes reality as participants cross the boundaries between ritualized world and the world outside of the ritual by momentarily framing everyone as if they were all model socialist citizens and only such. It reminds people, however fleetingly, of the existence of multiple and contradicting moral ideas of being a proper person that are a norm beyond the ritual. It also reminds people of how socialist morality had never been fully realized in life outside of such rituals no matter what promises the state had made or what interpretations of social reality the state might continue to offer. Performing memorial meetings presented an ironic contrast between the world of ritual and the world outside of ritual. As such, ritually constructed subjectivity is self-reflexive as well as normative. The bigger the contrast is between ritual framing and the everyday reality outside of ritual, the more reflexive a subject could be.

With its paleosocialist-like rhetoric, dying socialist in "capitalist" Shanghai (if you can forgive a simplification of China's market economy as capitalist for the benefit of the rhetorical contrast) then created a dissonant note in modern Shanghai's chorus. This was an unintended but potent act. Dissonance is here a challenge but not a rebellion; a dissonant note violently disrupts taken-for-granted harmony but does so only for a moment, and then it, too, is gone. Dissonance here provided a striking alternative in making everyone, for that moment, outwardly pretend that they were model socialist citizens. Performing memorial meetings therefore provided a potential critique of contemporary Chinese market governance in a market-driven reality by recognizing the impossible alternatives. As such, this ritually constructed subjectivity was productive because it created space for the living to gain a moment of self-reflexivity in thinking about who they were as people. Because the state itself now promoted market governance, its actual opposition was less linked to a triumph of capitalism or an embrace of liberal democratic values and more expressed by clinging to socialist rhetoric. In this sense, rather than seeing ritual as reproducing the social and the individual, ritual produces and transforms the social and the individual each time, and each time differently.

DYING RELIGIOUS IN A SOCIALIST RITUAL

In providing this account of the failure of personalized funerals and the resilience of the memorial meeting, I have purposefully worked in the previous chapters to leave an impression of a strong modernist and socialist presence at the end of life. Without a memorial speech and, thus, without a work unit or residence committee representative, a funeral simply cannot be a memorial meeting. As I discussed in the introduction, many scholars have documented the revival of reciprocal exchange and religious rituals since the beginning of the reform period in China. It was in this context that the continuity of memorial meetings with their distinct flavor of socialist ethics was puzzling.

However, memorial meetings as described in the last chapter rarely existed by themselves during my fieldwork. Rather, the vast majority of memorial meetings in Shanghai almost always contained "additions." These additions were rituals that emphasized relationality and religiosity based on the concept of afterlife and exchange between the living and the dead. These additional rituals ranged from presenting offerings to the dead to the funeral banquets they hosted. We can categorize these additions as belonging to popular religion even though the general public, including funeral professionals, considered these additions as customary or ordinary. By my estimation, approximately 90 percent of memorial meetings in both downtown and outlying Shanghai funeral parlors contained these additions. There were also some less common additional rituals that were more obviously Buddhist. These Buddhist additions usually existed as additions to the folk religious ritual additions. And yet, even with these additions, the socialist memorial meeting with the work unit representative's speech has remained the core.

But how is it possible to have religious variations of a secular and socialist funeral that deliberately and explicitly denies recognition of spirits or the afterlife? What did these kinds of rituals look like? How could urban Chinese revive relational and religious rituals without replacing or removing memorial meetings in the first place? Considering the fact that the CCP defined funeral parlors as public spaces rather than religious institutions, the existence of religious versions of memorial meetings is even more significant. In China, officially, activities in public spaces should not contain religious expressions—a distinction parallel to French secularism through the concept of *laïcité*.

With these ethnographic puzzles in mind, this chapter first describes the most common rituals Shanghai bereaved chose to add—rituals that were based on exchange among people as well as between humans and spirits. I then discuss some less frequent Buddhist additions and how people found ways to add these not yet routinized rituals to memorial meetings in funeral parlors. All this is to say that this chapter is an ethnography of additions rather than an ethnography of alternatives. This distinction is important because an ethnography of additions tackles a critical theoretical issue. That is, how do people live with incommensurable ideas of self and even alterity in our shared social lives where there are so many different normative forces at work shaping each of us as subjects?

This chapter demonstrates that what makes secular, socialist, relational, and religious ideas of person and death commensurable is the fact that these differences were dealt with within rituals. Ritual, as a particular kind of social action, created the conditions of possibility for living with differences. In the last chapter, I showed that memorial meetings momentarily frame perceptions and behaviors. Ritual here allows ritual participants to act as if they were all model socialist citizens living in an idealized socialist utopia. As such, ritually constructed subjectivity is both self-reflexive and normative. This chapter continues to develop the concept of ritually constructed subjectivity by tackling what characteristics of rituals make rituals particularly equipped to deal with different normative forces that shape subjectivity.

Adam Seligman et al. (2008) distinguish two modes of social actions in their work: ritual and sincerity. A ritual mode of social action gives people a common ground to act as if they were the same without actually being the same. They call this world framed by ritual a "subjunctive world." When following a ritual mode in ritual participation, people could modify their internal state, but they do not have to. Whether or not the internal meanings, feelings, and states of being are consistent with the externalized actions is unimportant if not irrelevant. Seligman and Robert Weller (2012) argue that such ambiguity in internal states created by ritual mode is the foundation for pluralism. In contrast, the sincerity mode refers to the urge to seek consistency between externalized actions and internal meanings, feelings, and being. Within this mode, what matters is whether participating in a ritual can help people reach a desired internal state. For example, the singing of a hymn is not itself the goal, but rather the singing of the hymn should be either reflecting one's belief or inculcating true belief in the hymn's words. Sincerity propels people to actively seek the world of as is by resolving the inconsistency between their externalized actions and their internal state. It is with this difference in mind that Seligman et al. (2008) argue fundamentalism has risen not because people embrace the ritual mode more even if they may have increased their ritual participation. Rather, fundamentalism has risen because some people felt the moral and emotional need to make the world "authentic" so that their lived reality is rendered consistent with the idealized world revealed in rituals. Given the power and prevalence of this sincerity mode in the United States and other parts of the world, it can be difficult to recognize its potential negative effects.

Building on the distinction between ritual and sincerity and the possibilities for religious pluralism each allows, I found two characteristics of memorial meetings that allowed people to deal with the coexistence of incommensurable ideas of self and death. The first is that these religious versions of memorial meetings were a kind of modular framing. In chapter 5, I already began to discuss Bateson's ([1955] 2000) concept of ritual framing. While the concept of ritual framing is theoretically productive, Bateson's analysis is nevertheless quite rigid. Recall his example of "this is play." In practice, the frame that distinguishes a playful fight from a real fight is not as clear-cut as Bateson's claim makes it appear to be. For example, sometimes people have different ideas on whether a fight was playful. Other times, a playful fight could easily turn into a real flight. Don Handelman (2006) thus proposes the concept of "fuzzy frame" to modify Bateson's overly rigid framing approach. Handelman suggests we treat ritual frames as porous while recognizing ritual's ability to frame perceptions and actions that distinguish rituals from nonrituals. With this idea of fuzzy frames in mind, I found that Shanghai residents transformed the original framing of memorial meetings into a set of modular frames in these religious versions of memorial meetings. This modular framing allowed Shanghai people to challenge the singular primacy of secular socialism while at the same time reaffirming its centrality.

The fuzzy and porous borders of ritual framing nevertheless lead us to question the efficacy of the framing in the first place. That is, how could ritual frame perceptions and actions in cases where the frame is too porous? Just pointing out the work of modular framing is not enough. Another characteristic of these religious versions of memorial meetings that increases the likelihood of having pluralist subjectivity was a particular view on ritual. I found that people who performed these types of additional rituals tended to see participating in memorial meetings as more about following externalized social convention. They did not participate in rituals to seek some sort of authentic representation of what they felt or what they believed nor to cultivate specific inner states of feeling and being out of the externalized actions. This attitude was crucial because while not all normative ideas of person and death contradicted each other in commemorating the dead in Shanghai, many did. However, for those people, no matter what they felt inside, as long as they did all the right things externally when they performed memorial meetings and their religious additions, then the contradictions between those different normative ideas of person and death did not matter. The interiority of individuals was not subjected to the normative governing forces as long as their focus was on the externalized commitment to social conventions. This chapter explains the above analytical concepts through ethnographic descriptions of folk religious and Buddhist additions to memorial meetings and their respective implications for the possibility of pluralist subjectivity.

Popular Religious Additions

Recall the structure of memorial meetings discussed in the previous chapter. An emcee's announcement and the farewell ceremony delineated the beginning and the end of the meeting. They marked the boundaries of this idealized socialist world in which everyone imagined themselves to be model socialist citizens. Prior to the Opening Up, funeral practitioners then zipped up the body bags (because coffins were not allowed as they were symbols of "feudalistic superstition") and pushed the deceased to the crematoria immediately after performing the farewell ceremony. During my fieldwork, however, this double farewell to the deceased and the family members of the dead was not the end of memorial meetings. If we use the language of music, the farewell ceremony was not a rest within memorial meetings. It was more of a fading out of one movement and a fading in of the next one. If the old movement was about socialism, then the new movement was about spirits, the afterlife, and social reciprocity.

After the very last group of people finished their farewell bowing, the immediate family members who had been standing next to the deceased formed a circle around the coffin. Although the tempo of this congregating act could be fast or slow, once the circle formed, the solemn atmosphere and highly restrained bodily movements that defined the modernist ritual suddenly broke down with an outburst of tears, weeping, stomping, kneeling, punching, or shaking on or around the plastic cover over the deceased. No choreographed harmony existed in this instant moment of change—only cacophony, chaos, and spontaneity. Bodies that were standing upright and straight just seconds prior all of a sudden lost their proper forms and postures. Sometimes, the outward expressions of grief and mourning that were repressed earlier came out similar to lava from volcanic eruptions. The grief swallowed both the modernist bodily movements and the socialist verbal utterances within a second as if they had not been performed as solemnly just moments earlier by the same bodies in the same space.

When it was time to stop this moment of crying, the funeral professionals broke the circle by opening the plastic cover that enveloped the coffin and then pushing the coffin to the center of the hall. This was now the time to place offerings. These offerings were neither commemorative objects, personal belongings of the deceased when they were alive, nor objects associated with the nation-state. There were no personal or national sentiments that connected the life of the deceased to these objects. Instead, they were prescribed religious objects. These objects were based on prior assumptions of the general existence of spirits and the afterlife after a biological death—exactly the kind of things that memorial meetings had denied.

If we panned, as a film director might, from shooting inside the meeting hall to the outside, we would see a vastly different world. The representative of the deceased's work unit and some of the funeral participants left the memorial meeting as soon as they performed the farewell ceremony. Other participants lingered outside the meeting hall to satisfy their nicotine urge or to resume socializing activities that had been "interrupted" by the beginning of the memorial meeting. Some of them stayed for quite a long time because they planned to attend the funeral banquet afterward. These people had to wait outside because the immediate family of the deceased (and anyone who wanted to stay inside the meeting hall) were still performing post farewell ceremony events.

Inside the memorial meeting hall again, the exact sequence of placing offerings varied from funeral professional to funeral professional. In general, the first step was to invite one child of the deceased to put a handkerchief and a wooden foldable fan in the deceased's right and left palms, respectively (although people only follow the right- and left-hand rule very loosely), to allow the deceased to use them in the afterlife. This step was taken despite the fact that Shanghai people no longer used cloth handkerchiefs (most people used tissues) or foldable fans. Both objects appeared to be traditional so that they provided an aura of invariance— one key characteristic of ritualized actions (Bell 1997; Rappaport 1999).

The child of the deceased, then, used a wooden comb to comb the deceased's hair three times before breaking the comb in half—one half was thrown to the floor, and the other was placed in the casket. The combing and the breaking of the comb symbolized the social ties between the generations and their consequent break with death. This breaking symbolically allowed the deceased to move on to the next world without lingering in this one. The combing and breaking of the comb showed a classic image of a rite of passage (Van Gennep 1960). In professional jargon, a comb, a fan, and a handkerchief together were called the "three minor things" (*xiaosanjian*).

After placing the three minor things, the funeral professional directed the bereaved to place afterlife consumer products and spiritual money (*mingbi*) into the coffin to enhance the joy of the deceased's afterlife. The former commonly included mahjong tiles, *maotai* liquor, cigarettes, and so on. All of these afterlife consumer products were made of paper. Spiritual money included cash that looked similar to Chinese yuan, Hong Kong dollars, US dollars, and Visa and Mastercard credit cards (all made of paper) or gold and silver ingots (*yuanbao*) made of plastic. Occasionally, people placed personal items used by the deceased, such as her or his glasses or favorite chess set. While I had expected such personal items to be more popular, this was consistent with my observations on the lack of personalization at the end of life in Shanghai.

After placing these objects, it was then time to add xibo—the most important type of spiritual money—into the coffin. Xibo were silver ingots made of tinfoil paper. People generally put enough xibo to cover the deceased's entire body except for the face. Xibo were used for a variety of rituals in Shanghai, whether for salvation rituals, wake keeping, ancestor worship, or (cremains) burial ceremonies. While I occasionally saw people choosing not to use the spiritual cash described above, almost everyone used xibo unless they were Protestants. In fact, a scholar in China even told me that although spiritual money is "superstitious," using xibo is "custom." While I am hesitant to agree with his categorization, his point nevertheless indexes the commonality of xibo.

After placing the xibo, funeral professionals asked the bereaved to go pick flowers from the flower baskets that were displayed on both sides of the meeting hall during the meeting. Chen Ting often specifically told the bereaved to pick one flower from each basket to allow the deceased to be accompanied by everyone's hearts—she was very good at conceiving of such satisfying details when directing rituals. Funeral brokers often asked the bereaved to pick the Chinese daffodils (*shuixian*) from each basket because they were usually the most expensive flowers in the baskets. They then put these flowers on top of the xibo. Through offering spiritual money and flowers, the living and the dead established specific debt relations and, thus, entered into a new set of reciprocal exchanges.

The time needed to place offerings varied depending on how calm the bereaved were. The more they cried, the more time would be needed. However, meeting halls were generally booked in one-hour time slots, and there was only a ten-minute break between funerals for the parlor's janitors to clean up and set up the area for the next family. Therefore, time management was important. If placing the offerings took too much time, experienced funeral professionals called in the state practitioners responsible for bringing in the coffin's lid before the bereaved finished. Once the coffin lid arrived, the bereaved knew that they had to finish placing the offerings in the coffin as soon as possible.

The coffin lid carriers, always men, also brought a hammer, four "descendant nails" (*zisunding*), and a "resting-in-peace covering" (*anxizhao*) along with them. Descendant nails look similar to regular long nails. Nailing them was said to work as protection and as a blessing for the descendants of the deceased. The descendant(s) of the deceased hammered down the first three nails through the lid into three corners of the coffin. However, the bereaved were instructed not to punch the fourth nail in all the way. Leaving the head of the nail standing out (or "rising out from the lid") resembled a "descendant outgrowing" (*zisunchutou*) and represented the protection by the deceased of an ongoing line of descendants. The nailing was purely symbolic because the coffin was not actually sealed and did not need to be airtight for the cremation. Either the children or grandchildren, both male and female, of the deceased performed the act of nailing. These four variables (children or grandchildren and males or females) were flexibly combined depending on the specific funeral professionals and their ad hoc judgments based on the situation of the grieving family.

Smart funeral professionals changed their rules based on their observations of the family politics also. For example, Chen Ting once made all four children of the deceased (one man and three women) do the nailing in one funeral. However, in another funeral, she made the grandchildren of the deceased do the nailing. She told me that this was because the deceased had three children but four grandchildren. Because funeral costs in Shanghai are generally split equally among children without regard for gender, she reasoned that this avoided making a particular child more important than the others during the ritual.

When the nailing ritual was complete, the funeral professionals draped a cloth resting-in-peace covering over the top and sides of the coffin and then directed the bereaved to accompany the deceased to the parking lot or crematorium, depending on which funeral parlor they were in. The resting-in-peace covering was a red cloth with a printed Chinese character that represented luck or fortune (*fu*). This cloth covered the coffin after it was (symbolically) sealed. This covering prevented the deceased from being exposed to light. Because the deceased was in a liminal stage, it was said to be vulnerable to the various spirits that fill the world. This act of covering someone who was in a liminal stage was also common in Chinese folk ritual practices. During my fieldwork, the resting-in-peace covering and the descendant nails were only used in one of the three urban funeral parlors in Shanghai. Both only became service items after the marketization of the funeral parlors.

Although I am pointing out the invented characteristics of the above two ritual practices, this does not imply that these religious objects were completely random inventions. For example, according to Master Gao, only one descendant nail (instead of four) was used before the Cultural Revolution. At that time, funeral professionals nailed the coffins themselves because they needed to be properly sealed and airtight because body burial was the main way of disposing of the body. Then, the descendent nail was a single large, long nail with a lotus flower attached to it. It was symbolically nailed in the center of the top edge of the coffin near the head. Additionally, instead of having the descendant perform the nailing, the maternal uncle of the deceased performed this act (for the role of maternal uncles in Chinese folk death ritual, see Martin 1973). Important here is that these seemingly "traditional" practices changed (and are changing) to fit the new circumstances of the time they were brought back. Overall, these contemporary folk death ritual practices all appeared to be traditional and were neither pure inventions coming from nowhere nor simply unchanging traditions inherited from the past.

This final journey was the mourners' last chance to send the deceased on his or her way (*song zuihou yicheng*). Although historically the processions from homes to graveyards were the most spectacular part of a funeral, funeral processions during my fieldwork were left as just a short walk. Shanghai funeral parlors offered their "ceremonial funeral procession" (*liyi chubin*) as a new service item to make this short walk more elaborate today. This military-style ceremonial funeral procession has coffin carriers wearing military-style uniforms and walking in goose step. People told me that this service item was borrowed from Taiwan. During the send-off, the bereaved who watch the coffin entering the hearse might stand, bow, or even kowtow to the deceased. They might also sob, weep, or do nothing. For this procession, funeral professionals usually offered no direction or restrictions to unify their movements.

Once the people who stayed inside for the post-farewell-ceremony rituals joined those lingering outside the hall again, they then went together to a restaurant either via a rented tour bus or by foot (if they opted for that funeral parlors' own on-site restaurant) for the funeral banquet. Before entering the restaurant, participants performed a cleansing ritual of crossing a fire to expel evil spirits (*guohuo*). Mourners tossed their black mourning armbands and condolence couplets into a small fire on the ground and then crossed over the fire with one leg. This ritual was done in an outdoor space, such as a sidewalk or parking lot. However, the chief mourners could not participate in this ritual because they were to remain in mourning longer than other funeral participants. In Shanghai, during my fieldwork, the most common ending date for mourning was the thirty-fifth

day after the death (counting seven days as one cycle, the mourning period usually contained five cycles).

As soon as the mourners entered the restaurant, the bereaved were served
sweet tea as a way to gain some good luck. Drinking sweet tea was a very common ritual in a variety of life cycle rituals among Han Chinese, not just in Shanghai but also in many other areas. After drinking sweet tea, the mourners sat
and enjoyed their banquet. Although funeral professionals usually accompanied
the bereaved to restaurants, they were not invited there to eat together. Their job
with the family ended when the banquet started. Overall, whether a funeral was
arranged through a funeral broker or a state practitioner, the above described
extra ritual acts were quite standardized.

Relational Subjectivity

When people moved from the original part of memorial meetings to the described popular religious additions, one of the most visible transitions was the
movement from a spiritless world to a world of spirits. Whereas the socialist civil
ritual was built on a set of assumptions that denied spirits and the afterlife, in
these post-memorial-meeting events, the most important goal was to take care of
the spirit of the deceased as if she or he was still alive to ensure a smooth transition into the afterlife. In this world of spirits, one of the most important priorities
was to please the deceased. Doing so included giving material wealth to the deceased by offering spiritual cash, paper-made mahjong tiles, maotai liquor, cigarettes, and gold and silver ingots, and by giving "face" (mianzi) to the deceased by
purchasing ceremonial funeral processions and a nicer hearse for sending them
off, for instance. Through the act of providing provisions (Stafford 1995), the relationship between the living and the dead was transformed into one of descendant
and ancestor. Ideally, these ancestor spirits would then grant prosperity to their
descendants. The construction of popular religious subjectivity was intertwined
with the construction of relational subjectivity in these post-memorial-meeting
additions. In the following sections, I analyze these processes of providing provisions through three kinds of exchange: affect, banquets, and flower baskets.

Affect   *gender*

The most dramatic change between the memorial meeting and post-memorial-
meeting additions was the transition of emotional regimes. In chapter 5, I described how individuals were expected to show solemnity and calm at memorial
meetings. This was in contrast to the older style of emotional regime that en-

couraged the outward expression of grief and mourning. As people performed the last step of memorial meetings, however, this modernist emotional regime started to break apart. In this sense, even though additional religious relational rituals mainly happened after the original memorial meetings, we nevertheless do see a crossover between those carefully maintained boundaries between memorial meetings and their religious and relational additions.

The release of emotion reached its peak when the bereaved formed a circle around the coffin after the last group of mourners performed their farewells. It was not uncommon for the bereaved's wailing to be accompanied by dramatic physical movements, such as shaking bodies, stomping, screaming, and even prostration. The transition from an emotional regime of solemn calm to one of highly emotional outward expressions of grief and mourning was a jarring part of the exit into the phenomenological and ontological world of "heat and noise" (renao) that marks all social occasions in Chinese public life, from night markets and temple festivals to weddings and traditional funerals. This hot and noisy atmosphere is one of the most important characteristics that structured and sustained popular religion in Chinese societies.

This change in emotional regimes was an entrance into relationality. The bereaved were expected to cry to different degrees according to how close they were to the deceased once they began such post-memorial-meeting events (even though they were not allowed to do so just prior to this). Externalized grief and mourning almost immediately became an important index of filial piety. A lack of outward expressions of grief and mourning during this post-memorial-meeting time implied an absence of affect, a breach of social propriety, and a denial of a social relationship. Recall my analysis in the last chapter: if stolid emotional expression and bowing were meant to deny the hierarchical family relationship during memorial meetings, then the opposite was required in post-memorial-meeting additions. This was also why I occasionally saw people prostrate themselves during these additions—something I almost never saw during memorial meetings. We can see the connection between externalized grief and proper relationality even more clearly when someone breached social propriety. For example, daughters-in-law were often the prime target of criticism for being unable to cry or unable to cry hard enough at their mother-in-law's funeral. Such conduct often provoked gossip, and this gossip very quickly moved from the emotional display itself to moral judgments of social relationships. As long as daughters-in-law could weep properly (which included an expectation of genuine facial expressions, ideally with tears), then their internal moral integrity and feelings would be more or less left alone.

Finally, this shift in emotional regimes marked the end of the structured order of the memorial meeting proper. No single requirement for mourning existed in post-memorial-meeting rituals since mourning here was a relational act. That is to say, after everyone performed the farewell ceremony, the family of the deceased stayed in the meeting hall, and the other people were free (within certain possible choices) to leave. This was in contrast to memorial meetings in which everyone was related as comrade to comrade and, thus, performing rituals differently was not needed. Such changes from memorial meetings to its additions revealed a shift from collectivism, where everyone did more or less the same thing at the same time, to a folk world in which many things occurred either simultaneously or at different times. Even as these key emotional displays continued inside, the funeral could already be over as far as one was concerned depending on one's relationship with the dead. The boundaries between relational religious rituals and everyday reality were porous in this sense.

Banquets

While the resurfacing of folk emotional regimes in memorial meetings (re)established religious and relational subjectivity within the secular socialist world through specific ways of expressing affect, affect was not the only way to establish relationality in urban Chinese funerals. Relationality also existed through gift exchange: the de facto method of constructing a relational self in Sinophone cultures. In contemporary Shanghai, gift exchange had only slightly changed its form and intensity despite it having been discouraged, if not prohibited, at the peak of the Cultural Revolution campaign.

One of the most widespread instances of gift exchange in memorial meetings was funeral banquets. While funeral banquets were banned at the peak of the Cultural Revolution, they returned to Shanghai people's public life as soon as state control over funerals lessened during the second half of the Cultural Revolution. By the time of my fieldwork, almost all memorial meetings ended with funeral banquets whether referring to popular religious, Buddhist, Protestant, or Catholic versions of memorial meetings. People who have different ideas of self and death generally had little problem in sitting down and banqueting together as long as they treated their participation in banquets as following etiquette and being a proper person.

The likelihood of conflict increased, however, when people felt the need to have some sort of consistency between their act of banqueting and their internal states. This need to clarify the nature of their relationships, feelings, or beliefs decreased the space available for ambiguity. A state practitioner who used to be a manager of a funeral parlor's restaurant once told me that he was surprised to find out, shortly after he first got that job, that mediating quarrels was one of his primary jobs. This was because death in Shanghai often involved conflicts over property division, especially regarding real estate property. Many elderly property owners gained their properties through work unit distributions rather than purchase. The subsequent high property values of these now freely bought and sold properties meant that the children of the deceased could completely turn around their financial situation if they successfully fought for their appropriate share of one. According to funeral professionals, quarrels over property only worsened as the real estate bubble in Shanghai continued to grow. Whereas memorial meetings might temporarily connect siblings in conflict, funeral banquets often became the site that allowed such conflicts to resurface. As Tang An told me, imagine that you had a few drinks of yellow rice liquor (*huangjiu*), you would be very likely to let all those repressed feelings come out. The moment people felt the need to be authentic and to pursue such consistency was the moment that differences had to be disambiguated and clarified.

One of the few funerals I know of that did not end with a funeral banquet was related to the death of a child. I interviewed the mother of the deceased, whom I met through a grief-counseling group in Shanghai. She had lost her only child approximately ten years before our interview. Her son was only ten years old when he died. She hired a funeral broker to arrange her son's funeral. This funeral was not a memorial meeting because no work unit or neighborhood committee gave a speech. When answering my inquiry about funeral banquets, she told me that she just could not imagine eating and socializing with people after her son's funeral, so they did not have one. She said that a funeral banquet only worked when the dead was an elder. What she was trying to say was that the pain inherent in the loss of a single child outweighed any other kind of loss under China's previous One Child Policy. This lack of a funeral banquet also echoed the tendency for many of those parents who lost their single child to completely withdraw from their kin and friendship networks. For her, her participation in a banquet had to be consistent with her internal state. Since she did not have the right kind of internal state, she did not want to have the ritual. Overall, whether we were talking about social conflicts in the first example or social withdraw in the second example, both examples of failed funeral banquets show how ritual loses its ability to create common ground when the need for authenticity and sincerity comes to outweigh the externalized commitment to social conventions.

Flower Baskets

Other than funeral banquets, another common gift exchange in memorial meetings was flower baskets. They existed in all memorial meetings regardless of differences in religion (or in the rare absence of it). Flower baskets were the primary and often the only decoration in the meeting halls in Shanghai. However, they did not exist for aesthetic reasons, at least not primarily. These baskets existed because they were records of *renqing wanglai* (lit., "human relationship interactions"). These baskets remained present throughout both memorial meetings and the additional post-memorial-meeting rituals. They were a good illustration of the fuzzy boundaries of ritual frames as people utilized these baskets for constructing socialist citizenship and religious and relational subjectivity all at once.

All flower baskets contained "mini couplets" (*xiaowanlian*). These couplets were the textual records of human relationships as they recorded the names of the gift giver, the receiver, and the kinship terminology that linked the two sides of the flower basket gift. For example, a mini couplet of a flower basket given to a grandfather by a grandson was as follows:

> Right: Deeply Mourn Paternal Grandfather
> Left: Respectively Given by Patrilineal Eldest Grandson Ma Wen and Grand Daughter-in-Law Jiang Mei

In general, these couplets articulated Confucian moral personhood—self was not only relationally but also hierarchically embedded. A person mourned for the loss of her or his paternal grandfather or maternal grandmother. The name of the deceased was not as important as the role of being senior kin to the gift giver. These kinship relationships could be entirely secular, or they could also involve spirits depending on the worldview of the direct descendants (although by no means am I suggesting that all the direct descendants of a particular deceased shared the same worldview).

These couplets on flower baskets were not only a "representation of the social" in a Durkheimian sense. Flower baskets were sites of creating relationality that allowed people to temporarily work out contradictions. One of the best examples was a memorial meeting I observed for a woman in her forties when she had died. She committed suicide at work by jumping out of her office window in a high-rise building. More than one hundred flower baskets had been booked for this funeral through Longevity. As soon as the florist delivered the flower baskets, Chen Ting began to arrange them based on the usual rules, and I was the assistant who made sure that the feet at the bottom of each basket stood at a diagonal with the edge of the floor tiles. When we were done, Chen Ting asked the sisters of the deceased to verify our arrangements. After checking, one of the sisters came to us and said, in a lowered voice, "I don't know how to say this. This is kind of embarrassing. My sister [the deceased] and her husband got divorced a long time ago. For several years since then, she had been seeing Mr. Lee, but they never got married. We called Mr. Lee 'Big Brother Lee.' Mr. Lee, as opposed to my sister's ex-husband, was more like family to my sister and me. Could you rearrange Mr. Lee's and my sister's ex-husband's flower baskets so that Mr. Lee's are in front?" Chen Ting said, "I understand. Which flower basket was sent by Mr. Lee?" One sister led us to the back of the line, where Lee's flower basket was.

In general, the closer a person was to the deceased, the more to the front her or his flower basket should be. Flower baskets of immediate family members of the deceased were placed in front. All baskets that addressed the deceased as friends were supposed to be at the back of the line. The couplets on the flower basket from Lee said, "Dear friend" (*zhiyou*). Meanwhile, although the couplets from the ex-husband's flower basket did not describe his relation to the deceased as husband or ex-husband, it described the other giver of the same basket as the daughter of the deceased. Because Lee's flower basket defined his relationship to the deceased as "dear friend," whereas the ex-husband's basket described his daughter's relation to the deceased as daughter to mother, of course Lee's basket was placed at the back of the line while the ex-husband's one was in front.

Chen Ting apologized for the mistake. Chen Ting then asked the sisters of the bereaved exactly where she should put Lee's and the ex-husband's flower baskets. The two sisters talked to each other for a while. They decided to put Lee's second, after the basket of the mother of the deceased. The third and fourth baskets were then their baskets. The fifth basket, the last one before those of other relatives and friends, was that of the ex-husband and their daughter. By moving Lee's basket to the front as the second basket, right after the basket of the mother of the deceased, the sisters of the deceased created the marital relationship for the deceased in public during her memorial meeting even though the deceased and Lee had never been officially married in life.

In addition to constructing Confucian moral personhood, these couplets were also used to sustain the relationship surrounding socialist citizenship in memorial meetings. This was accomplished by describing gift givers and receivers as comrades or members of a particular work unit. Both directly tied the deceased and the bereaved to the party and the state. In the following parts, I describe how socialist citizenship, too, was established through exchanging flower baskets by explaining how the living constructed hierarchical relationships between work units (with a twisted sense of irony here since comradeship was supposed to be based on equality).

To begin with, for memorial meetings organized by the family of the deceased, flower baskets based on kin and other personal ties were placed on the left (from the deceased's perspective) because the left side was the superior side (shangshou) in Shanghai. Flower baskets from work units were placed on the right side of the meeting, the inferior side (*xiashou*). When work units were the organizers of a memorial meeting, its flower baskets had to be on the left. However, as of my fieldwork, many professionals preferred to place the family's flower baskets on the left and work units' flower baskets on the right even when the work units were the organizers of a memorial meeting. This preference indexed the changing power dynamics between work units and families in making funeral arrangements in contemporary Shanghai.

No matter which side these work unit flower baskets were placed on, the general rule for arranging flower baskets on the work unit side was to place the deceased's last work unit first. This rule sounds straightforward but ended up being a lot more complicated when carrying it out in practice. There were at least three reasons that produced such complication. Firstly, the work units themselves changed a lot in Shanghai. Normal death (i.e., death at old age) meant that the deceased might have been retired for approximately twenty years, if not longer, before they died. In the past twenty years, however, many dramatic changes have happened to work units in Shanghai as a result of the market economic reforms. Many were transformed, partially privatized, or spun off into different companies multiple times since the reform. Secondly, many people today were hired again by a different work unit after their official retirement. This was especially the case for those who were relatively high up in an industry. In such a case, which is the deceased's final work unit, the one they officially retired from or the one they began working at next?

Finally, the unspoken rules of promotion and succession in China have also complicated work unit affiliations. In state organizations and companies, employees could generally only move up or stay at the same level—rarely did they ever move down. However, when a leader was about to retire, his or her work unit needed to sort out the succession issues before the actual retirement without demoting this person. Let me give a hypothetical example to illustrate this. Suppose the head of Funeral Parlor A was made the party secretary of Funeral Parlor B two years before he retired to solve a succession issue at Parlor A. This way, his successor could take over before his retirement while at the same time giving him a promotion as well. Having retired from Parlor B, this person then went on to work as a consultant on funerals for the Civil Affairs Bureau. For his funeral, his last work unit before retiring was Parlor B on the books as the party secretary. However, he had spent much more time (and was much more well known) as Parlor A's day-to-day leader. Moreover, after he retired, he continued to work for the Civil Affairs Bureau, which was itself the parent organization of both parlors, thereby providing a need for its own flower basket to be near the front. These complications meant that different people could have different claims regarding which basket should be placed as the first on the work unit side.

Overall, just as happened on the family side (and perhaps more so), arranging flower baskets on the work unit side involved clarifying and delineating the hierarchical relationships among institutions, among people who represented the institutions, and between them and the deceased or the bereaved temporarily. Sometimes these baskets represented the hierarchical relationships between different work units; sometimes the baskets created a specific hierarchy. No matter which, as long as the differences were dealt with as in the context of a memorial meeting, then it allowed participants to hold onto whatever they believed the correct hierarchy was without forcing everyone who participated in the same ritual to agree on one correct version of work unit hierarchy. The negotiations over the flower basket sequence could take even longer when the staff sent to supervise the flower basket arrangement by these respective institutions needed to call their superiors (or their superiors needed to call their superiors) to find a temporary resolution when different understandings of hierarchy arose. This is not even mentioning the fact that once a particular flower basket had to be moved, all of the other flower baskets after this one needed to be moved as well. As such, many state practitioners told me that arranging flower baskets for memorial meetings of important people in the largest meeting hall was one of the most time-consuming preparations. They sometimes had to spend the entire night before the funeral doing it.

Overall, whether we are talking about flower baskets on the family or work unit side, negotiations over the sequential order of flower baskets were a frequent occurrence. For example, if the deceased was a woman and her parents were still alive, should the flower basket of her own parents stand before that of her parents-in-law (patrilineal order) or vice versa? (During my fieldwork, privileging her own parents was the more common arrangement.) If the deceased had several children—some men and some women—should their flower baskets be arranged purely based on birth order or separated first by gender? Although funeral professionals knew the general rules and had their preferences for ordering arrangements based on their interpretation of the general rules, these rules were negotiated continuously on-site. Through the negotiation of every actor's idiosyncratic understanding of the general rules, human relationships were created, upgraded, and downgraded during memorial meetings in ways that might or might not correspond to those relationships in real life. In the performance of memorial meetings, however, different understandings of hierarchy could be momentarily put aside as a part of social convention.

In Shanghai, these human relationship interactions, articulated through flower baskets, were exchanged in three non-mutually-exclusive ways in the same memorial meeting. Firstly, a flower basket was a gift from the living to the dead. We saw this most commonly in those flower baskets presented by the direct descendants of the deceased to the deceased. Secondly, flower baskets were a gift among the living. Funeral participants (as either individuals or representatives of institutions) often decided to give flower baskets based on their connections to the mourners. In this way, though addressed to the deceased, the basket might be a gift to a particular bereaved family member. Finally, some of the flower baskets were also a return gift from the direct descendants of the deceased to other family members and friends as a sort of thank-you after the latter had given (or in anticipation of the latter giving) the former white envelopes (*baibao*) containing a condolence gift of cash.[1]

With regard to the white envelopes, such cash gifts were the most common form of gift giving for life-cycle rituals in Sinophone cultures. The color white here (rather than red for most other occasions) was because white was the traditional color of mourning. Once the direct descendants received white envelopes, then they were obligated to partially reciprocate such an exchange by buying flower baskets on behalf of white envelope givers. If the relationship between white envelope givers and the deceased (or the chief mourners) was too distant (which usually also indicated a lower amount of money inside the envelopes), if the amount of money given was small, or if the exchange happened, unanticipated, on-site at the meeting hall, then the chief mourners might simply write mini couplets for the giver without purchasing flower baskets on their behalf.[2] Every memorial meeting hall had several wrought-iron stands on which funeral professionals could hang those mini couplets that were not attached to flower baskets.

Having said that flower baskets were the return gifts for white envelopes, one of the first things I noticed during my fieldwork in Shanghai was a distinct lack of white envelopes in memorial meetings in Shanghai. In Taiwan, generally, the host family sets up a gift table at the entrance to the funeral. Someone from the hosting family is stationed at the table to formally receive the white envelopes, take the money out of them, calculate the exact amount of money given, and then record the name and the amount given in a gift book. There were no such tables in Shanghai funeral parlors, however.

At one funeral I attended, I suddenly noticed a funeral participant pushing his hand into a chief mourner's hand as they socialized before the meeting started. The former gave the latter some rolled-up white paper. After this act, they made eye contact, and the chief mourner said thank you and then put the roll of white paper into his pocket in the back of his pants. They then carried on their conversation as if nothing had just happened. The act of giving happened so quickly that it was almost unnoticeable. This furtive act was more similar to a drug dealer in Hollywood movies handing a bag of dope to a customer. Once I noticed this particular exchange, I began to see it repeatedly between various chief mourners and funeral participants in that memorial meeting (and many more later). During one instance in which I saw this act, a state practitioner happened to be standing next to me. I whispered to her and asked her to look at what was happening in these subtle, almost secretive acts of passing a roll of white paper. She looked where I pointed and then stared at me in disbelief.

"Those are baibao. They are funeral participants' expression of their condolences to the bereaved."

"Baibao!" I replied. "Why give white envelopes in such a secretive way?"

"Don't you give baibao in Taiwan?"

"Yes, we do, of course. But we have a gift table where someone takes the money out of the white envelopes, and then we make a written record of who gave and how much they gave. Giving baibao is not a criminal act. Why do you hide it?"

"Oh, your way is like our rural way. We urban Shanghai people do not do that."

I asked Chen Yu about this secretive manner of giving white envelopes. She first told me that people in her hometown (in rural Jiangsu) also set up a gift table for funerals (and other life rituals). She was kind of happy to find out that my Taiwanese way was more similar to her rural hometown way. She then said that Shanghai people did not set up gift tables at funeral parlors because they were too frugal and too concerned about other people knowing how frugal they were. A gift table would make Shanghai people "lose face" since everyone would know how much money you gave out for gift exchange on the spot. When I raised this question to a local Shanghainese, not surprisingly, he provided a very different explanation. He said that Shanghai people did not have gift books to record gift exchanges in public because they were more sophisticated. For him, being sophisticated meant being less direct. Giving money and counting it in public was too direct and, thus, almost vulgar. This was why, he explained, Shanghai's act of gift giving had to be subtle and unnoticed.

While both readings may (or may not) be statements of the feeling they experienced, I suggest a third reading is important here—one that takes into account the management of the frame of memorial meetings and their additional folk rituals. The rule for giving white envelopes in Shanghai was that these envelopes had to be given before the memorial meeting started. Many people, especially if they were close to either the deceased or the bereaved, gave their white envelopes in the two days following death at the deceased's wake, and most wakes were held at the deceased's home. During these visits, people would simply give the bereaved white envelopes and exchange a few words, or they could also offer incense and prostrations to the deceased's portrait—actions that were completely appropriate if happening in private homes.

However, not everyone could pay a visit during the wake. For those who could not do so, they needed to complete the giving of white envelopes during the short period before the official beginning of the memorial meeting. The problem here was that they were no longer at home. Rather, they were at a public space that was supposed to be devoid of folk practices. As such, a secretive manner of making an exchange (even though everyone else knew exactly what was going on) allowed people who were involved in the exchange (as well as the audience who witnessed the exchange) to see such acts as private and domestic instead of public matters. In the next section, where I discuss Buddhist additions, I again return to this method of carving out a domestic space within a state space and illustrate how it allowed conflicting ideas of person and death to be momentarily resolved. For our purposes here, this secretive manner was one way Shanghai people guarded the frame of memorial meetings and their religious additions.

As a whole, the more flower baskets the families received in the funeral, the more extensive was the family's network of gift exchange. Having many flower baskets made a public statement about the status of the deceased, the bereaved, their family, or all of the above. This was why one common thing people did before memorial meetings started was to browse through the mini couplets, especially those on the flower baskets. I saw many funeral participants making comments about mini couplets, such as "Oh, the party-secretary [of whichever organization] gave a flower basket," when looking around before the memorial meetings started. This relationality was also why the bereaved burned the mini couplets afterward—it was their way to notify the deceased of who had sent her or him a posthumous gift.

To sum up, almost all funerals contained the rituals of giving white envelopes, flower baskets, and funeral banquets. These examples showed the construction of relational subjectivity for both the dead and the living in the public domain. Conceptualizing the deceased as a relational subject was the most common type of addition observed in contemporary memorial meetings. Folk death rituals were entirely based on the beginning of (re)new(ed) exchanges between the living and the dead. This universal character testified to the well-documented foundational place of gift exchange in the social fabric of Chinese societies.

While much of the description of relationality to memorial meetings matches quite well with descriptions of the ongoing role that relationality has been shown to play in the world of the living, it is worth pointing out once again the lengths that the party-state went to particularly (but not uniquely) in terms of the death industry to eliminate these options for horizontal ties. Recalling chapter 1, I described how the state worked to undermine and eliminate native-place associations and nearly anything to do with ancestors and ancestor worship as key components of Funeral Reform. While even the reappearance of relational selves is intriguing here, and in resonance with descriptions of the return of religion more generally, what is more surprising was the way that such relationality was incorporated into and alongside the socialist ritual itself without challenging it and in no way attempting to replace it. It is in this sense that I describe these religious versions of memorial meetings as additions, not alternatives.

Buddhist Additions

In addition to the routinized rituals described above, some of the less routinized additions were distinctively Buddhist. Whereas the routinized additions happened immediately after the original part of memorial meetings, Buddhist additions often happened before the memorial meetings began. Some of the most common Buddhist rituals involved the use of the *dharani* flag, chanting Amitabha, or having monks in *kasaya*. Among these, participants would have been much more likely to run into a memorial meeting using the dharani flag than one with monks in the meeting itself. All the funeral brokers I knew regularly stocked dharani flags even though funeral parlors usually did not sell them. Regarding having monks in kasaya inside meeting halls themselves, among the seventy-five memorial meetings and numerous other parts of meetings I witnessed, I only saw this happen twice.

The likelihood of having Buddhist additions was linked to whether the death √ was abnormal. In the following sections, I provide two ethnographic vignettes that describe additional Buddhist rituals. The first was a story of how I first saw a dharani flag. In this vignette, the deceased was an elderly bachelor. For Han Chinese, dying as a bachelor without any descendants was one of the worst conditions of death (not to mention an unfilial act to one's own ancestors). The second was a story of the tragic death of a woman who died in a car accident and how her family members hired monks to chant at her memorial meeting. Both were considered to be abnormal deaths. According to Chinese popular belief, abnormal deaths might engender malicious ghosts and, at least, suggested extra difficulties that the deceased would encounter on their way to the next world. Therefore, they needed more help from the living on their route to salvation. Overall, I found that Buddhist ideas of self and death were particularly salient when a bad death was involved.

These Buddhist additions provide a particularly salient perspective from which to analyze how to add new ideas of the self that allow the living to conceptualize the dead as simultaneously a socialist citizen as well as folk religious and relational subject in their commemoration. Specifically, I found the most common technique used was to momentarily create a domestic and private framing within the public space that was supposed to be secular. Through the creation of a temporary space where people acted as if they were Buddhist within the world where people acted as if they were secular socialist citizens, Shanghai residents demonstrated how Buddhist subjectivity could become commensurable with secular socialist citizenship within the same memorial meeting. Bad deaths provided a powerful site from which to examine the experimental creation of new rituals within memorial meetings.

The Dharani Flag

A dharani flag was a yellow flag printed with red Buddhist sutra texts on it. The printed sutras on a dharani flag function to produce merit for the deceased on their postmortem journey. Liang Wan from Longevity once told me that "having a dharani flag to cover the body is similar to having the national or party flag covering the body." Thus, when a memorial meeting was finished, "just as you would not burn the national or party flag, you need to take the dharani flag out before closing the coffin for cremation. You use dharani flags to wrap around a cremains casket, like those who have national or party flags do." In this sense, each of these flags protected the deceased; they just did so by being associated with different sources of power.

The first time I saw a dharani flag was at an elderly bachelor's funeral. The younger brother of the deceased held a normal memorial meeting for his older brother. He made his only son hold the photographic portrait of his paternal uncle—a role usually played only by direct descendants of the deceased. He also invited the older brother's last work unit to send someone to give a memorial speech. The wife of the younger brother was a lay Buddhist. She was a part of an informal group of lay Buddhist friends who chanted and visited temples together. This group of six lay Buddhists came to this funeral even though they did not know the deceased personally. The charismatic leader of this informal lay Buddhist group was the sleepover friend who taught me in chapter 5 that her first day working in a factory was the date on which she joined the revolution. This bachelor's funeral was how I initially met her.

The deceased's younger brother's family and the lay Buddhists arrived together at the meeting hall. After the younger brother signed all the documents, the state practitioner led all these people to the body preparation room at the back of the meeting hall. In general, only direct family members of the deceased go to the body preparation room (in addition to funeral professionals and the occasional stray ethnographer). However, this time the Buddhists accompanied the family members to the back room. Once they were in the room, the charismatic leader got out her dharani flag. She draped it on top of the deceased's body. After laying down this flag, she began to chant Amitabha a couple of times while holding two hands palm to palm in front of her chest. In turn, the other people in the room began to do the same thing on their own, and their chanting was not collectively coordinated. This was the first time I had seen people placing dharani flags and chanting Amitabha in a funeral parlor. I secretly glanced at the state practitioner to see her reaction. The state practitioner did nothing.

The mourners stayed in the body preparation room a little longer than usual to allow the younger brother to take another close look at the deceased. Then, the state practitioner told them that it was about time to return to the meeting hall. After receiving this instruction, instead of walking back to the hall, the charismatic leader again started to chant Amitabha and made the palm-to-palm gesture again. However, this time, all of the women followed at once, and their chanting voices slipped into unison. Moreover, they did not just chant Amitabha once or twice but chanted a long chain, repeating Amitabha, in unison, which significantly raised the volume of the chanting such that it was high enough to be heard over the background noise. At this time of a rising resonating sound, the state practitioner stopped the chanting. She told them what they were doing was inappropriate. After they stopped, all of us returned to the meeting hall to wait for what would be an otherwise quite unremarkable memorial meeting (that also incorporated a popular religious addendum) to start. If chanting Amitabha in unison in a state parlor shows how the frame of these rituals was fuzzy, then the state practitioner's action showed that the state would indeed step in to guard that boundary at some point.

As they left, the charismatic leader did not take back the dharani flag. As a result, the dharani flag covered the body throughout the memorial meeting. This subtle action had a much stronger influence than it might sound because nearly all memorial meetings in Shanghai were open-casket ceremonies. Having a dharani flag that covered the dead then meant that a religious symbol visually occupied a place of prominence. Throughout the memorial meeting, even as work units and the bereaved narrated the idealized socialist citizenship that the deceased was said to embody, what people would see at the symbolic center was a dharani flag. There was perhaps no better image than this dharani flag to illustrate how porous the boundaries of these ritual framings were.

From this vignette, we also see how the state practitioner did not stop the bereaved when the family (along with their lay Buddhist friends) chanted as they draped the dharani flag on the coffin. They were able to do this because the body preparation room was behind the meeting hall and, thus, farther from the official public space. Only close family members and funeral professionals (and I) were in the back rooms. In addition, those sporadic and individual Amitabha chants were not easily apprehensible. People in the next body preparation room could likely not hear what was going on, let alone people in the meeting hall itself. All these factors allowed the chanting act to be conceptualized as a domestic ritual even though it occurred in a funeral parlor—a public space. However, as soon as the individual chanting became a collective act that allowed the chanting sounds to penetrate the walls of the body preparation room, this edge-ball play broke the bubble of the temporarily created alternative framing, and the state practitioner intervened.

Monks in Kasaya

The kasaya is a garment worn by practicing Buddhist monks. The first time that I saw monks in kasaya chant in memorial meeting halls was for a very unusual funeral. The deceased died in her early forties, and her husband was very wealthy—so much so that her husband was in a jail somewhere serving a corruption-related sentence when she died in the accident that night. In addition, although the family comprised local Shanghai people, they had acquired Hong Kong residency at the beginning of the Reform and Opening Up. Therefore, her death counted as the death of a Hong Kong person instead of as one of a Shanghainese. This meant the deceased was exempted from mandatory cremation and some other regulations. Finally, the deceased was not only rich (through her husband) but also famous in the entertainment business and in philanthropy in Hong Kong and Shanghai. Apparently, she even made it into fashion magazines every once a while as a glamorous celebrity. The combination of these factors—of being a Hong Kong resident, wealthy, and famous—meant that the family was able to push the edges of regulations quite far in the process of handling this sudden death. The family hired Chen Ting to be their funeral broker, and I followed this incident right from the beginning. Both the funeral broker and state practitioners gave this family much leeway when organizing her funeral.

This person's memorial meeting was held in the largest meeting hall at Huangpu Funeral Parlor. Although her family estimated that they would have "only" several hundred funeral guests (and therefore the second-largest hall would have been sufficient), they insisted on renting the largest hall because, as her sister told Chen Ting at our initial business meeting, "she deserved the best." Before the memorial meeting started, twenty monks arrived in the meeting hall wearing bright yellow and red kasaya. Such colors made this group of monks even more conspicuous in places such as Huangpu, where practicing monks were rarely seen and where the primary colors of the buildings were white and light gray. As soon as I saw the monks, I looked to Manager Liu, manager of the sales unit at Huangpu. He showed up for all the funerals held in the largest meeting hall. Not surprisingly, he had an expression of distinct disapproval on his face. As I walked over to be closer to Manager Liu to see what he would do next, he told me, "I am about to talk to the bereaved. In a place such as this [the largest hall], with a memorial meeting at this level [having so many upper-class people], it is very inappropriate [to have so many monks in kasaya]. They should at least wait until the meeting is finished [if they want to have monks perform rituals]."

Manager Liu first asked the monks to take a break in the resting room adjacent to the meeting hall to get them out of the public gaze. Then, he went to talk to Chen Ting about this issue. Chen Ting told Liu that the family originally told her that they wanted to perform a salvation ceremony after the meeting. She protested that she had only just found out that the family member who hired the monks insisted on having a short sutra chant performed before the meeting as well because the deceased had died so young and so suddenly. The soul of someone dying young is even more desperate for salvation and merit to ensure that she does not stay in limbo and linger in this world. Nonetheless, Manager Liu insisted that it was inappropriate to have monks in the meeting hall, especially in such a grand public space. After all, this largest hall was the same one that held memorial meetings of high-ranking party leaders.

For a while, I thought the issue had been settled and that the monks would not chant. Later, however, Chen Ting told me that Manager Liu had agreed to step back and allow a brief chant to be performed before the meeting for various reasons. First, it turned out that these monks were from the Jade Buddha Temple, one of the four most famous Buddhist temples in Shanghai. One rumor about this temple was that the late Deng Xiaoping himself visited the Jade Buddha Temple every Chinese New Year. This rumor showed the extra power that the Jade Buddha Temple was viewed as having. The leading monk at the temple personally knew the deceased. Otherwise, famous temples such as this one did not usually send their monks out to perform salvation rituals to funeral parlors. Secondly, one of the monks turned out to be a personal acquaintance of Manager Liu. These two factors added together prevented Liu from saying no.

Manager Liu, Chen Ting, and the son of the deceased came to a solution for doing this properly. They decided first to ask everyone to leave the meeting hall. They then would bring in the deceased and invite only the family members to reenter to join a short domestic salvation ceremony before the memorial meeting. When this was done, they then would invite everyone else again to start the public and official memorial meeting, as usual. However, because approximately three to four hundred guests were in attendance, executing this alternative plan was impossible. The funeral professionals managed to ask some people to leave the main portion of the meeting hall, but when the deceased came in, everyone (and not just family members) came back in as well (and many had never even left the hall as they were asked to in the first place). In the end, the twenty monks stood around the deceased to perform ten minutes of sutra chanting in front of all the funeral participants. When this salvation ritual ended, the emcee announced the beginning of the memorial meeting, pretending that the previous chanting and early entrance of the rest of the participants had not just happened. Through the power of officiating, the emcee smoothed over the social glitches (Goffman 1974) as if everything was as it should be. The remaining parts of the memorial meeting then proceeded as usual.

From this vignette, we can see that when Manager Liu saw a group of twenty monks in kasaya present and attempting to chant, he immediately removed them to the resting room to prevent them from being seen in the meeting hall. However, given the deceased's influential background, the status of the temple that these monks represented, and Manager Liu's having known one of the monks personally, he decided to compromise and allow them to perform a chanting ritual before the meeting started. The collaborative solution they came up with was to evacuate everyone from the meeting hall. This evacuation of funeral participants allowed whatever events were held in the same space later to be viewed as domestic rituals. By removing the crowd, the funeral professionals and the bereaved could (attempt to) turn a site of public mourning into a site of family mourning.

Though the funeral professionals and the bereaved did not execute their plan successfully in this case, this solution nevertheless indicated the assumption that it was possible to momentarily carve out an imagined space within a public, socialist, and state space. This way of framing through space and time allowed Shanghai people to add a not-yet-routinized religious ritual without denying the primacy of the meeting's secular socialist framing. During this Buddhist chanting ritual, the deceased was not a model socialist citizen even though the physical space was reserved for such. Instead, she was a wandering soul who needed the power of the Buddha to guide her on her incarnation journey. Even though the isolating strategy failed, the attempt to do so apparently made the chanting performance acceptable—it was as if the room had been cleared.

State "Complicity" in Buddhist Inclusions

These religious versions of memorial meetings diversified the secular framing of memorial meetings that constructed socialist citizenship. While it was technically illegal to have religion in public spaces, the temporary creation of private space within public space was by no means a resistance against the state. Funeral parlors themselves rely on the method of temporarily creating an imagined domestic space within funeral parlors to increase their profits. The best example here was of the wake-keeping rooms in Huangpu. I heard about these wake-keeping rooms when I first visited Huangpu during my preparatory fieldwork in 2009. During that visit, I talked to a Mr. Huang, who was relatively high up in the parlor, about Shanghai funeral parlors in general. Back then, I had yet to attend any funerals in China.

During our conversation, I asked him if religious activities were allowed in funeral parlors. He said that the law stated that religious activities were only allowed in religious spaces. However, as Huang went on to explain, because the bereaved had religious demands (*zongjiao xuqiu*), funeral parlors attempted to accommodate consumer needs as much as they could. For example, Huang said that several Western-style memorial meeting halls could be used for Protestant or Catholic memorial meetings. These meeting halls had stained-glass windows to resemble those in Christian churches, albeit without the Christian symbols. This religious ambiguity was a part of the design because, he told me, both Christians and non-Christians rented such Western-style meeting halls. I then asked Huang if any meeting halls existed for Buddhism or other religions. He said that some meeting halls were decorated with wooden windows that appeared more Chinese in style and could be used in this manner if the bereaved wanted to.

Huang sensed my curiosity for religion and then told me that one of the six wake-keeping rooms at the parlor was clearly Buddhist—the Jade Lotus Room. This room was decorated with statues of the Eighteen Arhats. According to Mahayana Buddhism, the Eighteen Arhats are disciples of the Buddha who ended the cycle of reincarnation and reached nirvana. However, Huang declined my request to visit this wake-keeping room during our interview and said that I would have a chance to do so after I officially started my fieldwork. A year after that interview, when I did start the long portion of my fieldwork, I visited the Jade Lotus Room several times.

At Huangpu, all of the wake-keeping rooms were located in the office building on the fourth floor. Unless people knew where they were going, it would have been highly unlikely for someone to just pass by and see the wake-keeping rooms. The Jade Lotus Room was rectangular, just like any of the other meeting halls in Shanghai funeral parlors. One short side of the room opened to the back hallway, where the body would arrive from the preparation room in the cosmetics unit. The other short side was adjacent to a separate lounge, where several Chinese-style wooden chairs and a shower room were provided. The bereaved could sit in the lounge as monks performed sutra chanting and salvation ceremonies in the room. They need not be constantly present because they only needed to offer incense and prostrations to the deceased at certain correct moments. They did not have to sit through the entire ceremony with the monks.

Extending from floor to ceiling along each of the two long walls of the room were nine dark-stained, wood-paneled display cases. Whereas the bottom three feet of the cases were intricately carved solid wood, in the alcove of the nine top portions were golden painted statues in a variety of poses standing on white marble blocks. These Eighteen Arhat statues oversaw all of the rituals that took place in the room. The impression they gave was quite striking—each was approximately two feet tall and lit with a single spotlight from above—and their golden color sparkled in the light and presented a strong contrast with both the dark wood paneling and the white of the floor and the ceiling. This feeling grew even stronger once I became familiar with Huangpu's environment because its architecture and interior design was everywhere else modernist and minimalist with much empty space and minimal decorations. As a result, the Eighteen Arhats in the Jade Lotus Room stood out even more as both religious symbols and almost extravagant decorations.

Although the Jade Lotus Room at Huangpu certainly stood out given its deliberate decorations, all three city funeral parlors allowed monks to chant in such separate, less accessible wake-keeping rooms rather than in their actual memorial meeting halls. Huangpu allowed people to hire monks to chant in their wake-keeping rooms as long as the bereaved hired these monks through the parlor. It is worth noting, however, that most ordained monks in Shanghai did not go out of their temples to perform rituals. To have a ritual performed, people had to go to temples instead, which was particularly true for monks based in famous temples. As such, the monks hired through Huangpu were also almost always nonpracticing professional monks—they were not ordained based on state rules. These unordained monks were people who provided Buddhist rituals as their livelihood. They might know how to chant, but they did not practice celibacy and might not even be vegetarians.

I once asked a state practitioner why people must hire monks through the parlor. He told me that if funeral parlors allowed the bereaved to hire their own monks, these monks might burn spirit money or light oil candles (instead of electric candles) inside the meeting halls. Funeral parlors would lose control over the ritual performance. Regardless of whether the funeral parlors' monks were real or fake, the fact that monks were not allowed in memorial meeting halls was strange to me in the first place because Protestant pastors and Catholic priests could enter memorial meeting halls with their followers. My funeral broker friends, however, found it in no way strange because parlors could make money by providing monks but could not very well do the same by providing priests or pastors. While the loss of control might be one reason for state funeral parlors to prohibit people from hiring monks themselves, the fact that salespeople in funeral parlors received commissions from selling chanting services probably contributed at least equally (if not more) to why funeral parlors forced the bereaved to hire monks through parlors themselves. Whenever I visited the main sales office at Huangpu, a note was always hanging on the whiteboard that showed how many Buddhist chanting services each salesperson had sold in the last month and how large a bonus they had earned respectively during the past few months.

The wake-keeping rooms and the monk rules at funeral parlors both showed how these Buddhist additions modified the original framing of memorial meetings without challenging it. Capitalist profits gave funeral parlors a motivation to incorporate religious additions into memorial meetings despite the fact that it was technically illegal to have religious activities in public spaces. As such, just like the maneuver between funeral brokers and state practitioners when they added not-yet-routinized Buddhist rituals to memorial meetings, funeral parlors themselves did the same thing. By pretending the existence of wake-keeping rooms were for domestic consumption only, and despite those rooms being physically located in public spaces, the state was also "complicit" in diversifying commemorations of the dead. The tricky attitude shown toward distinctively Buddhist practices in state funeral parlors revealed a unique relationship between the Chinese state and Buddhism. Whereas the state allowed Buddhism to exist within funeral parlors, Buddhism had to exist in specific ways. The articulation of Buddhist subjects had to be quiet, inclusive (as part of a socialist citizenship), and remain marginal.

Modular Framing and Pluralist Subjectivity

I have shown in this chapter two additional types of self that were commonly constructed in memorial meetings: relational and religious selves. These notions were embedded in reciprocal exchanges between the living and the dead as well as among the living. By allowing added rituals to exist after a memorial meeting, religious and relational additions became routine additions to the socialist civil funeral. The best evidence for this situation was the standardization of the entire set of rituals (including funeral banquets) that happened after the farewell ceremony. Through temporalization, popular religious and relational selves not only could coexist with the dominant secular socialist self but also maintained a more or less peaceful relationship with it.

Buddhist ideas of conceptualizing the dead, meanwhile, were less common in Shanghai. However, by creating an alternative space within the state space, Buddhist ideas of self and death could coexist alongside and within a secular socialist framing. In this temporarily created space, both funeral professionals and the bereaved perceived what they were doing as merely a domestic ritual even though this domestic ritual was being held in a public space and was observed by non-family members. In other words, if temporalization could routinize religious and relational additions within the framework of memorial meetings, then spatialization created the possibility for routinization to begin.

If we imagine a memorial meeting as a book of socialism, then Shanghai people performed religious and relational variations of socialist civil funerals by adding a preface and an appendix to the socialist book. Although the story that made the book was still about socialism, its preface and appendix were concerned with religious conceptions of the world, the deceased, and the afterlife, as well as with the reciprocal relationships between and among the living and the dead. Within the religious preface and appendix, various ideas associated with folk religions and Buddhism coexisted even though the specific ideas of person and death that were grouped as such were in contradiction. Through temporalization and spatialization, Shanghai residents transformed the frame of memorial meetings into a type of modular frame by adding folk religious frames to the secular socialist frame. A Buddhist frame, too, might be added. Banquets and gift exchange practices and their relational framing then added a final ingredient to this hybridity.

While the original socialist framing of the memorial meeting was more or less left intact without any frame disrupting another, there was nonetheless some crossover. Recall the transition from the last step of memorial meetings to the beginning of the folk ritual addition: at times, ritual participants would resume the folk emotional regime before they finished the farewell ceremony. Also, in the first Buddhist vignette, whereas the state practitioner successfully asked the bereaved to chant individually and only in the body preparation room, she did not remove the dharani flag as the body was moved into the public memorial meeting hall. As a result, the dharani flag covered the body in public throughout the memorial meeting. Finally, recall how in the second Buddhist vignette, state practitioners, funeral brokers, and the bereaved failed to clear the hall as they held a private Buddhist family ritual before the meeting started.

Having described the boundaries of these modular frames as fuzzy and porous, however, does not mean that no attempt was made to govern and maintain these boundaries. By contrast, as several of my examples show (especially concerning rituals that were not yet routinized), constant efforts were made to police (including the effort to not govern on the state side), define, and regulate proper behavior and, ultimately, to negotiate these boundaries. To follow the book metaphor again here, though, can we really describe a book as a book of socialism when there are only twenty pages about socialism and the remaining eighty pages of that book are about religion even if these pages are titled as preface and appendix? In this case, we can, precisely because of the centrality of those socialist pages. This is why these religious versions of memorial meetings were a modular framing rather than just a collection of rituals each with their own respective framing.

Consequently, although this pluralist construction of the self did not pose a challenge to the socialist citizenship, it did challenge the necessity of a collectively shared singular self. The logical inconsistencies in these different ways of conceptualizing the dead could coexist exactly because people who performed these kinds of rituals treated their action—participating in the memorial meeting—as merely following social convention. Their participation in ritual did not seek to elicit in them any specific internal states, and neither did such participation require the representation to others of their specific internal states. It was in the world of ritual and in their willingness to see their actions as metacommunicative in expressing a general acceptance of all social conventions that Shanghai people were able to construct dead bodies as spirits needing to be pleased, ancestors in kinship relationships with the living, and sources of pollution that needed to be managed. They also constructed reciprocal and relational types of subjectivity of dead bodies—a type of self that continued as the deceased was transformed by these exchanges into a beneficent ancestor all in one ritual.

These people might believe the content of their rituals, or they might not. The ritual might or might not authentically represent the deceased. The ritual might or might not make participants cultivate correct internality. The point is that there was no moral and emotional need to make their externalized actions consistent with who they were or what they believed. What mattered was that ritual participants did all the right things even though all these right things were logically incoherent, if not at times contradictory to each other. Pluralist subjectivity was possible exactly because all these differences were dealt with within a ritual act. To put it differently, the more people view participating in memorial meetings as merely following external social convention, the more likely for them to construct pluralist subjectivity for the dead. This particular view on rituals, armed with the modular framing the bereaved created largely through funeral brokers, is the foundation of pluralist subjectivity.

To sum up, I show here how pluralist subjectivity was made possible in the combination of modular framing and a perspective on rituals as merely following external social conventions. Such a combination allowed socialist citizenship to exist in conjunction with religious and relational subjectivities. In this sense, we might all come together to perform a set of acts of mourning without any need to believe in the same afterlife, god(s), or secular socialism. From the perspective of the ritual as a whole, we see the coexistence of secular socialist, relational, and religious ideas of person and death in contemporary urban Chinese funerals exactly because these differences were dealt with through ritual.

To take this argument a final step forward, this preface and appendix approach was not the only possible way to create a modular frame. Some Protestants attempted to transform memorial meetings in a different way wherein the denotative meaning of the meeting became more important than the frame of ritual. Just following social convention came to no longer be enough even under socialist authority (or exactly because they were under such authority). To use Seligman and Weller's (2012) phrasing, some Protestants were on their way to moving from a ritual mode of action to a sincerity mode of action in their participation in religious versions of memorial meetings. In the next chapter, I discuss such Protestant variations of memorial meetings, their contrasts with the socialist book and its religious preface and appendix approach, and some of the social consequences that occurred due to this different attitude toward what ritual is.

PLURALISM, INTERRUPTED

One afternoon, Chen Yu asked me if I wanted to attend a memorial meeting with her the next morning. A funeral broker from a different funeral agency, Lin Bingzhong, had hired her to be the videographer for a funeral that he was organizing. Early the next morning, we arrived at Huangpu from our respective homes. Not long after Chen Yu and I arrived in the parking lot, Lin Bingzhong drove in as well. He gave Chen Yu RMB 500 (USD 77) up front for her work that day because he might be too busy to pay her later since memorial meeting endings were usually quite chaotic. He told Chen Yu that this family had requested that the video recording start in the parking lot to record the arrival of the bereaved. Without such a specific request, the usual funeral recording only covered what happened inside the meeting hall, along with the final act of sending the body away.

We waited another twenty minutes or so before three buses filled with guests drove into the parking lot together. The first group to alight from the first bus was composed of members of a marching band who wore marine-like white uniforms. Three were percussionists, and the other four played a variety of wind instruments, such as the clarinet and saxophone. This was a bit unusual because all three parlors had their respective in-house bands. As such, in general, the bereaved needed to hire the in-house marching band. However, since this parlor was located outside the downtown area, there was always a bit more leeway in doing things.

The first person who got off the bus immediately after the marching band was holding the deceased's portrait. This indicated that he was the eldest son of the deceased. After him, more people got off from the first and second bus. All of them wore black armbands. As I previously described, black armbands (having replaced full mourning dress) were the standard form of mourning dress during my fieldwork. At this point, other than the fact that the marching band hired was not an in-house one, nothing seemed unusual about this funeral until I spotted the people who got off the third bus. Rather than wearing black armbands, these people all wore a white armband with a red cross on it. While it was a standard practice for Christians to wear white armbands in Shanghai, this was the first time I saw people wearing two different colors of armband in the same funeral. This was despite the fact that it was quite common to have some ritual participants who were Christian and some who were not in the same memorial meeting since conversion to Christianity in Shanghai at that time usually happened at an individual rather than household level. At that moment, I started to suspect that the immediate family members of the deceased were not Christian while most of the people on the third bus were. I later confirmed my speculation with Lin Bingzhong. He told me that the deceased was a devout Protestant, but none of her five children was. The deceased's wish was to have a Protestant memorial meeting.

In describing this particular Protestant version of a memorial meeting, I examine in this chapter how ritual's ability to allow people to live with difference starts to break apart. Specifically, I found that when people began to view performing rituals as making a personal statement of who they were and what they believed, then ritual's capacity to accommodate alterity started to diminish even though the ritual itself was still somehow a modular frame that contained different but coexisting ideas of self and death. To put it differently, if the last chapter was about how a particular view supports ritual's modular framing and its likelihood to facilitate pluralism, then this chapter explores a different attitude toward ritual and how this new attitude changes the modular framing of the rituals as well as reducing the likelihood to have pluralist subjectivity.

To be clear, when I talk about a decreased possibility for pluralism in this Protestant version of memorial meetings, especially in comparison to folk religious and Buddhist versions, I am not talking about "religious pluralism" here. Joel Robbins (2014) makes a useful distinction in his work between religious pluralism and what he calls "value pluralism," which serves as a good starting point for my discussion here. Religious pluralism refers to the relationships between people who identify themselves with different, more-or-less bounded religious traditions. It is about "how social units are defined and how they and their members relate to one another" (3). Values, however, are "ends that are culturally defined as worth orienting action toward" (3). The use of the word *culturally* here stresses how these values are shared and prescribed even when they serve as individual motivations. Such values are not random or spontaneous. Rather than exploring religious pluralism—relations between adherents of different religious beliefs (including atheists)—what I explore here instead are these conflicts of ethical values. These different values reflect different moral ideas of what being a proper person means. They are the moral compasses through which people seek to act as ethical subjects.

Robbins (2013) points out that social life almost always contains multiple often only partially realized values. As many values we hold are in conflict with each other, people must constantly negotiate and compromise between different values in the actions they take. Ritual, for Robbins (2014, 7), is one of the few, if not the only, mode of social action that fully realizes values "in unusually complete form" in ways that other social actions are unable to. Robbins runs through a good example on the values of honesty and politeness in academic conferences to illustrate this dynamic. For the most part, participants in academic conferences must constantly negotiate between the value of being honest and that of being polite. One exception to this happens when participants perform the ritual of applause after hearing a talk. This hand clapping ritual allows people to fully realize the value of politeness in that moment.

Robbins suggests that performing the applause ritual creates value pluralism. This is because enabling the full realization of the value of politeness within that ritual moment does not indicate a denial of the value of honesty—you clap for presentations you dislike. The ritual in some ways enables questions of honest reaction to be put aside for the moment. Moreover, for Robbins, each ritual fully realizes one single value at this smaller scale. With a whole range of rituals, our social world is thus able to accommodate seemingly incommensurable values. Ritual allows the temporary hierarchization of values as it fully realizes one value. In other words, ritual makes value pluralism possible because ritual provides the perfect singular realization of one specific value at one specific time (Robbins 2014).

However, what if there are ethnographic examples to show that ritual could realize more than one value? If some rituals indeed realize multiple values, is it still the case that just one value is fully realized, while others are realized only partially? Or is it possible that whether one value is more fully realized than another in any one ritual must remain forever undetermined? These questions about whether a ritual could realize one or more values are important because they directly relate to the critical question of value pluralism: What makes value pluralism possible? This chapter supports many things that Robbins argues, especially ritual's performative power to fully realize values that make value pluralism possible. However, we differ on one critical point—that is, ritual's ability to fully realize one singular value and such ritually embedded singularity being key to value pluralism. This chapter shows that what makes value pluralism vis-à-vis ritual possible, and possible in particular forms, depends more on how actors view what ritual is rather than ritual always reflecting only one singular value in a perfect form.

Specifically, in this chapter, I show that as some people attempted to make performing rituals into a way of speaking personal testimony of their inner states or as a way to cultivate correct internal states, ritual's modular framing then started to lose its power to accommodate alterity. As people started to ensure that values revealed in rituals were consistent with values outside of rituals, we saw an increase of social conflicts around the ritual. In the following sections, I continue to describe the Protestant version of a memorial meeting that I started at the beginning of this chapter. I then analyze how this Protestant version of memorial meetings created a pluralist subject through its modular framing. Meanwhile, however, I illustrate how this ritual was on its way to becoming one focused on personal testimony and detail the social consequences of this different attitude toward what participating in ritual entails.

A Protestant Version of the Memorial Meeting

In the parking lot, once everyone had alighted from the bus, they started walking together to the meeting hall. The marching band was in the lead, followed by the eldest son and other immediate family members, then distant family members and friends, and finally the Protestant group from the third bus. Because Chen Yu had to film this march, we kept running to stay ahead of everyone. After finding a proper distance between ourselves and the mourners, we then walked backward to face the crowd. As Chen Yu recorded the march, I helped her carry the equipment and camera cases. This ceremonial march from the parking lot to the meeting hall was a new experience for me at that time.[1]

After the band arrived at the meeting hall, they stood outside near the door to allow the deceased (via her portrait) to enter first. They continued to play to welcome the other funeral participants as the latter walked into the hall. Inside the meeting hall, once the funeral participants had signed in, they began to socialize with each other. Some walked around the meeting hall to read the mini couplets on the flower baskets. Meanwhile, Lin Bingzhong was talking through some last-minute preparations with the eldest son of the deceased, the state practitioner in charge of this meeting hall, and another man whom I did not know. This person wore a black button-down shirt and a pair of black suit pants. Although his dress was relatively formal, he was not wearing a uniform. I later found out that this man was a pastor. Not soon after they started the conversation, a much younger man joined this group discussion. He looked a bit timid and inexperienced. He turned out to be the representative of the deceased's work unit. From the conversation, I realized that he did not personally know the deceased. As I previously explained, this situation was fairly common.

Approximately twenty minutes later, the pastor tested the microphone. He, rather than Lin Bingzhong, would be the emcee even though most funeral brokers' cases would have the brokers themselves as emcee. Using the microphone, this pastor told the funeral participants that the memorial meeting was about to start and asked them to line up. As explained in chapter 5, the general rule was that immediate family members of the deceased stood in the first few rows and the work unit representative stood somewhere with them (see figure 7.1).

However, perhaps because participants were busy socializing with other people and, thus, did not hear the pastor's instructions or perhaps because the pastor did not make an earnest attempt to make people line up correctly, the participants lined up in a very unusual way. The first few rows split into right and left sections (from the deceased's perspective), in a 1:2 ratio. On the left was the family of the deceased, as is normal. However, people from the deceased's congregation occupied the first few rows of the right side. The timid work unit representative

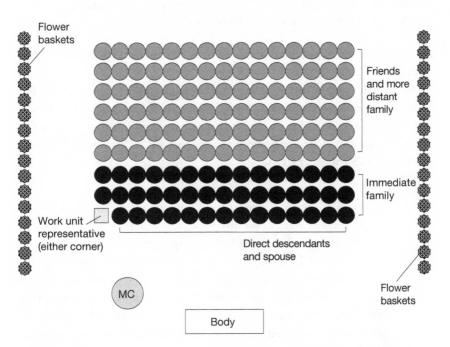

FIGURE 7.1. The normal lineup for memorial meetings. Used with permission from Matthew West.

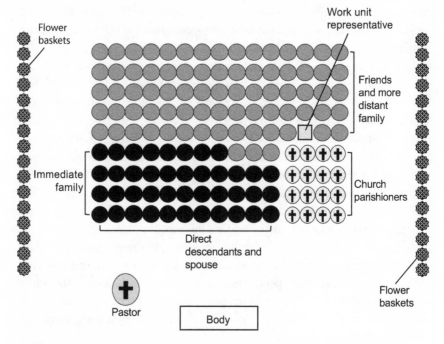

FIGURE 7.2. The actual lineup for this Protestant version of a memorial meeting. Used with permission from Matthew West.

was pushed all the way back to the middle rows, just behind the Christian crowd (see figure 7.2).

After all the people lined up, the pastor formally announced the start of the memorial meeting. In the description of the memorial meeting below, I have transcribed a selection of the speeches to give a sense of the quite different flavor of this meeting. I have also numbered the pastor's facilitations for the convenience of subsequent analysis.

The pastor (1):

> God loves everyone. . . . God is the creator of the universe. . . . God sacrificed his only son. . . . We are really happy that the family members of Sister Ma Donghua are willing to respect her religion and her wish to not have folk [*shisu de*] practices in her funeral such as burning [paper money], offering [sacrifices], and worshipping [ancestors]. We will also not have bowing today because Protestant funerals cannot contain "prostration and worshiping" [*guibai*]. We Protestants only submit ourselves to the holy God. . . . Today, we'll have hymn singing, prayer, a family member's thank-you speech, and the church's testimony. . . . Let us sing a hymn.

I want to point out three things here. First, in the list of funeral events, the pastor neglected to mention the work unit's memorial speech. Although probably an unintentional omission, seeing such an absence as a Freudian slip on the pastor's part that reflected the tension between the church and the state observed in Protestant versions of memorial meetings—on which I will elaborate—may not be too far-fetched. Second, singing hymns was accompanied by the marching band's music. However, clearly, only those who wore white armbands (the Protestants) were singing. The immediate family members who stood in the first few rows had a piece of paper with the lyrics on it in their hands. Some of them looked as if they were reading the lyrics when others were singing the hymns, but most of them appeared to be simply listening to the hymns. Either way, they did not sing as did Protestant participants. That said, they participated in the singing of hymns by agreeing to be there. They did this because they merely followed the social convention of Protestants rather than because they believed in Christianity or somehow felt that their participation could aid them in cultivating the specific kinds of internal states the songs taught. Finally, the pastor's opening—his combination of preaching and singing hymns—took a long time. He did not invite in the body of the deceased for a good ten minutes. Such a prolonged opening never happened in non-Protestant memorial meetings.

After the pastor gave the instruction to bring in the dead, a state practitioner pushed the deceased to the designated space in the middle of the hall. He then stepped to the side and remained more or less invisible in the meeting hall for the rest of the memorial meeting. The pastor then said the following:

The pastor (2):

> Today, we are here in the biggest memorial meeting hall of the Huangpu Funeral Parlor to have this funeral for Sister Ma Donghua. The people who came to join Sister Ma Donghua's funeral are her family members, relatives and friends, leaders and colleagues at her work unit, and her brothers and sisters from the congregation.
>
> Now I announce the beginning of Sister Ma Donghua's funeral. Please all commemorate her silently. Please play the dirge.
> [Playing "The Dirge"]

The pastor (3):

> Now we are going to pray to God. Please, everyone, close your eyes and pray to God.
>
> Dear holy Father, thank you for loving everyone in the world. ["Amen!" the church members said in unison.] You created the sky, the earth, and everything. ["Amen!"] You created us, your human beings.

["Amen!"] Your glory enlightens us. . . . When the work unit's representative gives his memorial speech, the bereaved's representative gives a
thank-you speech, and when we hear the church's testimony, you are
with us. You watch, lead, and guide us, similar to a shepherd taking care
of his flock! Now we invite the work unit representative to give the memorial speech.

The work unit representative came up and stood facing the deceased's portrait
and body. He bowed three times to the deceased. He then turned around and
bowed one time to the participants.

The work unit representative:

Comrades! Today, with extreme sorrow, we all come to this memorial
meeting to mourn Comrade Ma Donghua, a retired worker from the
Shanghai Machine Limited Liability Company (Co., Ltd.). Comrade
Ma Donghua died from failure to cure an illness. She passed away at
22:30 on March 22, 2011, at the age of seventy-seven.

Comrade Ma Donghua was born in Shanghai City on June 16,
1934. Prior to 1949, Comrade Ma Donghua stayed in her hometown to
help her parents with domestic affairs. Between July 1955 and 1965,
Comrade Ma Donghua worked in the Fuxin District Committee and
at the Shanghai Electric Factory. Starting in July 1968, she entered the
Shanghai Machine Factory to work in the administrative unit. She retired in June 1984.

Comrade Ma Donghua was born in the Old Society. During the decade before liberation, she followed her parents and experienced much
disturbance, hardship, and bitterness—like the other thousands and
hundreds of millions of workers' children. She experienced exploitation and oppression in the Old Society and had a difficult life. After
New China was established, she liberated herself [fanshen]. She joined
the construction of socialism fully, heartily, and with enthusiasm. She
devoted all of her youth and life to this, especially after July 1968,
when she entered the administrative unit in the Shanghai Machine
Factory. She worked hard and did her best to contribute from her
humble position. She retired in glory in June 1984.

After she retired, she never made excessive demands to the work
unit. Over twenty years of retired life, she overcame all of her difficulties herself without giving the work unit trouble. She showed excellent quality in being a retired worker. Who won't feel pain and
sorrow for her departure? Commemorating Comrade Ma Donghua
is to learn from her love for the party and for socialism, her hardwork-

ing ethic and endurance, and her selfless [*wusi*] spirit. The life of Comrade Ma Donghua was a laborious life, a life of dedication. We need to turn our grief into strength. From our working location, we each need to contribute to construct China as a well-off and harmonious society as early as possible.

Now, please allow me to represent the Retirement Committee of the Shanghai Machine Co., Ltd., and all employees in the Shanghai Machine Co., Ltd., to give deepest condolences to Comrade Ma Donghua. Comrade Ma Donghua, please let her rest in peace! It is March 26, 2011.

After the work unit representative went back to where he stood, the oldest son of the deceased came to the front. Note that he did not bow three times to the deceased before giving his speech. He "stared" at the picture for several seconds and then nodded to the audience.

The eldest son of the deceased:

This is the thank-you speech. Dear [work unit] leaders, relatives and friends, Protestant brothers and sisters, good morning. First, I am representing my family to thank you for coming to my mother's memorial meeting despite the busy schedules you have. Thanks to those Protestant brothers and sisters who visited and helped my mother while she was alive and sick. I give all of you my deepest gratitude. My dear mother was born on June 16, 1934. She entered the Shanghai Machine Factory in July 1968 to work in the cafeteria under the administrative unit. She retired in glory in June 1984 from the Shanghai Machine Factory. On February 23, 2011, she was admitted to the No. 5 People's Hospital due to her long-term illness with diabetes. Due to her illness deteriorating, she left this world forever at 22:30 on March 22, 2011. She passed away at the age of seventy-seven.

My dear mother was born into a poor worker's family. She worked diligently in her life without recognition from the world. She was conscientious, honest, and down-to-earth. She raised five children in her life. She helped her husband and taught her children. She was frugal and prudent in order to bring us up. She loved and cared about us all wholeheartedly. She taught us each how to be a person and how to lead the next generation to also become a proper person. She was a typical Chinese-style good wife and good mother.

Dear Mother, your departure made us feel so much pain and sorrow. Dear Mother, how could you leave so soon? It is just about time for us children to return your upbringing and love—how could you leave us forever without enjoying this? Your sons are crying. Your daughters are crying. Your departure is so bitter, and our hearts are in pain. Dear Mother, please leave without worrying. We will never forget your wish—your wish for us siblings to stay together and educate the next generation. We hope you are peaceful and cheerful in heaven [*tiantang*]. We hope to be your children again in the next life. My dear Mother, please rest in peace and have a good final journey.

Finally, I represent our family again to show our deepest gratitude to all of you who have come to her memorial meeting today.

He then turned around and "stared" at his mother's picture portrait for several seconds and then nodded to the audience before walking back to where he stood earlier.

The pastor (4):

Now, let us sing another [Christian] hymn.

Again, as in the beginning, one-third of the participants appeared deeply immersed in the hymn singing, whereas the other two-thirds were simply listening.

The pastor (5):

Yes, Jesus loves you [spoken in response to the last line of the lyrics in the hymn]. Jesus saves you. Our dear Sister Ma Donghua left all of those wonderful memories to us. We heard all these beautiful testimonies about her, whether from her family or her work unit. We need to know today that she was also a good example in the church. She was very pious in her beliefs. She went to church services; she also went to home prayer gatherings. With fellow brothers and sisters, she attended church gatherings, sang hymns, prayed, worshiped God, read the Bible, and listened to sermons. All these are beautiful testimonies and valuable treasures in the eyes of God. Today, we see these family members, relatives, friends, and leaders from the work unit respect this old lady and love this loving mother. We all feel sorrow for her departure.

What she has left to us is her faith. She found God, this unchanging God. . . . In today's China with a population of more than a billion, there are not many people who know God. Ma Donghua Sister was blessed because she had this chance to know the only one true God.

I have skipped here the portions of the pastor's preaching that involved narrating the life of Jesus, that there was only one God, that all other folk religious practices were idolatry, that God loves us and sacrificed his life to save us, that simple belief can save you too, and so on.

The pastor's preaching went on and on. I started to feel my legs getting sore. After all, I had been standing since I arrived in the parking lot (in addition to standing for more than an hour during my commute from home to the parlor). And I quickly noticed that I was not the only one who felt this way. I saw many people, especially those who did not wear Christian armbands, start to stretch their legs. They began with subtle stretching, but soon their actions became more obvious. More than this, some non-Protestant participants started to get restless and exchanged eye contact. Some even began whispering to each other. After all, a normal memorial meeting should be finished in twenty minutes. However, we passed the forty-minute mark, and the pastor had yet to invite the participants to begin the farewell ceremony.

I stood next to Chen Yu and faced the crowd from the front at that time. I saw that the Protestant participants were still very much concentrating on their pastor's preaching. Meanwhile, the faces of an increasing number of non-Protestant participants changed from showing seriousness (or indifference?) to obvious impatience. I could see such changes even among the immediate family members of the deceased. I felt an awkward atmosphere continue to build up, but the pastor kept preaching. Then, at some point, I accidentally made eye contact with the eldest son of the deceased. He subtly asked me over to him with his eyes. I looked around to make sure that he was indeed looking at me. The state practitioner and Lin Bingzhong were out of sight. By that time, Chen Yu stood on the other side of the meeting hall from me. Thus, I approached the eldest son as requested. He whispered to me to tell the pastor to finish his preaching soon because they were running out of time. Not knowing what to do and feeling that I should not talk directly to the preaching pastor, I left the meeting hall to find Lin Bingzhong. My guess was right—he was enjoying a cigarette outside. I told him about the chief mourner's request. He then tossed his unfinished cigarette, walked back to the meeting hall, and went straight to the pastor to say a few words to him. The pastor acknowledged Lin Bingzhong's reminder. However, he went on for another several minutes before finally announcing the beginning of the farewell ceremony.

We finally started the farewell ceremony—the last step of the official part of a memorial meeting. Recall that in a typical memorial meeting as described in chapter 5, people collectively bowed three times to the deceased before the farewell ceremony. Then, during the farewell ceremony, small groups of people approached and bowed another three times to the deceased. In this memorial meeting, however, as the pastor requested at the beginning of his performance, no personal nor collective bowing was to occur (in fact, up to that point, the work unit representative was the only person who bowed during the entire meeting).

As such, when performing their respective farewell ceremonies, some of the immediate family members and all of the Protestant participants did not bow. They simply stared at the deceased and then left flowers on top of her body. Other participants, however, bowed as usual when performing their part of the farewell ceremony—possibly because they were unclear about the Protestant rules, because they did know the rules and just forgot, or simply did not want to follow the no-bowing rule. In any case, without the act of bowing, the farewell ceremony went very fast.

Some people left the meeting hall after the farewell ceremony, but some stayed. As I described in the last chapter, this movement marked a change in modality from mourning as a collective act to a more folk-informed frame that enacts mourning as relational. The immediate family then formed a circle around Ma Donghua's coffin. Once the circle was formed, they suddenly started wailing loudly. This wailing was also consistent with the memorial meeting appendix in which we saw a change in the emotional regime from self-restraint to outward expressions of grief and mourning. The main difference in this Protestant version was that, as soon as the immediate family members started to weep, the pastor—who was not standing in the circle—gave the bereaved a withering look that appeared to be disapproval. Such a silent look of condemnation was not enough, however; the pastor then walked close to the bereaved and verbally reminded them that they should restrain themselves. The bereaved decreased their volume of wailing for several seconds but soon began crying loudly again. Lin Bingzhong, himself also clearly frustrated, then said to the bereaved, "Aren't you Protestants? Aren't Protestants not allowed to wail? Please stop weeping." However, the bereaved continued to wail. After all, they were not Protestants.

After a while, the bereaved's wailing gradually faded, and the state practitioner pushed the body to the middle of the meeting hall. In this meeting hall, the deceased's body rested on a bed during the memorial meeting instead of in a coffin (different funeral parlors had different ways of organizing these arrangements). Another practitioner pushed a white coffin into the hall along with a matching white lid. Painted on top of the white lid was a big red cross. Only Christians used white coffins in Shanghai. Lin Bingzhong directed the descendants of the deceased to move their mother's body from the bed to the coffin. Lin Bingzhong then asked the bereaved to pick flowers from the displayed flower baskets to put inside the coffin. Because no placing of xibo happened in this funeral, people just kept bringing flowers, as if they were xibo (the more the better). They brought so many flowers that Lin had to stop them in the end.

People continued to wail throughout this entire time just as I described in the folk funeral appendix in the last chapter. Meanwhile, Lin Bingzhong again felt a need to admonish them, "Don't wail. Protestants do not cry. Protestants are happy in times of death because your mother is now in heaven with Jesus. This is a good thing. She is in heaven now. No need to cry." Although Lin himself was not Christian, this comment did not reflect his idiosyncratic interpretation. It was common knowledge among funeral professionals regarding Protestant memorial meetings that Protestants could not (and should not) cry at funerals because funerals were supposed to represent a happy reunification with God.

When this part of the ceremony was finally over, a group of five people wearing marine-like white uniforms entered. They lifted the coffin onto their shoulders and marched in goose step while carrying the coffin from the meeting hall to the crematoria. Because this service resembled a secular military ritual, ceremonial funeral processions during my fieldwork were quite popular, disregarding religious differences, especially in suburban funeral parlors. Along with the marching band, we marched to the crematoria, which was located on the other side of the parlor. When we arrived at the cremator unit, the bereaved increased their wailing. A state practitioner then put the coffin into the cremator and pushed a button. We witnessed a conveyor belt send the deceased into a dark tunnel. Lin Bingzhong then led all the funeral participants (including those who had waited outside) to a nearby restaurant for their funeral banquet lunch. On the same day, the immediate family members picked up Ma's cremains after their meal.

Chen Yu called someone she knew at that parlor and asked him if he could give us a ride back to Longevity's office. She had seen this person driving into the parlor earlier. He told Chen Yu that he had just dropped off a body and had an empty car going back downtown. We were welcome to join him. This was the first time that I had sat in a hearse. Chen Yu sat in the passenger seat, and I sat in the solitary seat in the back. Right next to my seat was a stainless-steel board where a body would be (and had just recently been) placed. On my way from the parlor to Longevity's office, I did not speak much and, instead, stared at that steel board and tried to figure out exactly what and how I should feel about it and how I should feel about the Protestant version of a memorial meeting I had just witnessed.

Ritually Constructed Plural Subjectivities

Ma Donghua's memorial meeting showed that her funeral simultaneously constructed her as a socialist citizen holding a traditional Chinese female social role and as a devout Protestant through the sequential coexistence of the work unit representative's memorial speech, the eldest son's thank-you speech, and the pastor's preaching. Below I explain how Ma Donghua was commemorated as socialist citizen, Han Chinese woman, and Protestant in turn. First, the work unit representative's standard and stylized narrative described Ma Donghua as someone born in the Old Society, who experienced disturbances, hardship, bitterness, exploitation, and oppression and who then liberated herself after New China was established. Recall the memorial speech of Wang Dashan in chapter 5. These two speeches used the same narrative devices to delineate the life histories of the dead. Moreover, the embodied ethics of Ma Donghua and Wang Dashan are practically identical. As I analyzed in chapter 5, these socialist narratives construct the identity of the dead within a particular socialist imagination of time and person. Similar to Wang Dashan's funeral creating socialist subjectivity for him postmortem, by narrating this socialist idea of time, person, and ethics, Ma Donghua's funeral made her into a model socialist citizen at the end of her life. As far as the public was concerned, whether or not it was an authentic or sincere representation of who she was while alive, she was now a model socialist citizen in the public domain, at least momentarily.

One thing worth pointing out was that Ma Donghua's memorial speech further elaborated on the relationship between the socialist state and its citizen(s); the speech provided a concrete example that illustrates Ma Donghua's selflessness that we did not see in Wang Dashan's memorial speech. The work unit representative said, "After she retired, she never made excessive demands on the work unit. Over twenty years of retired life, she overcame all of her difficulties herself without giving the work unit trouble. She showed excellent quality in being a retired worker." In this narrative, a truly selfless socialist citizen not only devoted all of her productivity to the work unit but also asked for nothing in return once she lost her productivity. She was a true socialist citizen due to this selflessness even though the company she had worked for has since been privatized (it became a limited liability company).

This one-sided devotion was in stark contrast to traditional Chinese ideas of social relationships, including that between a ruler and his subjects that was essentially based on reciprocity. For example, the idea of filial piety was built on the assumption that parental provision created a debt relationship. Children were expected to taking care of their old and infirm parents just as the parents took care of them as equally infirm babies. Confucius's idea of the ruler-subject relationship was then an extension of filial piety. Overall, by describing Ma as a good retired worker, her memorial speech transformed her into a socialist citizen whose moral superiority was said to transcend the implied utilitarian nature of the traditional moral world. Whether or not Ma Donghua actually did not make demands after she retired was a different (and perhaps irrelevant) matter because this speech was most likely based on her company's memorial speech template. What mattered was the image that the speech projected.

Whereas the memorial speech made Ma Donghua into a socialist citizen sub-ject, the thank-you speech given by her eldest son remade her as both socialist and (Han) Chinese. Unlike the memorial speech, which was based on a singular ethi-cal source of socialism, this thank-you speech contained a variety of moral sources in conceptualizing the deceased. We can see this variety in several parts. First, the eldest son started his speech by thanking work unit leaders, relatives and friends, and Protestant brothers and sisters. His approach contrasted with that of the work unit representative who referred to everyone simply as comrades. This recognition of different identity categories articulated a shift from conceptualizing all funeral participants as undifferentiated (and individuated) socialist citizen subjects who were collectively and directly connected to the socialist state (everyone is a "com-rade") to differentiated groups of people whose identities were defined by their relationships to the socialist state (some are "leaders"), by kinship and other recip-rocal relationships (some are "relatives and friends"), and by religious affiliations distinguished by gender (some are "Protestant brothers and sisters").

Such differentiated recognition led to several coexisting conceptualizations of the deceased in the thank-you speech. The first conceptualizing framework was socialist subjectivity. This framework operated through the narration of Ma Donghua's socialist status categories and socialist ethics. In the second paragraph of Ma Donghua's thank-you speech, the eldest son said that she came from a "poor worker's" family. Moreover, he then described his mother as honest, down-to-earth, frugal, prudent, and so on. Just as Wang Dashan's thank-you speech echoed his memorial speech, so did Ma Donghua's thank-you speech also echo her memorial speech. Both the memorial speech and the thank-you speech used the same narrative techniques. However, we can also see a shift in how to con-ceptualize such socialist status and ethics in Ma Donghua's thank-you speech. Instead of presenting these standards solely in terms of socialism, by the end of the second paragraph, the eldest son illustrated his mother's merits by conclud-ing that these had "led the next generation to become a proper person" and that his mother was a typical "Chinese-style good wife and good mother." This con-clusion tacitly added onto and transformed a socialist interpretative framework into a Chinese cultural interpretative framework for understanding what these moral characteristics mean in being a person. Thus, the fact that Ma Donghua was honest, down-to-earth, frugal, and prudent was (also?) because she was a "typical Chinese woman."

The third paragraph of the thank-you speech shifted the voice from talking to the bereaved about the deceased to speaking directly to the deceased. The in-triguing part was that this paragraph was also a direct entrance into the tradi-tional Chinese moral world in which human relationships were defined again by reciprocity as described in the last chapter. The eldest son said, "It is just about the time for us children to return your upbringing and love—how could you leave us forever without enjoying this?" The evocation of return showed how the one-sided socialist social relationship has been submerged into a reciprocal relationship. Furthermore, the eldest son solemnly said, "Your sons are crying. Your daughters are crying." I discussed in chapter 5 that the externalized expression of grief and mourning was key to the traditional Han Chinese death ritual. This was so important that ritualized wailing and professional weepers were integral parts of traditional funerals. In chapter 6, I further discussed how funeral participants today experience a change in emotion regime in this transition. The mention of crying in Ma Donghua's eldest son's speech articulated this sequential transformation in emotion regimes and embedded such emotion regimes in reciprocal social relationships.

Ma Donghua was not only conceptualized as a typical Chinese mother who was hierarchically and reciprocally related to her children but also as a critical source of lineage continuity. The eldest son said, "We will never forget your wish—your wish for us siblings to stay together and educate the next generation." Ma Donghua's provision to her children was not only intended to elicit reciprocity between her and them but also to create lineage consolidation and continuity through the provision for (and of) "the next generation." This would be possible through her transformation into an ancestor. Hence, the eldest son said that she was now "peaceful and cheerful in heaven."

One thing worth mentioning is that the eldest son used the word *tiantang* for "heaven" here. Although this phrase typically refers to the Christian idea of heaven, the following sentence shows that this might not be the case. The son described how he and his siblings "hope to be your children again in the next life." The reference to the "next life" was based on the idea of reincarnation that is prevalent in traditional Han Chinese notions of death, afterlife, and heaven that have long been heavily influenced by Buddhism. In other words, we could say that the use of the word *tiantang* first constructed Ma Donghua as a Christian person. However, this Christian person was then immediately reconfigured into a traditional Chinese person—an ancestor who can take care of lineage consolidation, continuity, and who might be reborn into this world again.

Finally, in the last paragraph, the eldest son switched from talking to the dead to talking again to the living. Again, this format was standard for thank-you speeches. He stressed his gratitude to the people who came to his mother's funeral. Such etiquette created and recognized the debt relationship between the immediate family members of the deceased and other funeral participants, indicating that the immediate family members had a continuing obligation to attend fellow funeral participants' life rituals and participate in associated gift exchanges (whether through banquets or cash) to repay such a debt.

Overall, if we compare Wang Dashan's thank-you speech in chapter 5 and Ma Donghua's, we observe slight variations. The bulk of Ma Donghua's speech constructs her as a traditional Chinese mother more than as a model socialist citizen—for many possible reasons. For example, gender differences led to an emphasis on socialist citizenship, which might also be caused by a different choice of templates or whether the funeral broker or the family member chose the templates. I did not have the chance to confirm whether Ma Donghua's eldest son wrote his speech based on a template, but both Chen Yu and I felt that the speech sounded similar to a template-generated one. Nevertheless, as discussed, the odd part about the thank-you speech in terms of contemporary Shanghai life was never the presence of traditional Han Chinese ideas of person and death. In contrast, the strange part was the presence of socialism because socialism rarely defines the epistemological and ontological experience between parents and children in contemporary Shanghai (or, really, among coworkers either). What was important was that Ma Donghua's thank-you speech, ostensibly from her children's perspective, contained both folk and socialist frameworks in delineating "who Ma Donghua was."

Finally, the pastor's preaching performed the postmortem construction of a Protestant subjectivity of Ma Donghua. From the beginning, she was delineated as a "sister" to him and his congregation instead of as a comrade or a typical Chinese woman. To put this sister's life into context, it was important to first explain to the assembled participants who God was and God's relationship to Ma Donghua. Perhaps this is why the pastor immediately told funeral participants that "God is the Creator and he loved us so much that he sacrificed his own son" (see pastor 1). In other words, the conceptualization of a Protestant person was first and foremost based on a relationship to a Christian creator God. However, such an understanding is merely the first step. The next necessary step was to separate Ma Donghua from the rest of the people who had not yet been saved by Jesus Christ, which is why the pastor stressed how they (those who were saved) were happy that Ma Donghua's family members (who were not yet saved) were willing to respect her religion by rejecting the folk practices of burning (paper money), offering (sacrifices), worshiping (ancestors), and bowing (prostration and worshiping). By respecting her faith, Ma Donghua's remaining family distinguished her funeral from those of regular people. It is worth noting that the pastor used the word *shisu* when describing folk practices. This phrase has a double meaning in Chinese. In addition to meaning "folk," *shisu* is also the Chinese translation of the English word "secular" (as understood in the dichotomous sense of the sacred and the profane). In this sense, to distinguish themselves from the secular, Protestants needed to reject both the profane and other religions, such as popular religion and Buddhism.

Just as the work unit representative narrated the socialist ethics and the eldest son narrated both the socialist and traditional Chinese ethics that Ma Donghua embodied, so too did the pastor narrate her Protestant ethics: "She was very pious in her beliefs. She went to church services; she also went to home prayer gatherings. With fellow brothers and sisters, she attended church gatherings, sang hymns, prayed, worshiped God, read the Bible, and listened to preaching. All these are beautiful testimonies and valuable treasures in the eyes of God" (see pastor 5). As a result, whereas the work unit lost a good comrade and the family lost a good (Chinese) mother and a good wife, the church lost a good and faithful Christian believer. However, while losing a good Christian was already bad enough, there was something even worse. That is, "in today's China with a population of more than a billion, not many people know God." From that point onward, the pastor's narrative fully switched gears from commemorating Ma Donghua to introducing the salvation offered by Christianity to the funeral participants. This effort to convert is a critical point to which I return in the next section.

To sum up, Ma Donghua's funeral simultaneously constructed her as a socialist citizen, a mother embedded in Chinese kinship, and a Christian in the memorial speech, the thank-you speech, and the pastor's preaching, respectively. This was despite the apparently incommensurable values in these three ideas of person. The coexistence of these three speeches in one single ritual provides a lens through which to examine how religious variations of memorial meetings allowed for incommensurable ideas to become temporarily commensurable in public. Each of these speeches illustrates how the modular framing of religious versions of memorial meetings creates pluralist conceptualizations of the dead as analyzed in the last chapter.

Even though the immediate family members and the work unit did not believe in Christianity, by following the social conventions of the pattern of memorial meetings and standing during the singing of the hymns alongside the Protestant participants, together they made Ma Donghua a pluralist subject. Through the acts of "as if" (whether we are talking about the immediate family acting as if they were Protestants and model socialists, the work unit representative acting as if he was a Protestant and traditional Han Chinese, the Protestants acting as if they were both model socialists and traditional Han Chinese, or whatever a specific individual pretended to be), their acceptance of social convention establishes who they appear to be in public at that subjunctive moment. In other words, attending this Protestant memorial meeting allowed funeral participants to cross from one epistemological boundary to another in the public domain. Whether these people felt any ("authentic") ontological transformation was beside the point and irrelevant to the work of the ritual. This was consistent with my findings in the chapter 6 discussions of popular religious, Buddhist, and relational add-ons in memorial meetings.

Recall my analysis on the preface and appendix approach to additions in the last chapter. Despite the many similarities shared by all of these religious variations of the socialist civil funeral, be they about popular religious, Buddhist, or Protestant versions, readers might notice that this Protestant memorial meeting involved more than simply adding a preface or appendix to the socialist book in creating its religious version of a memorial meeting. In the following section, I focus on the unique character of this Protestant version of addition.

The Rewrite Approach

Pastor 2 shows that, similar to the thank-you speech (but unlike the memorial speech), the pastor's narration recognized different identities of funeral participants. Thus, "the people who came to join Sister Ma Donghua's funeral were her family members, relatives and friends, her leaders and colleagues at her work unit, and her brothers and sisters from the congregation." This recognition paralleled the pastor's recognition of the coexistence of the Church's testimony, the work unit's memorial speech, and the family's thank-you speech in the memorial meeting. However, this recognition was merely the first step. Pastor 3 shows us that when the pastor prayed, he asked God to watch over all of these differentiated groups. Almost unbelievably, he even asked God to watch over the work unit leader—the effective Chinese Communist Party representative—when giving his speech. In other words, rather than just adding preface and appendix to a socialist book, the pastor here was attempted to rewrite the book itself with Christianity.

The pastor's attempt to symbolically submerge these differentiated groups of people under the power of his Christian God appeared also in the structural changes he made to the memorial meeting itself. This new reconfiguration was best articulated when we examine the structure of this Protestant memorial meeting in comparison to that presented in chapter 5. Here, I have listed the completed procedures of Ma Donghua's memorial meeting. I have marked the newly added or changed Protestant steps in bold.

> **Preface: The pastor preaches and leads the assembled in collective hymn singing.**
>
> Step 1: The master of ceremonies verbally announces the beginning of the memorial meeting.
>
> Step 2: All commemorate the deceased in silence while playing the funeral dirge.

Step 3: The pastor prays.

Step 4: The work unit representative gives a memorial speech.

Step 5: The representative of the bereaved gives a thank-you speech.

Step 6: The Christians sing hymns, and the pastor preaches.

Step 7: All participate in a farewell ceremony **without bowing (step 5 in the original).**

Appendix: The assembled weep, place flowers inside a Christian coffin, and participate in a ceremonial funeral procession and funeral banquet.

As one type of religious variation of a socialist ritual, Protestant memorial meetings were still pluralist in the sense that the ritual itself still provided a modular framing for ritual participants to sequentially construct a variety of kinds of subjectivity. However, as this new structure shows, the pastor also changed the original steps of the memorial meeting by inserting hymns and prayers between each socialist step. Singing hymns in the beginning was especially powerful because of the length and the density of its effect. As mentioned, the opening hymns lasted approximately ten minutes, which was a long time considering that people only needed about three minutes to read a memorial speech or thank-you speech.

Furthermore, even though bowing was meant to be a modernist bodily movement that replaced the hierarchal relationships produced by prostrations, Protestants treated bowing and prostrations as the same thing. They rejected both because, as the pastor said, "Protestants only submit themselves to God." As the meeting proceeded, Ma Donghua's pastor also inserted Protestant Christian messages between each socialist step during his facilitation. As such, whereas the key elements of memorial meetings remained (including the socialist narratives in the work unit's memorial speech and the bereaved's thank-you speech), these were surrounded by a new, explicitly religious, and more aggressive framework. Such a reframing attempt was meant to change the base of commemoration from socialism to Christianity, albeit without removing socialism. This reframing was possible because the Protestant pastor was the emcee.

Whom the emcee was turned out to be much more important than it might at first appear. Before the decline of the work unit in daily life in Shanghai, work units and not families organized memorial meetings. As such, the work unit assigned its person as the emcee. This practice was consistent with the popularization of memorial meetings that resulted from the Cultural Revolution rehabilitation rituals. In fact, even at the beginning of marketization, state practitioners working in meeting halls were only in charge of meeting hall maintenance. One practitioner told me that when she worked in meeting halls in 1999, she took care of six halls. She mainly cleaned them up after meetings. However, by the time of my fieldwork, she took care of only one hall, was the default emcee for each funeral (unless a broker was involved), and no longer needed to clean up the meeting hall.[2] Today, the norm is for funeral professionals to be emcees.

When funeral professionals acted as emcees, they did not talk much. They said only enough to facilitate the memorial meeting by explicitly directing participants when to speak, bow, or walk around the coffin. However, when pastors were emcees, they not only spoke volumes but were also able to reframe memorial meetings through their performance. John, a pastor from a different Protestant church, told me specifically that by being an emcee, pastors could "encase the original framing [kuangjia] of memorial meetings with Protestantism." He told me that the ideal situation for Protestant memorial meetings was for the deceased's pastor to be the emcee. By being emcees, pastors were able to insert Christianity to encase the original secular socialist framing.

Why, then, was it so important for pastors to reframe the memorial meetings they emceed? It turned out that it was all because of proselytization. Being the emcee allowed the pastor to carry out a conversion sermon in memorial meetings. Pastor John said that, for Protestants, memorial meetings had three primary goals: "The first [goal] is to commemorate the deceased. The second is to console the bereaved. The third is to proselytize [chuanfuyin]." John was from one of the Three Self Churches (Sanzi jiaohui) in Shanghai—a state-authorized Protestant church. According to John, this meant that his congregation was less evangelical than the family churches then growing rapidly in the areas around Shanghai. However, although he represented a less evangelical church, John told me in no uncertain terms that proselytizing often ended up being the most important goal of having a Protestant version of a socialist funeral. John explained that Protestant memorial meetings were for the living. If the deceased had converted to Christianity when alive, having a Protestant memorial meeting would not influence their salvation. By the same token, if the bereaved organized an idolatrous or other non-Protestant ritual for the deceased, they could not "undo" their salvation. The deceased's salvation solely depended on their individual relationship with God. Because what the bereaved did (or did not do) could not affect the deceased's relationship with God, proselytizing to the living became the primary goal.

The move toward proselytizing is critical to analyzing the Protestant version of memorial meetings for two reasons. First, this move indicated a transition from only adding a preface and appendix toward a complete rewrite of the book of socialism and a replacement of it with Christianity. For the preface-appendix type of religious variations of socialist rituals, the deceased was conceptualized as a socialist citizen first and then as a religious and relational subject. Both the preface and appendix added to the socialist core had significantly restricted audiences limited to family and close friends of the deceased. The Protestant version cared less about the preface and appendix precisely because these parts included fewer potential converts. In rewriting the socialist book, the work unit's memorial speech (and the family's thank-you speech) became one more speech submerged into a proper Protestant Christian narrative of conceptualizing person, death, and salvation.

Meanwhile, proselytizing marked a shift from treating ritual as a public statement of accepting social convention to treating it as personal testimony about who the deceased was, what the bereaved should think and feel about who the deceased was, and, eventually, who the bereaved should be. Unlike other religious versions of memorial meetings, the Protestant variation strived to ensure that funeral participants received and understood the message of the ritual in correct ways and, thus, could act accordingly. Just committing to social convention was no longer enough; proselytizing required people to move in a way that allowed them to understand the words and actions and to be inspired to believe and achieve salvation. The mere commitment to social convention externally defeated the purpose of proselytizing. The goal of a Protestant socialist funeral was to convert and turn ritual participants into authentic and sincere subjects whose socialist identity was submerged into their religious identity.

Social Conflicts

What then are some of the social consequences of transforming ritual from being a public statement to a personal testimony? In many memorial meetings, a sensible tension existed between Christian and non-Christian attendees, between the pastor and the work unit representatives, or between attendees expecting a fifteen- to twenty-minute meeting and the pastor speaking for close to an hour. We saw these tensions at Ma Donghua's memorial meeting. When the eldest son called me over and told me to ask the pastor to stop preaching, doing so was certainly a breach of etiquette. In this case, this breach of etiquette did not turn into an actual conflict. However, the tension inherent in the Protestant memorial meeting sometimes did lead to real arguments. Let me relate one such incident that Chen Yu told me about.

At this funeral, the deceased was both a scholar and a Communist Party member. Following his wife's earlier conversion to Protestantism, he himself had a deathbed conversion. None of his children were Christian. As Chen Yu told the story to me, "When people are on their deathbed, they listen to anything." After he died, his children arranged a Protestant memorial meeting based on his final wishes. He passed away at the age of sixty-one, a relatively young age that meant some people in his former work unit still personally knew the deceased. Because he had been relatively young and influential, many people from his work unit came to the memorial meeting, including the leaders of the work unit. When the work unit people arrived and realized that the memorial meeting would be a Protestant one, they could not accept that format and insisted that the funeral professional, not the pastor, be the emcee. They said that the pastor could say whatever he wanted after the memorial meeting (i.e., how people who practiced Buddhism or popular religion carried out their religious ceremonies). The funeral professionals listened but refused to take a stance, stating instead that they had to do what the bereaved—as their customers—wanted.

Not being appointed emcee and only talking after the meeting was an unacceptable option for proselytizing because those who stay afterward were either already fellow Christians or people to whom the church already had access (such as the bereaved's immediate family). Therefore, the pastor refused the suggestion, saying that it was the deceased's wish for him to be the emcee. The work unit people became angry and replied that the deceased had been a Communist Party member his entire life. He was an atheist! He believed in Communism and not Jesus! He converted to Christianity because he was old and ill and vulnerable. The church people had tricked him.

At the beginning of the quarrel, the children of the deceased were not sure what to do because their father's wish was to have a Protestant memorial meeting. However, the work unit people then said that if the pastor was the emcee, all but one of them would leave. This remaining person would be the lowest-ranking member, and he would read the memorial speech. Additionally, the bereaved should also not even think about getting their father's funeral expenses reimbursed (Shanghai people usually received some reimbursement from the deceased's work unit). Whereas the threat of not providing funeral reimbursement was more about venting their frustrations, the work unit people nevertheless were warning the bereaved about the potential (and potentially deliberately caused) difficulties in handling money matters that could arise if they allowed the pastor to be the emcee. When the bereaved realized how serious the situation could become, they changed their minds. In the end, the work unit won. A state practitioner was the emcee at this funeral.

This incident was not an isolated case. Pastor John also told me that the most likely type of conflict in Protestant memorial meetings was between work unit and church. John said that, in the past, when this Protestant version of memorial meetings was first allowed in funeral parlors after the Opening Up, frequent conflicts occurred between the church and the bereaved's family because, as mentioned, conversion in Shanghai often happened at an individual instead of a household level. Back then, occasionally overly enthusiastic Protestant follow-ers attempted to perform a Christian service during a Protestant's funeral with-out obtaining the family's permission in advance, or they only received permission from one descendant when the deceased had several children (re-call the parallels here to the negotiation work of Funeral Reform in practice). Such a situation could spark serious incidents, including physical fights. After a few incidents, John's congregation decided to host only those funerals where the bereaved (and not just the deceased) invited them and to require the bereaved to first reach a consensus. Understandably, John's congregation made such a move because he belongs to one of the state-sanctioned churches. This new pol-icy removed the potential for conflict between the church and the family but still left the possibility of tension with work units.

Conclusion

In the previous two chapters, I described how Shanghai residents not only have decided to keep memorial meetings that memorialize everyone as model social-ist citizen but have also created seemingly paradoxical religious variations out of this secular and civil funeral. This was possible because they transformed me-morial meetings into a modular frame. This was done primarily by what I call a preface-appendix approach to create religious versions of secular socialist funer-als. For people who followed this preface-appendix approach, they tended to treat participation in rituals as a public statement of adhering to social conven-tion. When seeing ritual under this light, it matters less when there are funda-mental inconsistencies between different values in one ritual. This tolerance for ambiguity allows for differences of interpretation, belief, and practice to remain beneath their common actions. This common action, framed safely but produc-tively within a ritual world, allows incommensurable ideas to be commensura-ble and therefore also enables people to live with value inconsistencies and even alterity. As Robbins (2014) has said, it is exactly because these differences are ad-dressed in ritual that value pluralism is possible.

Building on these discussions, this chapter shows that some Protestants started to adopt a rewriting approach in their attempts to transform memorial meetings into a modular form. While the preface-appendix approach attaches religious-value-infused ritual practices either before or after memorial meetings, the rewriting approach reframes memorial meetings with religious and relational rituals. On the surface, while the former is more likely to appear in folk religious and Buddhist versions of memorial meetings and the latter is more likely to ap-pear in Protestant versions, this need not necessarily be the case. What matters here is that people who have adopted the rewriting approach tend to treat rituals as making a personal statement of who they are, what they believe, or as a mean to cultivate a desired internal state of being, feeling, and belief in participants. In other words, this view on ritual invokes a need to make sure that values revealed in rituals are somehow consistent with values outside of it. This view propels participants to pursue the world of as is. With this view on what ritual is (and should be), then what people perform in ritual, even if it is still only an idealized image, now needs to reflect the values they hold internally (or at least that they aspire to). Consequently, the idea that participating in rituals is merely about following external social conventions then becomes a target of moral condemnation for being insincere or inauthentic, if not outright hypocritical.

While both the preface-appendix and rewriting techniques allow value pluralism, the former gives more space for pluralism. We see such evidence especially based on the fact that the rewrite approach leads to more social conflict. This is because once people view ritual as a personal testimony, when the incommensurable values are dealt with within ritual, their differences need to be identified and hierarchized. As such, secular socialist citizenship, Confucian hierarchical motherhood, folk ideas of ancestors, and Christianity can be commensurable as long as the dead are constructed as Protestant first. When ritual becomes a site of personal testimony, the space available for ambiguity is diminished.

Ironically, while the Protestant version of memorial meetings with their reframing technique was more successful in confronting socialism and creating a measure of structural change in the ritual forms, this Protestant version also ended up moving closer to the very same type of thing that the high socialist version of the memorial meeting was—that is, the rewrite approach seeks a singular definition of person and death. As the recent history of memorial meetings has unfolded, Protestantism and high socialism have been alike in sharing the same vision of subject formation. In their respective imaginations of idealized ritual worlds, incommensurable values have to become commensurable through either silencing or hierarchizing the competing voices. In this sense, it was the modular preface-appendix approach that was the more radical; though it left the socialist memorial meeting itself relatively untouched, it spoke to the very different possibility of people holding multiple, simultaneous, and sometimes contradictory ethics. Whereas both Protestantism and socialism were most powerful in terms of changing and challenging the normative structures, they nonetheless narrowed the possibility for pluralism and pluralist subjectivity.

CONCLUSION

I began my fieldwork armed with an expectation that I would observe the rise of personalized funerals that commemorated the dead as market subjects and the revival of traditional death rituals that commemorated the dead as religious and relational subjects. While these expectations were based on a series of scholarly works on contemporary China, they also emerged out of scholars' contrasting epistemological positions on what subjects are and, therefore, how a subject becomes a subject. Scholars who emphasized the competition between market governance and authoritarianism tended to paint a picture of the triumph of individuals and the possibilities for liberal democracy under such an emerging market economy. Meanwhile, those who stressed the commensurability between market governance and authoritarianism pointed instead to the triumph of an authoritarianism that sustained market governance and market subjectivity. The former were more likely to echo a humanistic approach to subjectivity while the latter were more likely to echo a (post)structuralist view of subjectivity.

What I have done in this book is to trace the diversified trajectories of subject formation for funeral professionals, the bereaved, and dead bodies by treating these processes like "rhizomes" (Deleuze and Guattari 1987) in which the nodes that power flows through provide a perspective through which to see both governance and subject formation. Specifically, by identifying the circumstances under which more resonant or dissonant relationships between subjectivity and governance have developed, I trace how there were a range of possibilities both for subjects acting as agents and for them to become subjected to normative power. By identifying the intended and unintended consequences that developed between individuals and structures within which they were situated, I identify four trends in contemporary China.

Firstly, market governance did not necessarily produce market subjectivity. We see this clearly in my analysis of state practitioners as well as the funeral parlors' failure to promote personalized funerals. For state practitioners, funeral parlors attempted to transform state practitioners from being government officials responsible for implementing policies to being entrepreneurs who were self-motivated, risk-taking, and profit-seeking individuals. However, in practice, grassroots state practitioners instead became working-class subjects capable of initiating class-based action. Such dissonance between the market governance of death and market subjectivity existed because state practitioners, as members of a work unit in Shanghai, had personal or institutional memories of initiating collective actions. As such, ironically, although the state was purposefully trying to turn state practitioners into market subjects, the fact that they worked for the state allowed them to resist this governing power.

Regarding ordinary residents of Shanghai, officials wanted to cultivate the bereaved and the dead as market subjects by encouraging a new way of conceptualizing the dead—one that commemorated the deceased as unique individuals. However, neither state practitioners nor the bereaved were interested in such personalized funerals. This was because the marketization of death was so successful that profiteering had already become one of the main frameworks for understanding the funeral industry in China. As such, unconventional suggestions by funeral professionals, including promoting personalized funerals, were treated by the public as attempts to earn exorbitant profits. As it turned out, the deepening of the market economy did not necessarily entail a desire for or even the rise of market subjects. In fact, in this case, what happened was quite the opposite. The profit-making aspects of marketization prevented, rather than facilitated, the cultivation of market subjects.

Secondly, fragility is one condition of possibility for the creation of market subjectivity under authoritarian market economies. Private funeral brokers were fragile because they were socially marginal people in two senses. The first was related to their demographic characteristics, such as their educational level and migrant status. The second was related to the fact that they were self-employed individuals or working in small household businesses within the Shanghai funeral industry. These fragile people were morally ambiguous because there was little room or means for them to run their businesses, let alone demand for political and legal changes, other than by pushing the moral and legal boundaries of social norms under this authoritarian regime. As a result, private funeral brokers became self-managing market subjects even though the state had actively discouraged and disciplined such cultivation of entrepreneurship. At a structural level, this morally ambiguous fragility played a crucial role in creating structural change. With their edge-ball playing as a means to carve out areas beyond the parlor's control for their businesses, funeral brokers created a platform for religious morality to reenter contemporary urban death rituals that had earlier been solely defined by secularism and socialism.

Thirdly, as market governance became commensurable with authoritarianism in contemporary China, the potential for challenging authoritarianism came to exist not in market action or capital accumulation but in formalized, conventional, and repetitive ritualized acts. As described, instead of giving up memorial meetings and embracing personalized funerals as the state desired after the introduction of the market governance of death, the vast majority of people in Shanghai preferred to continue to perform memorial meetings. The fact that this happened in the context of externalized, standardized, repetitive, formalized, and conventional acts is important because the discrepancy between the reality of living under a market economy and the idealized socialist world as revealed in ritual shows that performing ritualized acts created dissonance. Ritual thus does not merely affirm or re-create the social. This ritually created dissonance, however, was not resistance. Rather, such dissonance momentarily denaturalizes reality by recognizing the complexity of everyday life and the irony of presenting an idealized and simplified socialist rhetoric. Because the authoritarian state itself promoted market governance, one possibility for questioning the state came to be expressed not by embracing capitalist or liberal democratic values but by clinging to time-honored socialist rituals. Moreover, as China has strengthened its authoritarian rule in silencing liberal voices in the years since my fieldwork ended, the most likely space to express discontent toward the state has come to exist in people's realization of how the CCP's promised utopia of equality has been broken. Just as nationalism is a double-edged sword for the Chinese state, socialist rituals, too, are like water—they can carry as well as overturn the boat.

The final trend I wish to highlight here is about the relationship between pluralist subjectivity and particular perceptions of ritual. I have shown here how the more people saw ritual as following externalized social convention, the more likely it was they could live with seemingly contradictory ideas of persons. Conversely, the more people treated ritual as personal statements expressing authenticity and sincerity, the less likely it was for them to live with alterity. This is because the desire and effort to express who the deceased truly was and what the deceased truly believed propelled people to rework incommensurable ideas and, thus, to notice their contradictions. As such, the conditions of possibility for pluralist subjectivity lay less in the meaning or content of ritual. Rather, plu-

ralist subjectivity was rather more dependent on the degree to which people
viewed rituals as shared social convention.

As a whole, my findings challenge the analytical framework of neoliberalism
for analyzing subject formation both inside and outside Sinophone studies. From
David Harvey's (2005) description of "neoliberalism with Chinese characteristics," to Li Zhang and Aihwa Ong's (2008) reference to "neoliberalism as technologies of self-subjectification," and to Wendy Brown's (2015, 21) definition of
"neoliberalism" as "a distinctive mode of reason, of the production of subjects,
a 'conduct of conduct,' and a scheme of valuation," many scholars have argued
that there has been a rise of neoliberalism and, through it, the production of neoliberal subjects. While the application of the "neoliberalism" label directly to
China has been contested in a political-economic sense due to the absence of
state deregulation in socialist China's market transition (Kipnis 2007; Nonini
2008), many scholars have continued to use neoliberalism in an ethical sense to
analyze the subject formation process in contemporary China (Hoffman 2006;
Rofel 2007).

Just as the political-economic version of neoliberalism is a sometimes subtly
odd fit for contemporary China due to its quite different starting position and
"transition" process, the ethical version too begins differently. As I describe in
the first chapters, the much earlier transition to socialism in cities was already
very much a policy of individualization as governance measures sought to remove the horizontal and alternative links between people and replace them with
a singular connection between autonomous individuals and the party-state.
With the shift from high socialism toward market governance, what some take
as a neoliberal turn, governance did indeed aim to introduce an idea of market
subjects. And yet, at this very time, we also see the dissonant ways that subject
formation occurred on the ground for funeral practitioners and the way funeral
brokers who did shift in resonance with this policy made room for the re-
introduction of relational and religious (i.e., nonautonomous individuals) ideas
of self alongside an autonomous but also ethically socialist (rather than market)
self enacted in the choice to maintain memorial meetings at the ritual center of
the funeral. Overall, trends one to three, as presented throughout the book, thus
challenge the claim that the CCP's pursuit of economic efficiency necessarily sub-
jugated individuals into self-enterprising subjects, as studies framed in terms of
neoliberalism and governmentality often have suggested. This look at the self at
the time of death also strongly suggests that the emergence of individualism in
China under marketization may have been overly generalized if not overstated.

This is not, then, to say that market governance in China is completely unrelated to ethical neoliberalism but rather that an approach that allows us to highlight the differences that make a difference is crucial for understanding the

contribution that China-based ethnographies can make to this theoretical perspective and its neighbors. Along this line, the concept of fragility developed in this book complements the concept of precarity that is usually associated with (late?) liberal democracies. In studies of neoliberalism that focus on the way that neoliberalism creates neoliberal market subjects, many scholars have discussed the role of precarity as produced in these new economic forms and productive of new forms of subjects (Allison 2013). By pointing out how the logic of authoritarian market governance works and the critical differences between the introduction of neoliberal-similar policies in liberal democracies and contemporary Chinese authoritarian market socialism, I show that we can better understand the formation of market subjects under authoritarian regimes by focusing on fragility, its moral ambiguity, and its productivity in creating structural change.

Finally, my use of ritually constructed subjectivity demonstrates the possibility of having self-reflexivity and normative structures at the same time in analyzing subject formation processes. This is because rituals are neither inside human minds nor inside structures (however structures are defined). It is in ritual where individuals act and feel—things that are critical to human agency as well as to the structural shaping processes of the subjectification of individuals. Far from ritual being an "empty" manifestation of social expectations or irrelevant to ideas of self, rituals and death rituals in particular are key sites of subject formation. The historical making of rituals gives a means of seeing their construction at the intersection of governance, political economy, the desires of participants (especially the hosts or, here, the bereaved), and especially of the (here, fragile) agency of the ritual experts who run them. From the ethnographies of the rituals as enacted then, we set on a fertile site to see the ritual framing techniques and enactment efforts of finalizing a public sense of the self of the deceased as well as, in their participation, a temporary redefinition of the self of participants. Perhaps most importantly, the concept of ritually constructed subjectivity is a means by which we might rethink the role of ritual and its role in creating pluralist subjectivity.

To sum up, by tracing the way different logics of power flowed through a variety of nodes of power, the concepts of resonance and dissonance allow us to explore both intended and unintended consequences in subject formation. The result of such explorations is a reevaluation of existing scholarly works on subject formation in contemporary China—an era that has been marked by the power of the market; socialist moral discourses of equality, sameness, and self-sacrifice; nationalism and patriotism; authoritarianism; and reciprocal exchange. Death rituals and their constructions of self are particularly productive because it is in death where the living (re-)create new identities of and for the dead in heterogeneous and interconnected ways.

The New Chinese Way of Death

On May 28, 2014, the *New York Times* journalist Didi Kirsten Tatlow published an article on the rumors that at least six elders committed suicide in Anqing City in Anhui Province after the Anqing Civil Affairs Bureau announced its determination to implement Funeral and Interment Reform in that small city. The rumors suggested that the suicides were precipitated after the local government confiscated the coffins that the elders had prepared (purchasing one's own coffin before you die has long been a customary practice for the elderly in many parts of China) as a first strike at enforcing mandatory cremation. This news article reported that the suicides were a way to both protest the changes and to get into their coffins and graves before the change went into effect. On August 2, 2018, four years later, a different *New York Times* journalist, Austin Ramzy, reported on how thousands of confiscated coffins and an exhumed corpses stoked fury in China because of the implementation of Funeral Reform in recent years.

These events are significant reminders that Funeral Reform, as I describe its history in Shanghai, was in no way a mere remnant of the past. As I've presented my work in a variety of forums since my fieldwork, I have repeatedly encountered people (both scholars and laypeople) who tell me that what I observed in Shanghai funeral parlors might simply be the result of the "fact" that funerals are "always the last thing to change" in any given society. According to this view, it was only a matter of time before people in Shanghai would move away from memorial meetings and their "paleosocialist" narratives and toward either individualist or religious memorialization. The assumption behind this prediction was the belief that the market economy either creates market subjects who are self-managing entrepreneurs (and, thus, leads to the desire for a personalized funeral) or somehow that the market is the antithesis of the authoritarian socialist state (and, thus, people would move toward having religious [antiatheist] death rituals). History, however, has not unfolded along either of these two lines. Indeed, officials high in the various Shanghai funeral bureaus often told me they saw Shanghai as on the cutting edge of reform, an example that would soon be followed by second-tier and third-tier cities as well. Funeral Reform has continued to be enacted in more and more places. It seems that soon I may no longer need to convince people that the Funeral Reform policies and memorial meetings belong to both the past and the present and are still evolving. The ways that the people of Shanghai managed death and performed death rituals during my fieldwork were contemporary responses to the economic reforms (albeit informed by historical realities), wherein state institutions have had to earn profits, boundaries of moralities have been contested, and different ideas of self flow in and out regardless of the apparently archaic appearance of these rituals. Memorial meetings might appear to be paleosocialist, especially considering the decline of work units since the introduction of economic reforms and especially to younger Chinese who have not yet had the misfortune of having to attend many funerals. However, the meaning of this commemoration and what this type of ritual did within society were rarely only socialist. Rather, they held very different meanings and outcomes depending on when and how these rituals were performed. In this sense, death rituals have changed rapidly over time. Funerals might not be the first thing to change, but certainly they also were not the last, especially given the intensity to which the Chinese government has historically privileged governance focused on funeral policies. Regardless of how invariant death rituals might appear to be, they change similar to other aspects of daily life at the intersectional nodes of a variety of agencies and a variety of structures of normative power.

I would like to end this book by proposing three possible directions for future studies on the anthropology of death in general and for Sinophone studies in particular. The first direction is about the technology of dead bodies. During my fieldwork, I observed two seemingly counterintuitive trends in the Shanghai funeral industry. The first was to explore more economical and environmentally efficient ways to handle human remains, such as condensing cremains into a ring or inventing a special fluid to entirely eliminate (dissolve) dead bodies. The second was to develop more humanistic and compassionate ways to handle dead bodies, such as providing special hair or spa treatments for the dead. Although both treated the materiality of dead bodies as the primary focus, the former aimed to erase corpses, whereas the latter hoped to extend the "life" of dead bodies. Biological death creates dead bodies that need to be taken care of regardless of the sociocultural contexts in which we conduct our research. I believe that studies in the realm of dead body technologies (including the attempts at being antitechnological) will further scholarly discussions on the facts of death.

Such a discussion on dead body management perhaps becomes even more important in the era of COVID-19. COVID-19 and its impact on death constitute probably one of the most urgent areas awaiting scholarly attention in the near future, not just in China but also in the world. A news article about death during the global pandemic in China from Reuters was titled, "No Farewells, No Ceremonies," on March 29, 2020. Prior to the outbreak of COVID-19, the bereaved would have to use cremains in funerals when the cause of death was one of a few specifically legally defined contagious diseases. The 2003 SARS outbreak established this policy in Shanghai. While open-casket funerals were more prestigious, a funeral with cremains could still be a proper memorial meeting as long as a representative from the deceased's work unit was present. However, because these deaths happened during the peak of COVID-19, the bereaved could not have any form of public commemoration since in-person gatherings were banned. This state of prohibition on memorialization recalls Master Gao's explanation of how Shanghai people did not know what to do in funerals once the Cultural Revolution began: he said that people could just "take a look and have a cry." Deaths that occurred at the peak of COVID-19 in China would not even have had this.

Consequently, although probably unintentionally, death under COVID-19 has become strangely similar to the politically problematic deaths that happened during the Cultural Revolution. In this kind of death, surviving family members could not have any form of public memorialization. Rubie Watson (1994) published a powerful article to describe how people used public mourning for political leaders as sites to mourn for their unmourned personal losses. In fact, for politically problematic deaths, it was not uncommon for the family members of those who were accused as counterrevolutionaries to find out about the death only after they were notified to claim cremains. As I discussed, this was why memorial meetings as a particular form of civil commemoration came to be used for political rehabilitation. As such, how will the living construct the self of those who died from COVID-19, if given that opportunity at all? Will we see further deritualization from this as the CCP's long-standing policy has hoped? Or, instead, will we see the revival of death rituals and of commemorations well after the fact of death? If this is the case, then will the bereaved have a stronger desire to construct the dead as individuals, socialist citizen subjects, religious subjects, relational subjects, or something else? In what ways will the politics around the pandemic's origins and China's early response affect the space available for such postdeath rituals and the form that they take? Moving outward, how did the pandemic change the relationship between individuals and the socialist state in relation to funeral professionals, the bereaved, and the dead? While we have seen sporadic news about funeral parlors coming from China, especially in Wuhan, where the initial big outbreak was located, scholars both within and beyond China's borders know very little, as of yet, about what happened on the ground.

A second possible direction to further explore concerns the power of the margins and the condition of fragility. In my research, I found that changes were not only initiated and implemented by powers at the center—in terms of both the original Funeral Reform efforts and in the decision to marketize funeral parlors during China's entrance into its market economy—but were also instigated and emerged in particular ways by and through powers at the margin, that is, private funeral brokers. Their fragile and marginal position showed how social change was neither a top-down nor a bottom-up process alone. Instead, certain social fields, including this kind of fragile middle, were caused by marginality similar to a node at which multiple, sometimes contradictory forces (including the brokers' own desires and personal innovations) moved in and out to make change happen. This is a keen reminder to all of us that social change toward more tolerance and diversity—and even change makers under authoritarian regimes—need not necessarily be inherently "liberal" or even "moral." Under specific circumstances, the best candidate to take down the hero may not be either Hercules or David but Eric Hobsbawm's (1969) bandits.

The third direction I suggest meriting further exploration is the directionality of cultural change and its relation to urbanization, perhaps the most important for studies of the People's Republic of China. Using the management of death and death rituals as examples, from Shanghai funeral professionals' perspective, Shanghai funeral rituals and funeral parlors are the future, not the past, of Chinese death ritual and the Chinese funeral industry. This statement is consistent with urbanization theorists who often see cultural change starting in urban centers and then dispersing outward to urban peripheries and rural societies. Meanwhile, studies on religious revival, at least in China and under the particularities of its selective governance, have made a case for the opposite directionality in cultural change. These scholars have observed many cases where religious and ritual revivals first started in rural societies (and usually remained more active there). Some of these religious trends then continue to spread to the urban periphery and then even to urban centers, while others might never leave rural territories. Either way, such contradictory views on change and urbanization show how death, death ritual, and dead bodies provide good sites for determining how culture changes between rural and urban areas, the manner in which such changes occur, and the sorts of consequences these changes entail in practice for the people in those places and their sense of self.

I began this book with the story of Prosperity, a funeral banquet restaurant that worshiped Chairman Mao, the said inventor of memorial meetings and the patron god of this restaurant. The story of Prosperity as a whole is a fitting fable for the complications of death ritual in urban China and the Shanghai funeral industry because it is an intriguing combination of atheist Mao as the only god able to control his martyred ghost followers, of a capitalist banquet business combined with Communist soldiers' spirits, and of competition between state funeral parlors and private funeral brokers. As an ethnography of funeral governance, this book has sought to disentangle the ways that changes in political, economic, and ritual structures of death interact with subject-formation processes. If dying socialist in "capitalist" Shanghai teaches us anything, then, it is the significance of attention paid to what happens in the middle, to the concepts of resonance and dissonance in understanding the interplay between subjectivity and governance.

Notes

1. CIVIL GOVERNANCE

1. Whereas guanqidian operated as full-time businesses, hongbaigang were more "amateur" in the sense that many people who worked there worked only part-time as carriers.

2. This type of organization was also very common in other urban areas and centers for international migrations. As Elizabeth Sinn (2003) describes, one of the original high-level organizations of Chinese residents in British colonial Hong Kong with any power was that of the Tung Wah Group of Hospitals that oversaw (as charity work) the receipt of coffins that were returning their residents home from living and working abroad.

3. In this document, page one contained the table of contents for this speech. According to the document, the first part of the talk was meant to summarize work done in 1959. The second part was to discuss the plan for 1960. The third part was a work evaluation based on work done in January and February of 1960.

4. Mao's vision of a socialist revolution was to overcome the barriers of "objective reality" through individual and, therefore, "subjective" efforts of the masses. The difference between "subjective" and "objective," in Chinese socialist jargon, is more similar to the difference between "social structure" and "individual agency" than that between "subjective" and "objective" in anthropology or social science.

5. Digging up coffins and converting cemeteries also happened before the Cultural Revolution in Shanghai. For example, the Shanghai Civil Affairs Bureau submitted a report to its supervising institution and a carbon copy to the rural committee of Shanghai on October 24, 1961. This report stated that, as early as the mid-1950s, a number of the FIA's charity cemeteries were converted to farmland by rural production brigades without the FIA's approval. At the time of this writing, a rural production brigade had just converted more than sixty mu into farmland, with only six mu remaining untouched. Moreover, "in the spring, peasants even dig out coffins to use them [their wood] to repair their houses, pig houses, or sheep houses. What is even worse is that the peasants do not even bury those bodies again afterward, so the bodies are left on the ground. Local residents are very upset" (Shanghai Civil Affairs Bureau 1961).

6. The Revolutionary Committee of the Municipality of Shanghai was the highest party and government authority between February 23, 1967, and December 1979.

2. MARKET GOVERNANCE

1. Among these county-level crematoria in Shanghai, five earned a profit and the remaining ten were at least barely able to balance their books. The exchange rate in 1983 was 1:2.61 USD to RMB, according to the World Bank's annual middle exchange rate for the US dollar to the Chinese yuan. The chart was accessed at "List of Renminbi Exchange Rates," Wikipedia, last edited November 9, 2021, http://en.wikipedia.org/wiki /List_of_renminbi_ exchange_rates.

2. Together, they earned RMB 9,430,000 (USD 3,367,857) in profit. The other 77 percent of crematoria lost a total of RMB 26,740,000 (USD 9,550,000). This exchange rate was based on 1:2.8 USD to RMB in 1984.

3. The exchange rate was 1:2.46 USD to RMB that year.

4. After Longhua Crematorium became its own financial unit, the Shanghai government designated RMB 315,000 (USD 128,048) as its annual budget to support its regular functions. This exchange rate was based on 1:2.48 USD to RMB from 1967.

5. In 1975, the exchange rate was 1:1.85 USD to RMB.

6. In that year, Longhua's annual income was RMB 913,200 (USD 493,621), and its total year's costs were RMB 751,490 (USD 406,210). In 1976, its profit rose to RMB 197,150 on RMB 862,740 of annual income. In 1977, its total income increased again to RMB 938,810.

7. Just to give a basis for understanding the meaning of these prices at that time, I provide numbers on funeral practitioners' income. In 1978, Longhua spent a total of approximately RMB 120,000 (USD 48,780) for personnel, including 162 employees. Their average salary was RMB 62.69 (USD 25) per month, meaning that renting a medium-sized meeting hall cost two-thirds of the monthly salary of a state practitioner working in a crematorium who received an average salary. Renting a large hall for half a day cost 40 RMB.

8. The Funeral Service Department here included the funeral service providing units, such as the cremation unit, the meeting hall unit, and the body transportation unit.

9. Longhua adopted several new business management methods between 1981 and 1984 as a prelude to introducing a contract responsibility system officially from the beginning of 1985.

10. Of them, 23 percent were women, and 68 percent were young people.

11. In 1986, the exchange rate was 1:3.45 USD to RMB.

12. In fact, the *Revised Mandarin Chinese Dictionary*, published by the Ministry of Education in Taiwan, specifically addressed the meaning of *tuochan* as leaving direct production jobs in China but not in Taiwan. See *Revised Mandarin Chinese Dictionary*, s.v., "tuochan," accessed March 10, 2017, http://dict.revised.moe.edu.tw/cgi-bin/cbdic/gsweb.cgi.

13. See *Cidian* [Dictionary], s.v. touchan, accessed July 8, 2014, http://cidian.xpcha.com/98568ebdu4u.html. Another online dictionary based in the PRC listed three meanings: (1) to transfer (production to other duties), (2) to take leave (for study or another job), (3) to dispose of property, and (4) to transfer assets (to avoid liability). See Chinese English Pinyin Dictionary, s.v., accessed April 8, 2022, https://chinese.yabla.com/chinese-english-pinyin-dictionary.php?define=tuochan.

14. The movement of urban youth to the countryside started as early as the 1950s. In 1962, this movement became nationally organized. This massive urban-to-rural migration reached a peak between 1966 and 1968.

15. At that time, nearly all jobs in China were assigned by the state, and there was no way to "apply" for just any job. Although theoretically this meant that everyone was assigned a position, sometimes positions did not become available for quite some time.

16. In terms of administrative category, FIS is a *shiye danwei* (public nonprofit unit), like funeral parlors, whereas the FIA/FIBA remained a *xingzheng danwei* (government bureau). Shiye danwei is a unique administrative category in China. Although many shiye danwei were converted into *qiye danwei* (private enterprises) when China adopted a market economy, funeral parlors (and FIS, for that matter) retained their shiye danwei status.

17. There is some linguistic irony here. In Taiwan, *xiahai* means "becoming a prostitute."

18. The tensions between the Religious Affairs Bureau and the Civil Affairs Bureau over the nationalization of the crematorium at Haihui Temple from chapter 1 provide another good example of this.

19. The list comprised (in order) real estate, elementary and middle school education, funeral and interment, publishing, automobile, glasses, telecommunication and

mobile phones, pharmaceuticals, studying abroad, and the online game industry. See http://finance.sina.com.cn/g/20040102/1440587719.shtml, accessed April 8, 2022.

20. Private entities can and do now own and operate cemeteries and funeral-related companies.

3. THE FRAGILE MIDDLE

1. These numbers were based on personal communications with state practitioners, including people on the ground and at the managerial level. Baoxin was located on the north side of Shanghai proper, whereas Longhua was on the south side. Because the neighborhood areas around Baoxin were more working-class, and those around Longhua were more middle- or upper-middle-class, class differences existed between the two parlors' customers.

2. In 2006, the trade association held its first annual training session for Shanghai funeral brokers and, in that year, gave licenses to seventeen funeral agencies (Mao 2006). In 2010, seventy-four agencies with 848 brokers joined the training, and each received a license. When I attended the training in 2011, there were ninety companies with 978 brokers. According to the head of FIS, this was the first time that there were more licensed funeral brokers than state funeral practitioners in Shanghai.

3. I have not put scare quotation marks here because he obviously did not feel that it was problematic to call such traditions superstitions. After all, there is no other vernacular term for popular religion.

4. Some officials believed that it was important to separate "superstition" (*mixin*) from "custom" (fengsu xiguan). Regarding how to make such a distinction, one scholar told me that many products sold on Funeral Avenue, such as "spiritual cash," paper-made TVs, paper security guards and maids, and paper houses, all meant to be burned to the deceased in the afterlife, were superstitious items, but xibo was not because it was traditional. Xibo were folded tinfoil papers that were also meant to be burned for the deceased's use in the afterlife and an important ritual object in popular religion in China.

4. INDIVIDUALISM, INTERRUPTED

1. According to my friends in the funeral profession, rumor had it that Zhou chose cremation and the scattering of his cremains because he was worried about what Mao might do to his body or cremains. Some friends even told me that Zhou's family secretly kept the last bit of his cremains and stored them in the Zhou Enlai Memorial Hall in Huai'an, Jiangsu. Huai'an was Zhou's hometown.

2. Officials told me that the first revolution happened between 1954 and 1982. In 1954, the FIA began to promote cremation, and 1982 was the year in which the Duhang Crematorium was built. This rural district was the last in Shanghai to have a crematorium.

3. Many of the same people who are supposed to persuade Shanghai people to give up keeping cremains, however, have been enthusiastically facilitating the dramatic flourishing of columbaria and cremains cemeteries since the marketization of death in the early 1980s. They did so because these places generated significant profit.

4. The story of the Ding family is a combination of two families whose business meetings I observed with funeral practitioners. The phone call occurred when I did an overnight shift with Li Shan. The face-to-face business meeting was one of the many business meetings that I observed during the day (face-to-face meetings only occurred in the daytime), when I did most of my fieldwork. Although representativeness is often not anthropologists' main concern, both cases described were fairly representative of the cases I saw throughout my time in the parlor. I have merged these into one case to give readers a more

coherent sense of how funerals were arranged between state funeral practitioners and the bereaved in Shanghai in general.

5. This phone number now is reserved for FIS's "private" funeral agency. FIS established its own funeral agency to compete more directly with private funeral brokers.

6. Taking one parlor as an example, its janitors, cooks, and security guards had different sets of uniforms. As far as I know, this parlor outsourced its janitorial and security guard jobs to different companies. Therefore, these people did not belong to this parlor and technically were not funeral practitioners.

7. I spent time at several funeral parlors in Shanghai. They each had their own lists. For example, Baoxin Funeral Parlor provided a list of fifty-eight couplets from which to choose. Bao Shan District Funeral Parlor provided a list of twelve choices. I have translated Longhua Funeral Parlor's list here.

8. In fact, Muslims in China did not use coffins when performing burials. This incorrect information was repeated frequently at the time I did my fieldwork in funeral parlors.

9. Related to this is that a person can "steal longevity" (*toushou*) by "begging" (*tao*) or even stealing longevity bowls. One day in Huangpu, a state funeral practitioner came to me and happily showed me a goody bag (with a longevity bowl) that he had just acquired by "begging." I asked him what was so special about this funeral. Funeral professionals frequently see longevity bowls, and the bereaved often give these to them to express their gratitude. I did not understand why he even bothered to "beg" for one. He said that the deceased was a nun who had died in her hundredth year. According to him, she was one of only a very few "real" nuns (real meaning that she had kept her vow of chastity) and had lived for so long. This meant that her longevity had an even greater magical power than ordinary longevity, which was why he requested a longevity bowl. He then added that he even saw random people trying to steal longevity bowls from her funeral.

5. DYING SOCIALIST IN "CAPITALIST" SHANGHAI

1. "Passionately loved the Homeland, Socialism, and the Communist Party" was from a short-lived propaganda campaign slogan.

2. A more elaborate version of modern mourning garments were coarse (almost burlap) clothes wrapped around participants' waists in addition to the black armbands— but I saw these burlap-like clothes only occasionally.

3. This Five Replacements campaign was a part of the Transforming Customs and Changing Habits Campaign I discussed in chapter 1.

4. Just as the professionals in charge of implementing Funeral Reform in this early period struggled to convince people to give up body burial for cremation in practice, there were also, of course, ongoing significant differences between this formal description of the layout of the ritual and what they looked and felt like in actual practice at that pre–Cultural Revolution time.

5. Such identity labels were ironic because, despite the CCP's efforts to remove religion and superstition, this political vocabulary was borrowed directly from Buddhist demonology.

6. DYING RELIGIOUS IN A SOCIALIST RITUAL

1. These baskets were purchased by the family member(s) organizing the funeral. Their couplets were chosen by the same family member(s) but written as though coming from the giver of the white envelopes and addressed to the deceased. The need for

such return gifts was the most common explanations that funeral professionals offered when they explained to the bereaved the necessity of buying flower baskets.

2. Longevity had one employee whose job was to write couplets based on the lists provided by the bereaved in advance. He also showed up at memorial meetings before their official beginning to write couplets.

7. PLURALISM, INTERRUPTED

1. Only Yishan City Funeral Parlor and suburban funeral parlors allowed the bereaved to perform this type of march. In fact, even the frequency of hiring bands varied across urban and suburban funeral parlors. Longhua, a parlor that primarily served middle- and upper-class customers, had the lowest band usage rate. Baoxin, located in a working-class area, had a higher band usage rate than Longhua. In both places, the only "marching" allowed was when they sent the body from the meeting hall to a hearse in the parking lot at the end of the funeral. Regarding Yishan and all other suburban funeral parlors, marching band usage rates were quite high, and people were allowed to march into the funeral parlors.

2. Cleaning jobs had been outsourced by the time I did my fieldwork due to cost concerns. Whereas the state practitioners in charge of the meeting halls received approximately RMB 3,000 (USD 479) per month, the outsourced cleaning staff were paid closer to RMB 1,000 (USD 159) per month and were not parlor (or state) employees.

References

Ahern, Emily Martin. 1973. *The Cult of the Dead in a Chinese Village*. Stanford, CA: Stanford University Press.

Allison, Anne. 2013. *Precarious Japan*. Durham, NC: Duke University Press.

Anagnost, Ann. 1994. "The Politics of Ritual Displacement." In *Asian Visions of Authority: Religion and the Modern States of East and Southeast Asia*, edited by Charles F. Keyes, Laurel Kendall and Helen Hardacre, 221–54. Honolulu: University of Hawaii Press.

Anton, Corey. 2001. *Selfhood and Authenticity*. Albany: State University of New York Press.

Ariès, Philippe. 1974. *Western Attitudes toward Death: From the Middle Ages to the Present*. Baltimore: Johns Hopkins University Press.

Aveline-dubach, Natacha. 2012. "The Revival of the Funeral Industry in Shanghai: A Model for China." In *Invisible Population: The Place of the Dead in East Asian Megacities*, edited by Natacha Aveline-dubach, 74–97. Lanham, MD: Lexington Books.

Ayres, Chris. 2010. "Clean Green Finish that Sends a Loved One down the Drain." *The Times*, February 27, 2010.

Barmé, Geremie. 1996. *Shades of Mao: The Posthumous Cult of the Great Leader*. New York: Routledge.

Bateson, Gregory. (1955) 2000. *Steps to an Ecology of Mind*. Chicago: University of Chicago Press.

Becker, Ernest. 1973. *The Denial of Death*. New York: Free Press.

Bell, Catherine M. 1997. *Ritual: Perspectives and Dimensions*. New York: Oxford University Press.

Bellah, Robert Neelly, Richard Madsen, William Sullivan, Ann Swindler, and Stephen M. Tipton. 1985. *Habits of the Heart: Individualism and Commitment in American Life*. Berkeley: University of California Press.

Bellocq, Maylis. 2012. "Dealing with the Dead: Funerary Rites in Contemporary Shanghai." In *Invisible Population: The Place of the Dead in East Asian Megacities*, edited by Natacha Aveline-dubach, 98–121. Lanham, MD: Lexington Books.

Bergère, Marie-Claire. 2009. *Shanghai: China's Gateway to Modernity*. Stanford, CA: Stanford University Press.

Bloch, Maurice, and Jonathan P. Parry. 1982. "Introduction: Death and the Regeneration of Life." In *Death and the Regeneration of Life*, edited by Maurice Bloch and Jonathan P. Parry, 1–44. Cambridge: Cambridge University Press.

Bourdieu, Pierre. 1977. *Outline of a Theory of Practice*. Cambridge, MA: Cambridge University Press.

Brown, Wendy. 2015. *Undoing the Demos: Neoliberalism's Stealth Revolution*. New York: Zone Books.

Bruun, Ole. 1996. "The Fengshui Resurgence in China: Conflicting Cosmologies between State and Peasantry." *China Journal* 36:47–65.

Butler, Judith. 2004. *Precarious Life: The Powers of Mourning and Violence*. New York: Verso.

Chan, Kin-man 2005. "The Development of NGOs under a Post-Totalitarian Regime: The Case of China." In *NGOs, Globalization and Political Change in Asia*, edited by Robert Weller, 20–41. New York: Routledge.

Chao, Emily. 1999. "The Maoist Shaman and the Madman: Ritual Bricolage, Failed Ritual, and Failed Ritual Theory." *Cultural Anthropology* 14 (4): 505–34.

Chao, Ji Zhou, and Han Jingti. 2005. *Xiandai Hanyu Cidian* [A modern Chinese dictionary]. Beijing: Commercial Press.

Chau, Adam Yuet. 2006. *Miraculous Response: Doing Popular Religion in Contemporary China*. Stanford, CA: Stanford University Press.

Chen, Chen, and Yang Liao. 2015. "Luo Lang: tashi zhongguojunleshiye mingfuqishi de yuanxun" [Luo Lang: A true pioneer in Chinese military music]. *Dongfang zaobao*, July 17, 2015.

Chen, Huawen, and Shujun Chen. 2008. *Wuyue sangzang wenhua* [Funeral and interment culture in Wu and Yue areas]. Beijing: Huawen Chubanshe.

Chen, Nancy N. 2003. "Healing Sects and Anti-Cult Campaigns." *China Quarterly* 174:505–20.

Cohen, Myron L. 1993. "Cultural and Political Inventions in Modern China: The Case of the Chinese 'Peasant.'" *Daedalus* 122 (2): 151–70.

Cousins, Mark. 2004. "The Asian Aesthetic." *Prospect Magazine*, November 21, 2004.

Davis, Deborah. 1995. "Introduction." In *Urban Spaces in Contemporary China: The Potential for Autonomy and Community in Post-Mao China*, edited by Deborah Davis, Richard Kraus, Barry Naughton, and Elizabeth J. Perry, 1–22. Washington, DC: Woodrow Wilson Center.

Davis, Deborah, and Stevan Harrell. 1993. "The Impact of Post-Mao Reforms on Family Life." In *Chinese Families in the Post-Mao Era*, edited by Deborah Davis and Stevan Harrell, 1–24. Berkeley: University of California Press.

Dawdy, Shannon Lee. forthcoming. "The Embalmer's Magic." In *The New Death: Mortality and Death Care in the 21st Century*, edited by Shannon Lee Dawdy and Tamara Kneese. Albuquerque: SAR and University of New Mexico Press.

Dean, Kenneth. 1998. *Lord of the Three in One: The Spread of a Cult in Southeast China*. Princeton, NJ: Princeton University Press.

Deleuze, Gilles, and Felix Guattari. 1987. *A Thousand Plateaus: Capitalism and Schizophrenia*. Translated by Brian Massumi. Minneapolis: University of Minnesota Press.

Drewal, Margaret Thompson. 1992. *Yoruba Ritual: Performers, Play, Agency*. Bloomington: Indiana University Press.

Durkheim, Émile. (1912) 1965. *The Elementary Forms of the Religious Life*. New York: Free Press.

Ebrey, Patricia. 1990. "Cremation in Sung China." *American Historical Review* 95 (2): 406–28.

——. 2005. *China: A Cultural, Social, and Political History*. Boston: Wadsworth.

Engelke, Matthew. 2019. "The Anthropology of Death Revisited." *Annual Review of Anthropology* 48:29–44.

Fan, Bitian. 1989. *Xiandai binzang gunali* [Modern funeral and interment management]. Beijing: Minzhengbu shehui shiwu si.

Fan, Jingsi, ed. 2000. "Dishiqizhang: Binzang guanli" [Chapter 17: Funeral and interment administration]. In *Shanghai Minzhengzhi* [Shanghai civil affairs gazetteer]. Shanghai: Shanghai Shehui Kexueyuan Chubanshe. Accessed April 9, 2022. http://www.shtong.gov.cn/Newsite/node2/node2245/node65977/node66002/index.html.

Farrer, James. 2002. *Opening Up: Youth Sex Culture and Market Reform in Shanghai*. Chicago: University of Chicago Press.

Fei, Hsiao-tung (Xiaotong). 1946. *Peasant Life in China: A Field Study of Country Life in the Yangtze Valley*. New York: Oxford University Press.

Feuchtwang, Stephan. 2010. *The Anthropology of Religion, Charisma, and Ghosts: Chinese Lessons for Adequate Theory*. New York: Walter de Gruyter.

Foucault, Michel. 1991. "Governmentality." In *The Foucault Effect*, edited by Graham Burchell, Colin Gordon, and Peter Miller, 87–104. Chicago: University of Chicago Press.

———. 2001. *Madness and Civilization: A History of Insanity in the Age of Reason*. London: Routledge.

———. 2003. "Technologies of the Self." In *The Essential Foucault: Selections from Essential Works of Foucault, 1954–1984*, edited by Paul Rabinow and Nikolas Rose, 145–69. New York: New Press.

Freedman, Maurice. 1974. "On the Sociological Study of Chinese Religion." In *Religion and Ritual in Chinese Society*, edited by Emily M. Ahern and Arthur P. Wolf, 19–42. Stanford, CA: Stanford University Press.

Geertz, Clifford. 1973. *The Interpretation of Cultures: Selected Essays*. New York: Basic Books.

Giddens, Anthony. 1991. *Modernity and Self-Identity: Self and Society in the Late Modern Age*. Cambridge: Polity.

Gladney, Dru C. 1991. *Muslim Chinese: Ethnic Nationalism in the People's Republic*. Cambridge, MA: Harvard University Press.

Goffman, Erving. 1973. *The Presentation of Self in Everyday Life*. Woodstock, NY: Overlook.

———. 1974. *Frame Analysis: An Essay on the Organization of Experience*. New York: Harper & Row.

Golas, Peter J. 1977. "Early Ch'ing Guilds." In *The City in Late Imperial China*, edited by G. William Skinner, 555–80. Stanford, CA: Stanford University Press.

Goossaert, Vincent, and David A. Palmer. 2012. *The Religious Question in Modern China*. Chicago: University of Chicago Press.

Handelman, Don. 2006. "Framing." In *Theorizing Rituals*, edited by Jens Kreinath, Joannes Augustinus Maria Snoek, and Michael Stausberg, 571–82. Leiden, Netherlands: Brill.

Hansen, Mette Halskov, and Rune Svarverud. 2010. *IChina: The Rise of the Individual in Modern Chinese Society*. Copenhagen: NIAS.

Harvey, David. 2005. *A Brief History of Neoliberalism*. New York: Oxford University Press.

Hatfield, Donald J. 2009. *Taiwanese Pilgrimage to China: Ritual, Complicity, Community*. New York: Palgrave Macmillan.

Henriot, Christian. 2016. *Scythe and the City: A Social History of Death in Shanghai*. Stanford, CA: Stanford University Press.

Hertz, Robert. (1907) 1960. *Death and the Right Hand*. Glencoe, IL: Free Press.

Hinton, William. 1966. *Fanshen: A Documentary of Revolution in a Chinese Village*. New York: Vintage Books.

Hobsbawm, Eric. 1969. *Bandits*. New York: New Press.

Hochschild, Arlie Russell. 1983. *The Managed Heart: Commercialization of Human Feeling*. Berkeley: University of California Press.

Hoffman, Lisa. 2006. "Autonomous Choices and Patriotic Professionalism: On Governmentality in Late-Socialist China." *Economy and Society* 35 (4): 557–70.

Honig, Emily. 1989. "Pride and Prejudice: Subei People in Contemporary Shanghai." In *Unofficial China: Popular Culture and Thought in the People's Republic*, edited by E. Perry Link, Richard Madsen, and Paul Pickowicz, 138–55. Boulder, CO: Westview.

Howell, Jude. 2004. "New Directions in Civil Society: Organizing around Marginalized Interests." In *Governance in China*, edited by Jude Howell, 143–71. Lanham, MD: Rowman & Littlefield.

Hsu, Francis L. K. 1971. *Under the Ancestors' Shadow: Kinship, Personality, and Social Mobility in China*. Stanford, CA: Stanford University Press.

Huang, Meizhen, Qikui Liu, and Xiaojian Wang, eds. 2005. *Shanghai Tongzhi* [Shanghai general local history]. Vol. 43, *Shehui shenghuo* [Social life]. Shanghai: Shanghai renmin chubanshe.

Ikels, Charlotte. 2004. "Serving the Ancestors, Serving the State: Filial Piety and Death Ritual in Contemporary Guangzhou." In *Filial Piety: Practice and Discourse in Contemporary East Asia*, edited by Charlotte Ikels, 88–105. Stanford, CA: Stanford University Press.

Jernow, Allison Liu. 1994. "Don't Force Us to Lie: The Struggle of Chinese Journalism in the Reform Era." In *Maryland Series in Contemporary Asian Studies* 1994 (2): art. 1. https://digitalcommons.law.umaryland.edu/mscas/vol1994/iss2/1/.

Jiang, Yarong, and David Ashley. 2013. *Mao's Children in the New China: Voices from the Red Guard Generation*. New York: Routledge.

Jing, Jun. 1996. *The Temple of Memories: History, Power, and Morality in a Chinese Village*. Stanford, CA: Stanford University Press.

Katz, Paul R. 2007. "Orthopraxy and Heteropraxy beyond the State: Standardizing Ritual in Chinese Society." *Modern China* 33 (1): 72–90.

Kawaguchi, Yukihiro 2012. "Traditional Funerary Rites Facing Urban Explosion in Guangzhou." In *Invisible Population: The Place of the Dead in East Asian Megacities*, edited by Natacha Aveline-dubach, 123–37. Lanham, MD: Lexington Books.

Kipnis, Andrew. 1997. *Producing Guanxi: Sentiment, Self, and Subculture in a North China Village*. Durham, NC: Duke University Press.

——. 2007. "Neoliberalism Reified: Suzhi Discourse and Tropes of Neoliberalism in the People's Republic of China." *Journal of the Royal Anthropological Institute* 13 (2): 383–400.

——. 2008. "Audit Cultures: Neoliberal Governmentality, Socialist Legacy, or Technologies of Governing?" *American Ethnologist*. 35(2): 275–89.

Kipnis, Andrew, Luigi Tomba, and Jonathan Unger. 2009. *Contemporary Chinese Society and Politics*. New York: Routledge.

Kristof, Nicholas 1989. "Shanghai Journal: At the Cutting Edge of China's New Journalism." *New York Times*, January 16, 1989.

Laderman, Gary. 2003. *Rest in Peace: A Cultural History of Death and the Funeral Home in Twentieth Century America*. Oxford: Oxford University Press.

Li, Anxing. 2008. "The Meaning of Cabianqiu" [Cabianqiu deyi yi]. *Lexicographical Studies* 5:153–55.

Li, Bosen and Cheng Long Xiao ed. 2014. *Green Book of Funeral (2012–2013)*. Shanghai: Social Sciences Academic Press (China).

Lindholm, Charles. 2008. *Culture and Authenticity*. Malden, MA: Blackwell.

Link, E. Perry, Richard Madsen, and Paul Pickowicz. 2002. "Introduction." In *Popular China: Unofficial Culture in a Globalizing Society*, edited by E. Perry Link, Richard Madsen, and Paul Pickowicz, 1–9. Lanham, MD: Rowman & Littlefield.

Liu, Huwy-min Lucia. 2011. "Substance, Masculinity, and Class: Betel Nut Consumption and Embarrassing Modernity in Taiwan." In *Charismatic Modernity: Popular Culture in Taiwan*, edited by Marc L. Moskowitz, 131–48. New York: Routledge.

——. 2022. "Making a Living From Death: Chinese Funeral Workers under the Market Economy." In *The New Death: Mortality and Death Care in the Twenty-First*

Century, edited by Shannon Lee Dawdy and Tamara Kneese, 241–58. Santa Fe: School for Advanced Research Press.

Liu, Shaoqi. 1952. *How to Be a Good Communist.* New York: New Century.

Liu, Xin. 2000. *In One's Own Shadow: An Ethnographic Account of the Condition of Post-Reform Rural China.* Berkeley: University of California Press.

———. 2004. *Rhetoric of the Chinese Cultural Revolution: The Impact on Chinese Thought, Culture, and Communication.* Columbia: University of South Carolina Press.

Lu, Qiguo. 2013. "Laoshanghai de binzang yu gongmu" [Funeral industry and public cemeteries in the Old Shanghai]. *Chengshibao,* June 28, 2013, A5.

Lu, Xiaobo, and Elizabeth J. Perry. 1997. *Danwei: The Changing Chinese Workplace in Historical and Comparative Perspectives.* New York: M. E. Sharpe.

Lu, Xiaohong, and Xiangdong Zheng. 2011. *Shiyong binzang liyi ji aiji wenshu* [Practical guides to funeral and interment ritual and eulogy]. Shanxi: Shanxi kexue jishu chubanshe.

Luhrmann, T. M. 2006. "Subjectivity." *Anthropological Theory* 6 (3): 345–61.

Madsen, Richard. 2003. "Catholic Revival during the Reform Era." *China Quarterly* 174:468–87.

Malinowski, Bronislaw. 1948. *Magic, Science and Religion, and Other Essays.* Boston: Beacon.

Martin, John. 1997. "Inventing Sincerity, Refashioning Prudence: The Discovery of the Individual in Renaissance Europe." *American Historical Review* 102 (5): 1309–42.

Mao yi. 2006. "'Fang xin' binzangzhongjie gongbu" [Announcing legal funeral brokers]. Xinwen chenbao, December 6, 2006. http://news.sina.com.cn/o/2006-12 -06/021010690893s.shtml.

McQuaid, Jim. 2012. Personal communication.

Metcalf, Peter, and Richard Huntington. 1991. *Celebrations of Death: The Anthropology of Mortuary Rituals.* Cambridge, MA: Cambridge University Press.

Ministry of Civil Affairs. 1982. *Minzhengbu guanyu jinyibu jiaqiang binzanggaige de baogao* [Ministry of Civil Affair's report on the further improvement of Funeral and Interment Reforms]. Shanghai: Library of the Chinese Funeral and Interment Profession.

———. 1989. *Fanbaojun fubuzhang zai dierci quanguo binzang gongzuohuiyi shang de baogao* [The vice minister Fan Baojun's report on Funeral and Interment Reforms]. Shanghai: Library of the Chinese Funeral and Interment Profession.

———. 1996. *Binzang guanli* [Funeral and Interment Administration]. Beijing: Zhongguo shehui.

Mitford, Jessica. 1978. *The American Way of Death.* New York: Simon and Schuster.

Moskowitz, Marc L. 2011. *Dancing for the Dead: Funeral Strippers in Taiwan.* Columbia, SC: Daunting Head Productions.

Mueggler, Erik. 2001. *The Age of Wild Ghosts: Memory, Violence, and Place in Southwest China.* Berkeley: University of California Press.

Nedostup, Rebecca. 2010. *Superstitious Regimes: Religion and the Politics of Chinese Modernity.* Cambridge, MA: Harvard University Press.

Nonini, Donald M. 2008. "Is China Becoming Neoliberal?" *Critique of Anthropology* 28 (2): 145–76.

Oxfeld, Ellen. 2010. *Drink Water but Remember the Source: Moral Discourse in a Chinese Village.* Berkeley: University of California Press.

Palmer, David A. 2007. *Qigong Fever: Body, Science, and Utopia in China.* New York: Columbia University Press.

Parish, Steven M. 2008. *Subjectivity and Suffering in American Culture: Possible Selves.* New York: Palgrave Macmillan.

Pei, Minxin. 1998. *From Reform to Revolution: The Demise of Communism in China and the Soviet Union*. Cambridge, MA: Harvard University Press.

Ramzy, Austin. 2018. "Thousands of Confiscated Coffins and an Exhumed Corpse Stoke Fury in China." *New York Times*, August 2, 2018.

Rappaport, Roy A. 1999. *Ritual and Religion in the Making of Humanity*. Cambridge, MA: Cambridge University Press.

Rawski, Evelyn. 1988. "A Historian's Approach to Chinese Death Ritual." In *Death Ritual in Late Imperial and Modern China*, edited by James L. Watson and Evelyn Rawski, 20–36. Berkeley: University of California Press.

Reddy, William M. 2001. *The Navigation of Feeling: A Framework for the History of Emotions*. Cambridge, MA: Cambridge University Press.

Robbins, Joel. 2012. "Cultural Values." In *A Companion to Moral Anthropology*, edited by Didier Fassin, 117–32. Malden, MA: John Wiley & Sons.

——. 2013. "Monism, Pluralism, and the Structure of Value Relations: A Dumontian Contribution to the Contemporary Study of Value." *HAU: Journal of Ethnographic Theory* 3 (1): 99–115.

——. 2014. "Religious Pluralism and Value Pluralism Ritual and the Management of Intercultural Diversity." *Debates do NER* 15 (26): 1–21.

Rofel, Lisa. 2007. *Desiring China: Experiments in Neoliberalism, Sexuality, and Public Culture*. Durham, NC: Duke University Press.

Schirokauer, Conrad. 1989. *A Brief History of Chinese and Japanese Civilizations*. New York: City College of the City University of New York.

Schmalzer, Sigrid. 2016. *Red Revolution, Green Revolution: Scientific Farming in Socialist China*. Chicago: University of Chicago Press.

Seligman, Adam, and Robert P. Weller. 2012. *Rethinking Pluralism: Ritual, Experience, and Ambiguity*. New York: Oxford University Press.

Seligman, Adam, Robert P. Weller, Michael J. Puett, and Bennett Simon. 2008. *Ritual and Its Consequences: An Essay on the Limits of Sincerity*. Oxford: Oxford University Press.

Shanghai Civil Affairs Bureau. 1953. *Guanyu binzang gongzuo jixiang yijian cheng shifu wen* [Shanghai Civil Affairs Bureau's opinions on funeral governance]. Shanghai: Library of the Chinese Funeral and Interment Profession.

——. 1954. *Jieguan shanghai meishang wanguo binyiguan juti fangan (caoan)* [Plan to take over Wanguo Funeral Home]. Shanghai: Library of the Chinese Funeral and Interment Profession.

——. 1956. *Shanghai shi minzheng gongzuo guihua* [Annual work plan for Shanghai civil affairs governance]. Shanghai: Library of the Chinese Funeral and Interment Profession.

——. 1961. *Guanyu chuanshaxian yanjiaqiao dengchu yizhongdi fenmu beijue qingkuang he chuli yijian de qingshi baogao* [A report on the damages to charity cemeteries in Yanjiaqiao in Chuansha County]. Shanghai: Library of the Chinese Funeral and Interment Profession.

——. 1966. *Guanyu quxiao gongmu pinghui fenmu de qingshi baogao* [A report to cancel all cemeteries]. Shanghai: Library of the Chinese Funeral and Interment Profession.

——. 1996. *Shanghai minzhenggongzuo fazhanbaogaoshu* [The book of development of Shanghai civil affairs work]. Shanghai: Library of the Chinese Funeral and Interment Profession.

Shanghai Funeral and Interment Administration. 1956. *Guanyu ge gongmu yeyu nongye shengchan de baogao* [Regarding the amateur agricultural production in each public cemetery]. Shanghai: Library of the Chinese Funeral and Interment Profession.

——. 1960a. *Shanghai binzang shiye de yixie qingkuang* [The general condition of the Shanghai funeral and interment industry]. Shanghai: Library of the Chinese Funeral and Interment Profession.

——. 1960b. *Zhu eryuedi siyang baogao* [Report on raising pigs at the end of February]. Shanghai: Library of the Chinese Funeral and Interment Profession.

——. 1960c. *Linian siwang tongji qingkuang biao* [The statistical table of deaths]. Shanghai: Library of the Chinese Funeral and Interment Profession.

——. 1962. *Guanyu shiqindan gongsi zai Anping Gongmu sheli de yangjichang sunhuai fenmu qingkuang* [Regarding the Shanghai City Poultry and Egg Company's chicken raising in the Anping Cemetery and its damages to tombs]. Shanghai: Library of the Chinese Funeral and Interment Profession.

——. 1964. *1957 nian zhi 1963 nian huotuzang shengjiangshu bijiaobiao* [The increase and decrease in cremation between 1957 and 1963]. Shanghai: Library of the Chinese Funeral and Interment Profession.

——. 1978. *Qingkuang jianjie* [Introduction to funeral and interment management]. Shanghai: Library of the Chinese Funeral and Interment Profession.

——. 1984a. *Guanyu shiqu lianghuozangchang gengming de tongzhi* [Regarding changing the names of the two city crematoria]. Shanghai: Library of the Chinese Funeral and Interment Profession.

——. 1984b. *Zhenfenjingshen, maikaigaigebufa* [Stepping forward to the reform]. Shanghai Funeral and Interment Administration. Shanghai: Library of the Chinese Funeral and Interment Profession.

——. 1985. *Shanghai longhua binyiguan qingkuang jianjie* [Introduction to Longhua Funeral Parlor]. Shanghai: Library of the Chinese Funeral and Interment Profession.

——. 1987. "Dishiyizhang: Binzang shiye" [Chapter 11: Funeral and interment industry]. October 29, 1987. Shanghai: Library of the Chinese Funeral and Interment Profession.

——. N.d. *Shanghai minzhengshi xiabian chugao* [Shanghai civil affairs gazetteer, part 2, Draft]. Shanghai: Library of the Chinese Funeral and Interment Profession.

Shanghai Funeral and Interment Service Center. 2010. *Shanghai Funeral Museum.* Shanghai: Shanghai Funeral and Interment Service.

Shanghai Funeral Service Station. 1955. *Guanyu loushi chuli de xuanchuan ji cheshi shou fe biaozhun wenti baoqing heshi* [Regarding the propaganda of handling exposed bodies and fees for collecting bodies]. Shanghai: Library of the Chinese Funeral and Interment Profession.

Shanghai zangsu shihua wanguo binyiguan. 2003. Shanghai zangsu shihua wanguo binyiguan [History of Wanguo Funeral Home]. *Shanghai caifeng*, 26–27. Vol. 4. Shanghai: Shanghai caifeng yuekanshe.

Shanghai Religious Affairs Bureau. 1957. *Guanyu chuli haihuisi huozangchang jingguo qingkuang he jinhou chuli yijian* [Regarding the incident of the Haihui Temple's Crematorium and its solution]. Shanghai: Library of the Chinese Funeral and Interment Profession.

Sinn, Elizabeth. 2003. "The Tung Wah Hospital Committee as the Local Elite." In *Hong Kong: A Reader in Social History*, edited by David Faure, 211–67. Hong Kong: Oxford University Press.

Siu, Helen F. 1989. *Agents and Victims in South China: Accomplices in Rural Revolution.* New Haven, CT: Yale University Press.

Skinner, G. William. 1977. "Introduction: Urban and Rural in Chinese Society." In *The City in Late Imperial China*, edited by G. William Skinner and Hugh D. R. Baker, 253–74. Stanford, CA: Stanford University Press.

Stafford, Charles. 1995. *The Road of Chinese Childhood: Learning and Identification in Angang*. Cambridge: Cambridge University Press

———. 2000. *Separation and Reunion in Modern China*. Cambridge: Cambridge University Press.

Standaert, Nicolas. 2008. *The Interweaving of Rituals: Funerals in the Cultural Exchange between China and Europe*. Seattle: University of Washington Press.

State Council of the People's Republic of China. 1982. *Guowuyuan pizhuan minzhengbu guanyu jinyibujiaqiang binzanggaige gongzuode baogaode tongzhi* [State Council of the People's Republic of China's notification and transmission of the Ministry of Civil Affair's report on further improvement of funeral and interment reform]. Shanghai: Library of the Chinese Funeral and Interment Profession.

Steinmüller, Hans. 2013. *Communities of Complicity: Everyday Ethics in Rural China*. New York: Berghahn.

Sutton, Donald S. 2007. "Ritual, Cultural Standardization, and Orthopraxy in China: Reconsidering James L. Watson's Ideas." *Modern China* 33 (1): 3–21.

Suzuki, Hikaru. 2000. *The Price of Death: The Funeral Industry in Contemporary Japan*. Stanford, CA: Stanford University Press.

Szonyi, Michael. 2007. "Making Claims about Standardization and Orthopraxy in Late Imperial China: Rituals and Cults in the Fuzhou Region in Light of Watson's Theories." *Modern China* 33 (1): 47–71.

Tang, Zhenchang, ed. 1988. *Shanghai shi* [The history of Shanghai]. Shanghai: Shanghai renminchubanshe.

Tatlow, Didi Kirsten. 2014. "Elderly Suicides Reported after City Announces Phase-Out on Burials." *New York Times*, May 28, 2014.

Taylor, Charles. 1989. *Sources of the Self: The Making of the Modern Identity*. Cambridge, MA: Harvard University Press.

Toulson, Ruth. forthcoming. "Grief Transformed: New Rituals in a Singaporean Chinese Funeral Parlor." In *The New Death: Mortality and Death Care in the 21st Century*, edited by Shannon Lee Dawdy and Tamara Kneese. Albuquerque: SAR and University of New Mexico Press.

Trilling, Lionel. 1972. *Sincerity and Authenticity*. Cambridge, MA: Harvard University Press.

Turner, Victor Witter. 1969. *The Ritual Process: Structure and Anti-Structure*. New York: Aldine de Gruyter.

Van Gennep, Arnold. 1960. *The Rites of Passage*. Chicago: University of Chicago Press.

Verdery, Katherine. 1999. *The Political Lives of Dead Bodies*. New York: Columbia University Press.

Wakeman, Frederic, Jr. 1988. "Mao's Remans." In *Death Ritual in Late Imperial and Modern China*, edited by James L. Watson and Evelyn Rawski, 254–88. Berkeley: University of California Press.

Wang, Fuzai. 2007. *Binzang wenhuaxue: siwang wenhua de quanfangwei jiedu* [Funeral cultural studies: A comprehensive study of funeral culture]. Hunan: Hunan renmin chubanshe.

Watson, James L. 1988a. "Funeral Specialists in Cantonese Society: Pollution, Performance, and Social Hierarchy." In *Death Ritual in Late Imperial and Modern China*, edited by James L. Watson and Evelyn Rawski, 109–34. Berkeley: University of California Press.

———. 1988b. "The Structure of Chinese Funeral Rites: Elementary Forms, Ritual Sequence, and the Primacy of Performance." In *Death Ritual in Late Imperial and*

Modern China, edited by James L. Watson and Evelyn Rawski, 3–19. Berkeley: University of California Press.

Watson, Rubie S. 1994. "Making Secret Histories: Memory and Mourning in Post-Mao China." In *Memory, History, and Opposition under State Socialism*, edited by Rubie S. Watson, 65–85. Albuquerque: SAR and University of New Mexico Press.

Wei, Yahua. 2004. "2003 nian zhong guo shi da bao li hang ye" [The top ten industries with exorbitant profits in China in 2003). http://finance.sina.com.cn/g/20040102 /1440587719.shtml.

Weller, Robert P. 2006. *Discovering Nature: Globalization and Environmental Culture in China and Taiwan*. Cambridge, MA: Cambridge University Press.

Whyte, Martin King. 1988. "Death in the People's Republic of China." In *Death Ritual in Late Imperial and Modern China*, edited by James L. Watson and Evelyn Rawski, 289–316. Berkeley: University of California Press.

Wolf, Arthur P. 1974. "Introduction." In *Religion and Ritual in Chinese Society*, edited by Emily M. Ahern and Arthur P. Wolf, 1–18. Stanford, CA: Stanford University Press.

Wu, Jingrong, and Zhenqiu Cheng. 2001. *Xinshidai Hanying Dacidian* [New Age Chinese-English dictionary]. Shanghai: Commercial Press.

Xiang, Mingsheng. 1992. *Binzangxisu zhinan* [Funeral customs guide]. Shanghai: Shanghai wenhuachubanshe.

Xijin Funeral Parlor Funeral Service Team. n.d. *Huozang xuanchuan* [Promoting cremation]. Shanghai: Library of the Chinese Funeral and Interment Profession.

Xu, Dabiao, and Runliang Xu. 1999. "Shanghai binzangye and baoxing binyiguan" [Shanghai funeral and interment industry and Baoxing Funeral Parlor]. In *Shanghai difangzhi* [Shanghai local gazetteer]. Shanghai: Shanghai renmin chubanshe.

Yan, Hairong. 2003. "Neoliberal Governmentality and Neohumanism: Organizing Suzhi/Value Flow through Labor Recruitment Networks." *Cultural Anthropology* 18 (4): 493–523.

Yan, Yunxiang. 1996. *The Flow of Gifts: Reciprocity and Social Networks in a Chinese Village*. Stanford, CA: Stanford University Press.

———. 2003. *Private Life under Socialism: Love, Intimacy, and Family Change in a Chinese Village, 1949–1999*. Stanford, CA: Stanford University Press.

Yang, C. K. 1961. *Religion in Chinese Society: A Study of Contemporary Social Functions of Religion and Some of Their Historical Factors*. Berkeley: University of California Press.

Yang, Fenggang. 2005. "Lost in the Market, Saved at McDonald's: Conversion to Christianity in Urban China." *Journal for the Scientific Study of Religion* 44 (4): 423–41.

Yang, Mayfair Mei-hui. 1994. *Gifts, Favors, and Banquets: The Art of Social Relationships in China*. Ithaca, NY: Cornell University Press.

Yu, Shuenn-Der. 2004. "Hot and Noisy: Taiwan's Night Market Culture." In *The Minor Arts of Daily Life: Popular Culture in Taiwan*, edited by David K. Jordan, Andrew D. Morris, and Marc L. Moskowitz, 129–149. Honolulu: University of Hawaii Press.

Zhang, Li. 2001. *Strangers in the City: Reconfigurations of Space, Power, and Social Networks within China's Floating Population*. Stanford, CA: Stanford University Press.

Zhang, Li, and Aihwa Ong. 2008. "Privatizing China—Power of the Self, Socialism from Afar." In *Privatizing China: Socialism from Afar*, edited by Li Zhang and Aihwa Ong, 1–19. Ithaca, NY: Cornell University Press.

Zhao, Dingxin. 2009. "The Mandate of Heaven and Performance Legitimation in Historical and Contemporary China." *American Behavioral Scientist* 53 (3): 416–33.

Index